DEFOE IN EDINBURGH
AND OTHER PAPERS

Other Books by Paul H. Scott

1707: The Union of Scotland and England (1979)
Walter Scott and Scotland (1981)
John Galt (1985)
In Bed with an Elephant (1985)
The Thinking Nation (1989)
Cultural Independence (1989)
Towards Independence: Essays on Scotland (1991)
Andrew Fletcher and the Treaty of Union (1992)
Scotland in Europe: A Dialogue with a Sceptical Friend (1992)

Edited:
The Age of MacDiarmid (1980) (With A.C. Davis)
Sir Walter Scott's The Letters of Malachi Malagrowther (1981)
Andrew Fletcher's United and Separate Parliaments (1982)
A Scottish Postbag (1986) (With George Bruce)
Policy for the Arts: A Selection of AdCAS Papers (1991) (With A.C. Davis)
Scotland: A Concise Cultural History (1993)

Contributions to joint volumes in:
Scott and his Influence (1983) (Ed. by J.H. Alexander and David Hewitt)
Cultural Policy in Europe (1984) (Ed. by M. Anderson and L. Dominguez)
The History of Scottish Literature, Vol. 3 (1988) (Ed. by Douglas Gifford)
Byron and Scotland (1989) (Ed. by Angus Calder)
Edwin Muir: Centenary Assessments (1990) (Ed. by C.J.M. MacLachlan and D.S. Robb)
Reference Guide to Short Fiction (1994) (Ed. by Noelle Watson)

DEFOE IN EDINBURGH
and Other Papers

PAUL H. SCOTT

TUCKWELL PRESS

For Laura

First published in 1995 by
Tuckwell Press Ltd
The Mill House
Phantassie
East Linton
East Lothian EH40 3UC
Scotland

Copyright © Paul H. Scott 1995

British Library Cataloguing-in-Publication Data
A catalogue record for this book
is available on request from the
British Library

The Publishers acknowledge subsidy from the
Scottish Arts Council towards the publication
of this volume

Typeset by Light Technology Ltd, Fife

Printed and bound by
The Cromwell Press Limited,
Broughton Gifford, Melksham, Wiltshire

Contents

INTRODUCTION

Several of the papers in this collection are the results of attempts to satisfy my own curiosity about people or events that were often the subject of tantalising allusion, but not of adequate explanation. It is, for instance, well known that Daniel Defoe was in Edinburgh during the long debate on the Treaty of Union. What did he do there and why? I could not find a satisfying account of this in any of the books about either Defoe or the Union and therefore did my best to find out. The first essay in this book is the result. Similarly with John Macky and John Leyden. They appear frequently in footnotes, memoirs and the like, but they seemed to be mysterious and shadowy figures. I felt that I had to find out more.

Although some of these essays are therefore historical, they generally have a bearing on the challenges and opportunities which now face us in Scotland. Some are about Italy, France, Ireland or India but they have their connections with the main theme as well. That theme is explicit in *Cultural Independence*.

Since several of the essays first appeared in *Blackwood's Magazine*, I should like to offer my respects to that periodical, which had such a long and distinguished life, and to regret the passing of a medium which offered more generous space than you can now usually find in any magazine or review. Acknowledgement is due also to the editors of the other periodicals and newspapers where some of these essays first appeared.

P.H.S.
Edinburgh

PART ONE

From Defoe to Muir

I

Defoe in Edinburgh

'We have all had *Robinson Crusoe* read aloud to us as children,' said Virginia Woolf in one of her essays. 'It never occurred to us that there was such a person as Defoe, and to have been told that *Robinson Crusoe* was the work of a man with a pen in his hand would either have disturbed us unpleasantly or meant nothing at all.' No doubt Crusoe is more familiar to most of us than the man who wrote the book, although Defoe lived a long, crowded life with a pen almost constantly in his hand. He was full of ideas, and for him, to think, to write and to publish were all part of the same process, which seems to have been as natural to him as breathing. His output was phenomenal, about 500 works of diverse kinds, and continuous journalism, including a newsletter, *The Review*, which appeared three times a week for nearly ten years, and of which he wrote virtually every word himself. Most of his writing was didactic and polemical, because he had an irresistible urge to influence people and events. In our day, he would never have been off the television screen. He wrote his novels, *Robinson Crusoe*, *Moll Flanders* and *Roxana*, in the comparative tranquillity of his sixties. He was one of the inventors of the novel; but he spent most of his restless energy, with the same originality and plausibility, in journalism, propaganda and intelligence.

It has long been well known that Defoe played a role in Edinburgh politics in the winter of 1706 to 1707, at the time of the debates in the Scottish Parliament which led to the approval of the Treaty of Union. Unlike his *Journal of the Plague Year*, this was no figment of his imagination. It was an official, although secret, mission for the English Government, unusually successful for such undercover work, and surprisingly well documented. First of all, there was the public record published by Defoe at the time, or shortly afterwards, which admitted that he had been in Edinburgh and had been involved in the Union transactions. Even when he was in Edinburgh, he continued to send his copy to London for *The Review*, which for two years spoke of little else but the Union. He wrote at least eight pamphlets about it, two while he was still in London and the rest in Edinburgh. All were anonymous, as was the custom of the time, but six were transparently his. Two were under heavy cover where he pretended to be Scottish. If all of this was not enough, in 1709 he published a massive *History of the Union Between England and Scotland*, in nearly 800 pages folio. Even this, as we shall see, was not the end of it.

Two years after the vote, Defoe felt able to boast a little about some of his activities in the *History*: 'I had the honour to be frequently sent for into the several Committees of Parliament, which were appointed to state some difficult points relating to equalities, taxes, prohibitions, etc. 'Tis for those gentlemen to say, whether I was useful or not.' He tells us that proposals which he made on the beer tax 'stand in the Treaty of Union in his very words'. He had been 'eye witness to much of the general transaction, and furnished, by the best hands, with every most secret affair in the carrying it on'. But even in the *History*, he still pretended that he was an enthusiastic amateur, employed by no one:

> My curiosity pressed me to take a journey thither; and being by all my friends to whom I communicated my design, encouraged to think I might be useful there to prompt a work that I was fully convinced was for the general good of the whole island; and particularly necessary for the strengthening of the protestant interest, I was moved purely on these accounts to undertake a long winter, a chargeable, and, as it proved, a hazardous journey.
>
> I condemn, as not worth mentioning, the suggestion of some people of my being employed thither, to carry on the interest of a party. I have never loved any parties, but with my utmost zeal have sincerely espoused the great and original interest of this nation, and of all nations, I mean truth and liberty, and whoever are of that party, I desire to be with them.

He took the same line in *The Review*; he had been 'unsent, unemployed and not only unrewarded, but unsupported'.

It was too good a secret to keep for long. Defoe let the cat out of the bag in 1715, when he published his *Appeal to Honour and Justice*, an essay in self-justification. Here he admitted that he had been 'employed in several honourable though secret services' by Harley and Godolphin. Since they were, in succession, the leading ministers of the English Government and the chief architects of the Union, it should not have been difficult for people to put two and two together. John Clerk of Penicuik, a member of the Scottish Parliament, drew the right conclusion in his *Memoirs*. Defoe, he wrote, was 'sent to Scotland by the prime minister of England, the Earl of Godolphin, on purpose to give a faithful account to him from time to time how everything past here. He was therefore a Spy amongst us, but not known to be such, otherways the Mob of Edinburgh had pulled him to pieces'.

The truth about Defoe's mission in Edinburgh was revealed beyond all doubt only at the end of the last century, when the Historical Manuscripts Commission published the papers of the Duke of Portland. Among them were nearly 200 letters from Defoe to Robert Harley, including his reports from Edinburgh. They show that Defoe, in precise contradiction to his denial, was sent, employed, and rewarded and supported, if not very generously or punctually. He had to keep on reminding Harley of the dangers and costs of the job, and the needs of his large family; but he kept hard at work, infiltrating, persuading, observing and writing. He sent a secret report every week. So to the thousands of pages about the Union which Defoe wrote for publication, we have to add some hundreds more written for the private information of the Government. Seldom has one man written so much about one event.

How did this robust, independent, radical, dissenting and courageous upholder of the rights of the common man find himself in exactly the position he affected to despise: that of the paid Government agent? To understand this, we have to go back several years before 1706. Defoe was born in London *circa* 1660 to a respectable, puritanical, dissenting, and indeed Presbyterian, family in a modest way of business. After a sound education at a school for the sons of dissenters, he went into business on his own account in the City. He was not only in 'hosiery', as it amused his detractors to recall, but also in the import of wines, overseas trading ventures, and the manufacture of bricks and tiles. He was no misplaced Bohemian, trapped in commerce against his will, but a genuine enthusiast, who would rather have been a successful merchant than anything else. 'All his life he looked with admiration on the great merchant,' as one of the best of his biographers, James Sutherland, says, 'and celebrated with eloquence and complete sincerity the glories of trade. There is much of this enthusiasm for the merchant in the varied writings of Defoe; he comes nearest to being a poet when he writes in impassioned prose about the expansion of English commerce.' As often happens with enthusiasts, he was better at writing about it than practising it. His expansive ideas and his lust for speculation outran his prudence. By 1692 he was bankrupt. He had a wife and seven children to support, and it was an age when you could be imprisoned indefinitely for debt. For the rest of his life Defoe was plagued by creditors.

In this crisis, since he was excluded from trade, he decided to try to earn his living by writing. This is a desperate enough expedient at any time. It was even worse in the early eighteenth century for someone like Defoe who had a taste and talent for polemics. You could be attacked and cudgelled to death by thugs hired by your opponents, as happened to one of Defoe's rivals, John Tutchin. You could be prosecuted by the Government, as happened to Defoe himself. In 1703, *The Shortest Way with the Dissenters*, an ironic pamphlet attacking the high Tories, offended the Establishment. He was sentenced to stand three times in the pillory, pay a fine of 200 marks and be detained in prison at the Queen's pleasure.

The man to whom Defoe turned in this extremity was a Scotsman, William Paterson, who had some similarities of temperament. He was another stimulator of 'projects', among them the Bank of England, which may perhaps be counted as a success, and the Scottish colony at Darien, which was certainly a disaster. He supported the idea of Union, encouraged by a discreet Court pension, and was in the confidence of Robert Harley, then at the height of his power. In April 1703, Defoe wrote to Paterson from Newgate Prison to plead for his intercession with Harley: 'Nor is there anything so mean (which I can honestly stoop to do) that I would not submit to to obtain her Majestie's favour.' Defoe had already shown that he was a formidable controversialist, and Harley saw the advantage of having such a man on his side. He hardened his resolve by leaving him in Newgate for another six or seven months and then ordered his release. Defoe overwhelmed him with gratitude. He was 'the Gratefullest wretch Allive, . . . Ready to Dedicate my Life and all Possible Powers to The Intrest of So Generous and So Bountifull Benefactors'. Perhaps he did not know that Harley himself had started the investigation which had led to his arrest.

This sounds like abject and humiliating submission, even if Defoe had the excuse of desperation. But great as the gulf was between the wealthy, powerful Minister and poor, down-trodden Defoe, his relationship with Harley rapidly became one of collaboration rather than servitude. They shared a common outlook. Like Defoe, Harley was by birth and education a Whig and a dissenter. By degrees, he had become the leader of the moderate Tories; but Defoe too had moved from the extremes to an advocacy of moderation. 'The Moderate Men of both Partyes are the Substantial part of the Nation,' he said in one of his letters to Harley. Most of the policies of the Government which Defoe supported in *The Review*, launched a few months after his release from prison, were in line with his own convictions, and this was true also of the proposal of Union with Scotland.

Not content with writing alone, Defoe began to agitate for additional employment. At first, his suggestions were modest.

Perhaps he could be given an appointment in the Auditor's office: 'Matters of Accounts are my particular Element, what I have Allways been Master of.' Soon, he was being lavish with advice on the whole range of foreign and defence policy. He had ideas for the reorganisation of government, and urged Harley to become, in name as well as in fact, Prime Minister. He had a scheme for an office of secret intelligence at home and abroad. He wanted to see 'the foundation of Such an Intelligence as Never was in England . . . Intelligence is the Soul of all Publick bussiness'. He proposed that the Government should build up secret sources of information not only in the whole of Europe, but in England itself. They should collect information about the attitudes and political affiliations of leading men, including the clergy. There was a special need in Scotland. 'A Settl'd Intelligence in Scotland, a Thing Strangely Neglected There, is without Doubt the Principall Occasion of The present Missunderstandings between the Two kingdomes. In the Last Reign it Caus'd the king to have Many ill things Put upon him, and worse are Very likely to follow.'

Defoe was also concerned about security, another instance of the strangely twentieth-century cast of his mind. 'I have been in the Secretary's Office of a Post Night when Had I been a French spye I could ha' Put in my Pockett my Lord N – ms letters directed to sir Geo: Rook and to the Duke of Marlebro' Laid Carelessly on a Table for the Doorkeepers to Carry to the Post Office. How many Miscarriages have happen'd in England for want of Silence and Secresy.' Harley, to his cost, disregarded this advice. Less than four years later, a clerk in his office, William Greg, another Scotsman, was discovered passing correspondence to the French. He was condemned to the barbarous penalty for treason, but before he was executed he was kept in Newgate for 100 days in the hope that he might inculpate Harley in exchange for his life. He refused and Harley survived.

Defoe was less original than he supposed in his ideas about intelligence. Harley shared his taste for deception and the cloak and dagger. He already had agents, even in Scotland; the same William Greg had been one of them. In Defoe, Harley recognised a kindred spirit, well suited to this sort of work. He proposed at first to send him to Hanover; but in the end his first missions were to the eastern counties of England in 1704, and to the Midlands and the South-west the following year. Then, in September 1706, Harley ordered Defoe to Edinburgh, where the Parliamentary debates on the Treaty of Union were about to begin. Harley was as dilatory in sending instructions as he was with money, so Defoe drafted his own. From the first, he proposed a more active role for himself than merely collecting information:

However, That if my Notions are wrong, I may be Set Right by your
Instructions, I beg leav, tho' it be beginning at the wrong End, to Set
Down how I Understand my present bussiness – as foll.

1. To Inform My Self of the Measures Takeing Or Partys forming
Against the Union and Applye my Self to prevent them.

2. In Conversation and by all Reasonable Methods to Dispose
peoples minds to the Union.

3. By writeing or Discourse, to Answer any Objections, Libells
or Reflections on the Union, the English or the Court, Relateing to
the Union.

4. To Remove the Jealousies and Uneasyness of people about Secret
Designs here against the Kirk &c.

Defoe pressed for confirmation. He did not want to be 'your
Messengr without an Errand, your Ambassador without Instructions, your Servant without ordrs'. Harley responded in a letter
which reached Defoe when he was already in Edinburgh. Only the
first page has survived, but it is enough to show that Harley agreed
that Defoe was to be a propagandist and persuader as well as a spy:

Instructions

1. You are to use the utmost caution that it may not be supposed
you are employed by any person in England: but that you came there
upon your own business, & out of love to the Country.

2. You are to write constantly the true State how you find things,
at least once a week, & you need not subscribe any name, but direct
for me under Cover to Mrs Collins at the Posthouse, Middle Temple
Gate, London. For variety you may direct under Cover to Michael
Read in York Buildings.

3. You may confidently assure those you converse with, that the
Queen & all those who have Credit with her, are sincere & hearty
for the Union.

4. You must shew them this is such an opportunity that being
once lost or neglected is not again to be recovered. England never
was before in so good a disposition to make such large Concessions,
or so heartily to unite with Scotland, & should their kindness now
be slighted.

Defoe found Edinburgh in a state of fury and indignation against the
terms of Union which had been negotiated in London. The streets
were in a constant uproar. He sent Harley a vivid description:

I had not been Long There but I heard a Great Noise and looking
Out Saw a Terrible Multitude Come up the High street with A
Drum at the head of Them shouting and swearing and Cryeing Out
all Scotland would stand together, No Union, No Union, English
Dogs, and the like.

I Can Not Say to you I had No Apprehensions, Nor was Monsr
De Witt[1] quite Out of my Thoughts, and perticularly when a part of
This Mob fell upon a Gentleman who had Discretion little Enough
to say something that Displeased them just Undr my Window.

He Defended himself bravely and Call'd Out lustily also for help to
the Guard who being within Hearing and Ready Drawn up in Close
Ordr in the street, advanc't, Rescued the Gentleman, and took the
person he was Grappld with prisoner.

The City was by this time in a Terrible fright. The Guards were
Insulted and stoned as they stood, the Mob put out all the lights, no
body could stir in the streets, and not a light be seen in a windo' for
fear of stones.

No doubt Defoe had grounds for nervousness, and we have seen
John Clerk's testimony to the same effect. 'A Scots Rabble is the
worst of its kind,' Defoe said, but it was a rabble which seems to
have used its tongue more than its hands. There is no record that
anyone was killed or seriously hurt during the long tumult against
the Union. Even if Scottish troops were brought into the streets
of Edinburgh, and an English force assembled in readiness at the
Border, Defoe was a little fanciful in saying: 'I ran as much Risq
of my life as a Grenadr in storming a Counterscarp.' The thought
that he might be exaggerating did occur to his masters in London.
'I have often observed,' Godolphin commented to Harley, 'that he
gives you the worst side of the picture.'

The truth is that Defoe, so far from being torn apart by the mob,
was soon accepted everywhere in Edinburgh in various guises, even
as a helpful adviser to parliamentary committees and the Assembly
of the Church. He boasted to Harley:

I am Perfectly Unsuspected as Corresponding with anybody in
England. I Converse with Presbyterian, Episcopall-Dissenter, papist
and NonJuror, and I hope with Equall Circumspection. I flatter my
Self you will have no Complaints of my Conduct. I have faithfull
Emissaries in Every Company And I Talk to Everybody in Their
Own way. To the Merchants I am about to Settle here in Trade,
Building ships &c. With the Lawyers I Want to purchase a House
and Land to bring my family & live Upon it (God knows where the
Money is to pay for it). To day I am Goeing into Partnership with a
Member of parliamt in a Glass house, to morrow with Another in a
Salt work. With the Glasgow Mutineers I am to be a fish Merchant,
with the Aberdeen Men a woollen and with the Perth and western
men a Linen Manufacturer, and still at the End of all Discourse
the Union is the Essentiall and I am all to Every one that I may
Gain some.

Again I am in the Morning at the Committee, in the Afternoon in

the assembly. I am privy to all their folly, I wish I Could not Call it
knavery, and am Entirely Confided in.

This is a remarkable performance and it is astonishing that even
Defoe was able to get away with it. He must have played up
his Presbyterian upbringing for all that it was worth. He could
claim, from his pillorying and imprisonment, to be a martyr for the
cause, and a victim of English persecution. Alternatively, with some
damage to his pride and his capitalist pretensions, he could represent
himself as a refugee from an English debtors' prison. He had a facility
which was later the strength of his novels, for getting inside the
skin of assumed characters. He had great mental agility and an easy
flow of colloquial, amusing conversation. His nerves were strong,
and his interest in people and their problems inexhaustible. All of
these must have helped. Even so, he was unmistakably English,
and before leaving London he had been writing in support of the
Union from a distinctly English point of view. *The Review*, in which
most of this work appeared, was known to be his. Two pamphlets,
though anonymous, were part of a series which he more or less
openly acknowledged. The people of Edinburgh must have been
a great deal more tolerant than Defoe usually admitted, and the
Parliamentarians and Ministers of the Kirk, whose confidence he
abused, must have been trusting to the point of gullibility. No one
seems to have questioned his pose, as he described it in one of his
pamphlets, as 'a stranger that strives to speak impartial truth, and
has not one shilling to gain or lose, let it go which way it will'.

This series of pamphlets had the general title of *An Essay at
Removing National Prejudices*. The first two parts were published in
London and addressed to an English audience; the subsequent four,
published in Edinburgh, dealt with the controversy as it developed
inside and outside the Scottish Parliament. Defoe was too good a
propagandist to allow consistency to spoil a good argument, and
there are blatant differences between his approach to one audience
and the other. Presumably he relied on the poor communications
between the two capitals. In London, he was concerned with English
prejudices, which were certainly strong. Before Defoe, there was
hardly any English comment on Scotland which was not full of
hate and contempt and the Scots reciprocated. 'Never two nations',
in Defoe's words, 'had such inveteracy and aversion to one another
in their blood.' So, in London, he argued that the advantage of the
Union would be 'wholly on England's side'. By ending the threat
of intervention from the north and gaining Scotland's 'inexhaustible
treasure of men', it would increase the power of England and enable
her to make 'a different Figure in all the affairs of Europe'. The

addition of Scottish Presbyterians to the English dissenters could not, by sheer arithmetic, be a threat to the Church of England. 'I confess that I cannot speak with the same assurance that there is the same safety to the Scots.' The alternative to Union was war, which would be 'the most bloody, implacable and cruel, that ever happened between the Nations'. It was true that England had increased so much in wealth and strength that she should be able to crush Scotland; but 'there are such circumstances attending Scotland, and which render her a Nation which the other Powers of Europe will so gladly espouse, that we have unforseen Events to encounter with in such a Break'. He added the additional argument in *The Review* that the Union would mean a real increase in English trade. 'A new and vast Ocean of Wealth and Trade shall be laid open in the North.'

In Scotland, he needed the precise opposite of these arguments and this he duly produced. In London, he had cast doubt on the safety of the Scottish Church establishment after the Union. In Edinburgh, he denied that it was under any risk. He assured his Scottish readers, in defiance of the English doctrine of parliamentary supremacy, that the guarantees in the Treaty were secure for all time, for the Church, the economy and everything else. In London, he had warned his readers of the danger that Scotland without the Union might form alliances to the disadvantage of England. In Edinburgh, he poured scorn on this idea, especially in a pamphlet, *The Advantages of Scotland, by an Incorporate Union with England*, in which he pretended to be Scottish and even used some Scots words. In particular, he derided any suggestion of a revival of the old alliance with France: 'Did not they on every Falling out they had with England, engage us in their Quarrel, by which we sacrificed Millions of Men and Money to their Interest. All that time we were in League with them, they made mere Tools of us, and blew us up to a greater Loss, by their Deluding Arts, than ever England felt from the Force of their Arms.' About this point at least—opposition to France and Jacobitism—Defoe was entirely sincere. The Glorious Revolution of 1688 and William's resistance to French ambitions were the core of his political philosophy.

Despite the force of the anti-Jacobite argument, especially with the Church, Defoe had to face the awkward fact of what he called the 'general aversion' to the Union. 'The people cried out, they were Scotsmen, and they would be Scotsmen still "No incorporating union" was the word.' The Scottish Parliament was flooded with addresses against the Union from all over the country without a single one in favour. How was he to explain this away? His fifth and sixth essays were largely devoted to the attempt. He was driven to the rather desperate argument that only those with the very restrictive property qualifications entitling them to vote in elections had any right to express views on questions before Parliament. Those 'who have no Right to elect Representatives . . . can have no Right to direct those who they have no part in constituting . . . they are meddling with what they have no Right to be meddling with, nor are any way concerned in'. The addresses 'ought rather to be call'd Bold Declarations in opposition to Legal Authority'. It was an argument which came strangely from Defoe, of all people. In 1701, in one of his most courageous acts, he had delivered *Legion's Memorial to the House of Commons*, with its resounding claims for the rights of the people above those of Parliament: 'For Englishmen are no more to be slaves to Parliament than to a King. Our name is *Legion* and we are many. You are not above the People's resentments! The People of England, whom you serve, do REQUIRE and DEMAND.' He was consistent in one respect: on that occasion Defoe's objection was that the House of Commons were resisting the prosecution of the war against France.

So far, I have hardly mentioned any of the economic factors which some historians have represented as the prime cause of the Union. Defoe, with his passion for trade, might have been expected to be alive to all the possibilities. 'Writing upon trade', he said in the last issue of *The Review*, 'was the whore I really doted upon and designed to have taken up with.' In London he had argued that the Union would open up new markets to English trade. How did he see it from the Scottish point of view? The provisions of the Treaty affecting customs and excise, export duty and the like, were detailed and complicated and inevitably took up much of the time of the parliamentary debate. (It is one of the many similarities to the debate on joining the EEC.) Here Defoe was in his element, and this gave him his entrée to the parliamentary committees. On the wider question of the economic consequences, opinion in Scotland was divided. Some people saw substantial advantage in having access to the English and colonial markets, but many had misgivings. The Convention of Royal Burghs, which could claim to speak for the trading community (although Defoe disputed that), were opposed to the Union. They argued that 'the most considerable branches of our Trade are differing from those of England, and are, and may be yet more, discouraged by their laws'. Others were in favour of preserving the traditional pattern of Scottish trade with France, the Low Countries and Scandinavia, and thought the Colonies a poor substitute. While the question in the Scottish Parliament was still open, Defoe attacked all of these arguments, especially in one of his pamphlets written in an assumed role, *A Letter Concerning Trade from Several Scots-Gentlemen that are Merchants in England, to their*

Country-Men that are Merchants in Scotland. (The trick still works. A modern historian, T. C. Smout, in a book published in 1963, *Scottish Trade on the Eve of the Union*, refers to the pamphlet as though it were genuine evidence of the views of Scottish merchants in London at the time.) In this and other pamphlets, Defoe insisted that the Union would be of benefit to Scottish trade. He was on strong ground in arguing that England was the only possible market for the main Scottish exports of cattle and linen, after the loss of the European markets in consequence of England's wars with France and Holland. He was contradictory about trade with the Colonies, arguing both that it would be beneficial and that there was no point in Scotland keeping an overseas Trading Company (which the Treaty proposed to abolish) because she had insufficient production or consumption to sustain it.

Defoe did not seem to have been convinced by his own arguments about the economic consequences, and he took quite a different view once the vote in Parliament had been safely accomplished. In the Appendix to his *History of the Union* he was unusually neutral: 'Whether, upon the whole of these alterations in trade, Scotland is gainer or loser, I must acknowledge, it is a difficult point to resolve at so small a distance from the finishing the Union.' In the Dedication to Queen Anne, he argued, for once, that 'the little articles of commerce' were comparatively unimportant:

> Whatever loss some may allege Scotland suffers in this Union, in matters of commerce, in removing her parliaments, in lessening the conflux of her nobility and gentry to Edinburgh, in taxes, and in carrying away her people, things which time may remedy and repay her for with interest; yet this the most prejudiced man in Scotland must acknowledge they have in exchange, and which, if they know how to value it, is worth all they have paid or can pay for it; I mean Liberty in its due and best extent, religious and civil.

Twenty years later, in the third volume of his *Tour Thro' the Whole Island of Great Britain*, published in 1727, he acknowledged that an increase of trade and population in Scotland, 'reasonably expected upon the Union', was 'not the case, but rather the contrary'.

Defoe's *History* is a strange combination of documents, narrative and commentary. It is massive in length and badly needs pruning and rearranging. The heart of it is the official record of the Treaty negotiations in London in the summer of 1706, and the minutes of the debates in the Scottish Parliament during the following winter from October to January, both interspersed with comment. It gives the full text of the Acts of Union in both countries and a wide selection of other documents, which are still a useful source. 'A very exact History,' John Clerk wrote in his *Memoirs*, 'there is not one fact in it which I can challenge.' This is true as far as it goes, even if Clerk was an interested witness; the distortion is in the omissions. The minutes of the Scottish Parliament were admirable for clarity and brevity, but they recorded only what was proposed and rejected or adopted, not the speeches nor even a summary of the arguments. In spite of the length of the book, Defoe did little to make good the deficiency. 'I shall not name persons . . . not thinking it necessary to make this history a satire upon any one family.' With this curious explanation, he reported very few speeches. Apart from official statements, he gives only two by Seton of Pitmedden in favour of the Union, and two by Lord Belhaven, the most emotional of the speakers against it. He never mentions Fletcher of Saltoun, the main intellectual strength of the opposition, and his name appears only in the voting lists in the minutes. He makes no reference to the most extraordinary part of the whole debate, the way in which the intentions of the opposition were repeatedly frustrated by their nominal leader, the Duke of Hamilton. He plays down the independence and assertiveness of Parliament from 1703 to 1705, and makes no attempt to explain how the same Parliament with the same members became so supine in 1706. He ignores the whole question of 'management', the polite word for bribery, without which this transformation cannot be understood. Defoe does not suppress all the arguments against the Union, but he takes care always to have the last word. It is rather as Samuel Johnson said of his parliamentary reports: 'I took care that the Whig Dogs should not have the best of it.' Defoe does the same for the dogs opposed to the Union. At the same time, where he can do it without spoiling his argument, he avoids offence to Scottish feelings. On such matters as the Darien Scheme and the English Aliens Act of 1705, he supports the Scottish, rather than the English, case. Perhaps with his tongue in his cheek, and in flat contradiction to his letters to Harley, he flatters the Commission of the Church Assembly, 'the general proceedings of that reverent body being always tempered with modesty, calmness and discretion'. Was he trying to make the book acceptable in Scotland, or did he in fact find the country congenial?

Certainly, in his letters to Harley he did his best to give the impression that he disliked the Scots in general and the ministers of the Kirk in particular. 'They are a hardened, refractory and Terrible people,' he said of the ministers. 'Scrupulous and Positive' and, piling adjective on adjective, they were 'Unaccountable people, Humorous, Jealous, Partiall, Censorious, Haughty, Insolent, and Above all Monstrously Ignorant'. Of the aristocracy: 'I never Saw So

Much Trick, sham, pride, Jealousy, and Cutting of Friends Throats.'
The 'poorest and Meanest people' were 'Surly, Haughty, Vain'. He
explained to Harley that he had written a poem in praise of Scotland,
'an odd subject to bear a panegyrick', only to persuade the Scots that
he was a friend to their country. But how frank was he in all of this?
I suspect that it is to be taken in the same way as his constant harping
on the dangers and expenses of the job, his frenzied activity, his
successes in penetration, and his care to conceal his relationship with
the English Government. He was anxious to convince his uncertain
and irregular paymaster that he was earning his reward and that his
loyalties were in the right place.

There are good reasons to suppose that Defoe found Scotland
more congenial than he admitted to Harley. Some of his letters
to a friend, John Fransham, a linen-draper in Norwich, survive,
and in them Defoe tells a very different story: 'This people are a
Sober, Religious and Gallant Nation, the country good, the Soil in
most places capable of vast improvements and nothing wanting but
English Stocks, English Art and English Trade to make us all one
great people.' He said much the same in his *Tour Thro' the Whole
Island of Great Britain*. There was nothing wrong with the Scots if
only they would take Defoe's advice.

I think that James Sutherland is right when he says that Defoe's
'work in Scotland was the most satisfactory achievement in his
oddly private and obscure public life'. Defoe was a politician by
instinct; he had an urge to shape events and tell people what to
do. Edinburgh gave him his best opportunity. Never again was he
so close to the centre of great affairs. It indulged too his taste for
excitement, mystification and masquerade. In other ways he could
feel at home in Edinburgh. As a dissenter, Sutherland says, he was in
England 'something of an outsider all his life'. Presbyterianism was
dissent in England, but in Scotland the national Church. More than
this, there was much about the cast of Defoe's mind which would
have found a response in Edinburgh – his radicalism, rejection of
pretence, down-to-earth practicality and common sense, his range of
interests and seriousness of purpose. All of these are qualities more
native to the soil of Edinburgh than London.

It is therefore no surprise to find that Defoe tried to persuade
Harley to give him a permanent post in Scotland. At first, on 2
November 1706, he wrote to say that, as part of the deception, he
was pretending that he wanted to settle in Scotland. By 2 January
1707 he was asking in earnest: 'If nothing better can be found out
for me I Could Wish you will please to Settle me here after the
Unions. Perhaps I might do her Majestie a Service of One Sort
while I was in an office of a Different Face, but of that hereafter.'

On 21 May, his request was more straightforward: 'I Am Inform'd Sir the Custome house is Settled for this Country. Is there No Room for an Absent Servant to be admitted?' On 31 October, six months after the Union had come into force and Harley had left him without recall, instructions or funds, Defoe proposed a compromise: 'It is my Humble Opinion That the best way to Make me Truly Usefull in The Affair I am Upon is to have me be 8 Month here and 3 Months in London Each year. And the One Month Travailling between, Goeing Various Roads, I shall perhaps do More Service Than all the Rest.'

In the end, Defoe was disappointed in his hopes of respectable office. As is often the way in these matters, others who had done less gained the prizes. 'I know some,' Defoe said in *The Review*, 'that are gone to London to sollicit the Reward of what they had no hand in. I might have said, are gone to claim the Merit, of what I have been the single Author of.' His secret work in Scotland did not end when he eventually returned to London at the end of 1707. In February 1708, as a delayed consequence of the Greg affair, Harley fell from office, and Defoe was transferred to the service of Godolphin. He was back in Scotland in 1708 and 1709 to report on Jacobite intrigue. Few of his letters from this period have survived, and it must have been something of an anticlimax after the excitement of the Union debate. One paper which still exists is a well-argued case for the establishment of a naval base in the Forth estuary above Queensferry, advice which was eventually followed 200 years later when the Rosyth Dockyard was built. As always, he had his own business interests on the side. In 1709, he launched an Edinburgh edition of *The Review*, and the following year acquired two other newspapers there, the *Edinburgh Courant* and the *Scots Postman*. There are hints in his letters that his talk of setting up factories was more than part of his cover story.

What did Defoe achieve in Scotland? His barrage of pamphlets and the steady supporting fire of *The Review* were unlikely to have had much effect on the vote in the Scottish Parliament. The same members had been debating the same questions for four years and even Defoe could hardly hope to change their minds. The decisive shift in the balance of votes was achieved in the autumn of 1705, long before Defoe appeared on the scene, and by methods other than rational argument. He may, at the most, have reassured some waverers by his work in the committees on tax matters. There is no indication that his propaganda affected the people at large, but they were disregarded in any case. He probably helped to reconcile the ministers, 'the Rigid and Refractory Clergy, who are the worst Enemies of the Union', on whom he concentrated his efforts. But

I think that his real achievement went beyond any contribution he might have made to the approval of the Treaty. He was an enthusiast for the idea of a Union which was to be more than a political arrangement. 'Tis the Nature of Union,' he said in *The Review*, 'to preserve, not destroy; to secure, not endanger; to confirm, not undermine.' He believed, if few other Englishmen did, that England and Scotland both ceased to exist in 1707, as the Treaty said, and was replaced by a new enlarged entity of Britain, inhabited by 'one great people'. It was not his fault if the English stubbornly remained English and the Scots, if they tried a little harder to be British, remained Scots. He did not see that the Scots were unlikely to be attracted to his notion that the merging of the two nationalities could be achieved simply by the Scots adopting English ways. Where his approach may have had more permanent results was in his appeal for mutual tolerance and understanding between the two ancient enemies. That may now seem commonplace enough, but it is difficult to find any sign of it before Defoe.

(Blackwood's Magazine; October 1977;
No 1944: Vol. 322)

NOTE

1. The Dutch statesman who, along with his brother, was torn to pieces by a mob in the Hague in 1672.

2

'Bought and Sold for English Gold'

For an event which had such drastic and long-lasting consequences, it is astonishing how much ignorance and misunderstanding there is about the nature and causes of the Union of 1707. You might expect people to be curious about something so unusual and unexpected. How did it happen that a country, which had defended its independence for hundreds of years with determination and endurance, appear suddenly to surrender without much struggle?

Hume Brown, whose *History of Scotland* was for years the standard work, suggested that we had turned our eyes away by 'unconscious instinct' from a period which reflected so badly on our national reputation. He was referring of course to the humiliation of members of the Scottish Parliament yielding to bribery and intimidation and selling the independence of their country for paltry sums of money. Much of the evidence that this is indeed what happened became available only long after the event, but the facts were well enough known at the time and they lived in oral tradition. Robert Burns understood. As he wrote:

> 'We're bought and sold for English gold,
> Such a parcel of rogues in a nation.'

So did Sir Walter Scott. In his *Tales of a Grandfather* he expresses his outrage at the whole sordid business in strong language over more than thirty pages: 'a total surrender of their independence by false and corrupted statesmen despised by the English and detested by their own country'.

English historians, on the whole, have tended to focus more on their satisfaction at the outcome than enquire too closely into the methods. Recently the distinguished English historian, Christopher Hill, was honest enough to admit that 'Scotland was bribed and swindled into Union with England in 1707'. This is true as far as it goes, but how it came about is a fairly complex story.

Scotland had been disastrously weakened in 1603 when James VI, by a dynastic accident, became also King of England and departed to London. The loss of the royal court and royal patronage was a heavy blow to the prestige and prosperity of Edinburgh, but the political effects were even more serious. Scotland was still nominally independent with its own Parliament, Government and laws, but it now shared a king with England. He and his successors came increasingly under the influence of their English ministers. This mattered a great deal at that time because the monarch still exercised personally, or through his advisers, most of the executive functions of government. He made foreign policy, peace and war. All government income was collected and disbursed in his name. He made all government appointments, including the officers of state who were the ministers of the Scottish Government.

These senior officials were usually members of the Scottish nobility who formed more than a third of the one-chamber Scottish Parliament. Often they were rich in land, but poor in money and government appointments were the only way they could earn any. This made them dependent on the approval of the English court. They knew that their appointments were conditional on their accepting instructions from London.

The foreign policy carried out in the name of the king was English policy, on which Scotland was not consulted. Very often it was contrary to Scottish interests. English wars with the Low Countries and France, for instance, destroyed traditional Scottish trade. Scotland contributed men and money to these wars, but was forgotten again in the terms of the peace. Only very small forces were maintained in Scotland itself and by the end of the seventeenth century it was virtually without means of defence.

The 'Glorious Revolution' of 1688–89 restored to the Scottish Parliament freedom to discuss and resolve as it pleased; but its power was still largely nominal because the rest of the royal prerogatives remained in place. This suited England very well. By means of the joint monarchy they had achieved the domination over Scotland which had been their objective since the thirteenth century. Without the trouble of occupying the country they could prevent its becoming either a military threat or a rival in trade.

In Scotland, however, this semi-independence, which systematically frustrated Scotland from promoting her own interests, became increasingly intolerable. It was analysed with particular clarity by Andrew Fletcher of Saltoun, so robust a defender of the Scottish case that he has been known ever since as the Patriot. In his pamphlets and speeches in Parliament he described 'the miserable condition to which this nation is reduced by a dependence upon the English court' who treated it 'more like a conquered province than a free independent people'.

Matters came to a head over the Scottish colony at Darien. As King of Scotland, William assented to the Scottish Act which established the trading company. As King of England, he did his best to sabotage it and prevent it from raising capital in England or the Continent. In a great outburst of patriotic fervour, virtually everyone in Scotland with any savings invested them in the company. All of this was lost when the colony failed disastrously, partly because the site was ill-chosen and partly because of English hostility. To make matters worse, these events coincided with a series of poor harvests in Scotland between 1695 and 1699 which led to actual famine.

It was in this unhappy situation that a new Parliament was elected in Scotland in 1703, the Parliament which continued in being, meeting for a few months each summer, until it voted for its own dissolution in approving the Treaty of Union in 1707. To speak of an election is an exaggeration. Of the three estates who sat and voted together, the Lords were there by hereditary right, the representatives of the burghs were chosen by their self-perpetuating closed corporations, and those of the shires by the lairds out of their own number. Parliament in Scotland, as everywhere at the time, therefore represented only an infinitely small part of the population.

When this Parliament first met in May 1703 it immediately turned its attention to the most pressing problem of the time which, then as now, was the constitutional position of Scotland. Events in England had presented an opportunity of escape from subordination to the English court. When Queen Anne succeeded to the throne in 1702, all her children had died and she was unlikely to have any others. The English Parliament had solved the succession to their satisfaction by an Act which settled it on Sophia of Hanover and her issue. Not for the first or last time, they had forgotten about Scotland or taken it for granted. Scotland had not been consulted and was in no sense bound by the English Act.

The Queen's letter to the new Scottish Parliament therefore asked, apart from the supply of money, for their acceptance of the same succession as in the English Act. Parliament did not propose to yield. Fletcher proposed that either Scotland should choose a different successor or, if the same one, then all power should be effectively transferred from the Crown to Parliament itself. The Act of Security, which eventually emerged, included the substance of Fletcher's proposals. It provided that the Scottish successor to Anne was not to be the same as the English, unless conditions of government had been established which secured Scottish independence 'free from English or any foreign influence'. Also, men of military age were to be armed and trained.

In face of this resounding declaration of independence, the court and their chief representative in Scotland, the Duke of Queensberry as Commissioner, had lost control. They refused royal assent to the Act and continued their efforts to recruit more support through patronage. As an example, Seton of Pitmedden, who became one of the most skilful debaters on the side of the court, sold his services for a pension of £100 a year. The longer a Parliament lasted, the better chance the court had to buy votes in this way.

In the following session of 1704 the court tried again with a new Commissioner, the Marquis of Tweeddale. They failed again and Parliament passed once more the same Act of Security. This time it was given royal assent on the advice of the English Treasurer, and effectively first Minister, Godolphin, probably because he was anxious that the Scottish Parliament should vote supply.

At this point the English Parliament reacted and there was talk of war. There was bound to be Jacobite resistance to the Hanoverian sucession and an independent Scotland in alliance with France could become a threat. Both Houses passed the Aliens Act, an ultimatum with sanctions. Unless Scotland accepted the same succession by 25 December 1705, Scots would be treated as aliens in England and made incapable of inheriting property. The import of Scottish cattle, sheep, coal and linen (the main articles of trade) would be prohibited. The Act also authorised the Queen to appoint commissioners to 'treat and consult' with Scotland 'concerning the union of the two kingdoms'.

Union had been discussed many times since 1603, usually on the personal insistence of the monarch, without much enthusiasm from any one else. There was no expectation in 1705 that it was any more likely to come to anything than in the past. It was also a vague term, capable of many interpretations. Much confusion has been caused by the curious failure of historians to notice that the words, 'union', 'treaty' and 'federal' (a word which the Scots were about to use) were generally used in the early eighteenth century in different senses from those which they have since acquired. Union meant an association of any kind for any common purpose or simply the absence of discord or dissension. 'Treaty' very often meant negotiation as distinct from agreement. 'Federal' (from the Latin word for treaty) meant only pertaining to an agreement or treaty. There was therefore not necessarily anything new or alarming about this aspect of the English Act.

In the 1705 session of the Scottish Parliament the Commissioner was the Duke of Argyll. The Queen's message once again asked for the settlement of succession and supply but added a recommendation of union as a means of composing the differences between the two nations. For two months Parliament insisted on discussing other matters, including once again Fletcher's ideas for the limitation of royal power. In August the House was at length brought to discuss the English proposal for negotiations on union, providing their insulting ultimatum was withdrawn. A clause designed to safeguard independence was defeated by two votes. There was a startling turn of events on 1 September. The Duke of Hamilton, who led the opposition, had assured his followers that there would be no vote that day. After many of them had left the House, he suddenly proposed that the nomination of commissioners should be left to the Queen. The court party seized the opportunity and it was so decided.

This was not the last time that Hamilton deliberately sabotaged the efforts of his own side. Indeed the English historian, G.M. Trevelyan, says not unreasonably that he was the chief instrument of the 'almost miraculous' passage of the Union, but he does not explain why he behaved with such duplicity. In fact, there is plenty of evidence that he too had been bribed and that he was consciously playing a double game. For example, James Johnstone, Lord Clerk Register, who was in a good position to know, wrote from London on 13 January 1705: 'I have had suspicions, but now I am certain, that Duke Hamilton is tampering by means of Harley with the Lord Treasurer . . . He must have his debts payed.'

Hamilton's action meant, of course, that there was now no possibility of a genuine negotiation, since both teams would be picked by the English court. Only one man was included on the Scottish side who was not already one of their supporters. He was George Lockhart of Carnwath, who was included because he was related by marriage to one of the English Whig Lords who hoped to win him over. This attempt failed but it gave Lockhart a ring-side seat which he put to good use in writing his *Memoirs*, the fullest and frankest contemporary account of the events which led to the Union.

The so-called negotiations in London lasted from 16 April to 22 July 1706. At first, the Scots made a token stand in favour of a federal arrangement, by which they meant an agreement between the two kingdoms which would preserve the independence and separate Parliaments of both. The English refused to discuss anything but what was now called an 'incorporating union', in which the two kingdoms would become one with one and the same parliament. From the nature of the Scottish delegation it is not surprising that they capitulated at once. 'You see that what we are to treat of is not in our choice', the Scottish Secretary of State, the Earl of Mar, wrote to William Carstares in Edinburgh.

The Treaty which resulted still required the approval of both Parliaments. It purported to abolish both Scotland and England and replace them with a new entity, Great Britain, with one and the same British Parliament. In fact, the English Parliament and everything else in England was to continue undisturbed, apart from the addition of a few Scottish members. Scotland was to have forty-five members in the Commons. England, which then had five times the population, had 513 and Cornwall alone forty-four. The Scottish Lords were no longer to have a place by right in Parliament, but sixteen of them were to be elected to sit in the Lords.

This reduction of Scotland to political impotence was a bitter pill to swallow, but it was sweetened by a number of measures skilfully designed to appeal to the selfish interests of the classes represented in the Scottish Parliament. The Scottish legal system, the rights of the Royal Burghs and the hereditary jurisdictions of the landowners were all preserved. The Lords were given all the privileges of the English Peers, except an automatic seat in the Lords, but including exemption of imprisonment for debt, which was of more practical use to many of them. Most ingenious of all was the 'Equivalent', a sum of £398,065 10 shillings. This was to compensate Scotland for accepting liability for a share of the English National Debt, but it was also simultaneously to serve a number of other purposes, creative accounting of a high order. The first call on the money was to repay, with interest, the share holders of the Darien company. Since probably most members of the Scottish Parliament had been impoverished by the collapse of the company, this was a very strong inducement. Then the Equivalent was to be repaid from the imposition of English customs and excise duties on Scotland. As Sir Walter Scott wrote: 'In fact, the Parliament of Scotland was bribed with the public money belonging to their own country. In this way, Scotland herself was made to pay the price given to her legislators for the sacrifice of her independence'.

The Treaty was received in Scotland with outrage and indignation. In Parliament, with Queensberry again as Commissioner, the debate lasted from 3 October 1706 to 16 January 1707, against a background of continuous public protest. Parishes and burghs all over Scotland petitioned against the Union, and so did the Convention of Royal Burghs on behalf of the trading community. Even the leaders of the court party admitted in their private correspondence that the great majority of the people were utterly opposed to the Treaty.

In the course of the debate the opposition of the Kirk was countered by an Act, considered as an integral part of the Union, which guaranteed the Church of Scotland for all time. A group of Lords who had previously supported Fletcher were won over on the understanding (subsequently ignored) that they would have charge of the distribution of the Equivalent. £20,000 were sent up from London to buy a few more votes. In the end, the Treaty was approved. Fletcher is reported to have said that the country was now fit only for the slaves who had sold it.

The episode of the £20,000 was afterwards discovered by George Lockhart when he was a member of a parliamentary enquiry as a member of the new British Parliament. It was confirmed many years later when a letter from the Earls of Glasgow and Seafield came to light. They certified that they could not give details of the disbursement without bringing the management of Parliament into discredit. They end with the request that Queensberry (who had the largest share) should burn the letter after he had read it to the Lord Treasurer. Godolphin evidently insisted on keeping it as a receipt because it remained in his family papers until they were sold to the British Museum in 1892.

But the members who voted for the Treaty had another excuse, the threat of invasion. Already in July 1703 Godolphin sent a polite, but unmistakable, threat of military intervention to Seafield. He reminded him that England had greatly increased in wealth and power and this was at a time when Scotland was impoverished and defenceless. The English Government sent troops to the border during the final debate. Some years afterwards Sir John Clerk of Penicuik (who had been reluctantly recruited to the Union side by his patron, Queensberry) recorded his view that the main reason for the acceptance of the Treaty was that otherwise the country would have fallen under English domination by right of conquest.

It certainly had little to do with trade. If anything, such considerations pulled in the opposite direction. Many of the petitions against the Union argued that it would be highly damaging to Scottish trade. They were right. It took Scotland about forty years before she began to recover by her own exertions from the effects of the Union. The theory that Scotland had bargained away her independence for access to a wider market was invented about 1850 by Hill Burton and Macaulay who were trying to find a respectable explanation.

The Treaty of Union was not a bargain of any kind. It was a fake negotiation and an imposition by a strong country on a smaller neighbour when it was particularly weak and vulnerable. It was a ruthless and calculating application of power to secure the northern border of England and keep Scotland in subjection. It was not accepted by the Scottish people, who made their rejection of it very clear, but by an unrepresentative Parliament which was bribed and intimidated into submission.

(*Chapman*, No. 69, Autumn 1992.)

3

Andrew Fletcher, a Scottish Pioneer
of the European Idea

Andrew Fletcher of Saltoun, who lived from 1653 to 1716, has long been known in Scotland quite simply as 'the Patriot'. This is a distinction accorded to no one else in Scottish history, not even to Wallace or Bruce. It is a recognition of the courage, integrity and determination with which Fletcher struggled to defend the independence of Scotland during the five years of debate, intimidation and pressure which led to the ratification of the Treaty of Union in 1707. Fletcher's qualities were all the more outstanding because English intimidation and bribery were so pervasive and because so many other members of the Scottish Parliament succumbed.

Fletcher did not cultivate popularity. He had a quick temper and did not conceal his scorn for people who failed to meet his own high intellectual and moral standards. Even so, he was almost universally admired by his contemporaries, including political opponents. One of his political allies, George Lockhart of Carnwath, said that any man who wished to 'serve and merit well of his country' should take Fletcher's 'courage, zeal and constancy as a pattern' and think himself sufficiently rewarded if he obtained the character of being like Andrew Fletcher of Saltoun. John Macky, a Hanoverian agent and about as far removed politically from Lockhart as possible, praised Fletcher's courage, learning, honour and principles and concluded that he would 'lose his life readily to serve his country; and would not do a base thing to save it'. Somewhat later, David Hume described Fletcher as 'a man of signal probity and fine genius'. Sir Walter Scott said that he was 'one of the most accomplished men and best patriots that Scotland has produced in any age'.

More recently, Fletcher has acquired an additional reputation as a bold and original thinker and as an important contributor to the development of political ideas. Several of his contemporaries said that he was a republican. Although Fletcher said that a hereditary monarch was as absurd as a hereditary professor would be, he did not so much advocate the abolition of monarchy as the transfer of its powers to Parliament. We have still not achieved this because, under the British system, many of the secretive and irresponsible powers of the royal prerogative are now exercised, not by Parliament, but by Ministers. The future Prime Minister, Ramsay MacDonald, as a young journalist, in an article which he wrote in 1893, recognised that Fletcher in one of his pamphlets had sketched a rudimentary outline of the welfare state. It was this pamphlet which caused the first breach in the virtually unanimous approval of Fletcher. It led T. B. Macaulay, in his *History of England*, first published in the middle of the nineteenth century, to denounce Fletcher for advocating slavery. In this he has been gratefully followed by more recent writers, anxious for their own political purposes to find an excuse to attack Fletcher. The great historian had failed, in this one instance at least, to take account of the circumstances and the climate of ideas in which Fletcher wrote.

Still more recently, historians of political ideas, mainly in America, have rediscovered Fletcher as an essential link in the evolution of thought in the Aristotelean and Florentine humanist tradition. They regard him as having a clearer understanding than any of his predecessors of the nature of the modern state and of the importance of economic factors. Fletcher's ideas on this last point led directly to the economic theories of David Hume and Adam Smith. This is not the only respect in which Fletcher's ideas can be seen as one of the foundations of the Scottish Enlightenment.

Fletcher's ideas on international relations were even more revolutionary. He was far ahead of his time in advocating international co-operation in place of rivalry and hostility. As far as I know he was the first advocate, in the interests of peace, prosperity and cultural diversity, of a European-wide system of small, autonomous, but interdependent, countries. He followed the ancient Scottish tradition of study and work in other countries in Europe, although in his case it was mainly as a political exile. The great library, which he collected throughout his life, systematically included books on every European country. He was familiar with many of the languages and wrote one of his pamphlets in Italian.

Andrew Fletcher succeeded his father as Laird of Saltoun, in East Lothian, not far from Edinburgh, when he was only twelve. The estate of fine farming land was prosperous and produced a good income. Lairds were a powerful class in Scotland socially and politically, at least until they began to be displaced by the industrialists and businessmen in the nineteenth century. A law of 1567 provided for the lairds in each shire to elect one or two of their number to represent the shire in Parliament. They were very often lay members as elders in the General Assembly of the Church of Scotland at a time when it played a central role in the affairs of Scotland. They had responsibilities for the upkeep of the local church and manse, the roads, the school and poor relief. Most of the advocates and judges, often the backbone of the intellectual life of the country, were lairds or the sons or brothers of lairds.

They also tended to be well educated. As early as 1496 an Act of Parliament in the reign of James IV required the eldest sons of barons and freeholders to be sent to grammar school from the age of eight or nine, to remain there until they had 'perfite latyne' and then spend three years at university to acquire knowledge of the law. Very often this education included a period of study in France, Holland or Germany. Early in the nineteenth century, Dugald Stewart, Professor of Moral Philosophy in Edinburgh University and one of the most celebrated university professors of his time, wrote this explanation of the astonishing outburst of intellectual enquiry in the Scotland of the eighteenth century, the Scottish Enlightenment:

> It deserves to be remarked, as a circumstance which throws considerable light on the literary history of Scotland during the latter half of the eighteenth century, that, from time immemorial, a continued intercourse had been kept up between Scotland and the Continent. To all who were destined for the profession of law, an education either at a Dutch or French university was considered as almost essential. The case was nearly the same in the profession of physic; and, even among the Scottish clergy, I have conversed, in my youth, with some old men who had studied theology in Holland or in Germany. Of our smaller country gentlemen, resident on their own estates, (an order of men which, from various causes, has now, alas! totally vanished,) there was scarcely one who had not enjoyed the benefit of a university education and very few of those who could afford the expense of foreign travel, who had not visited France and Italy. Lord Monboddo somewhere mentions, to the honour of his father, that he sold part of his estate to enable himself [his eldest son] to pursue his studies at the University of Groningen. The constant influx of information and of liberality from abroad, which was thus kept up in Scotland in consequence of the ancient habits and manners of the people, may help to account for the sudden burst of genius, which to a foreigner must seem to have sprung up in this country by a sort of enchantment, soon after the Rebellion of 1745.

Fletcher's early education was in good hands because his father in the last years of his life appointed a remarkable man as tutor to his sons and a companion to himself in his own favourite studies of mathematics and philosophy. This was Gilbert Burnet, afterwards in turn Professor of Theology in Glasgow, chaplain to King William and Bishop of Salisbury. He was a man of great energy and liberal principles and he had enlighted ideas on education. Among other books he wrote *A History of My Own Times*, one of the liveliest of historical memoirs, which is an important source of information on the period.

From this point onwards there are gaps in our knowledge of Fletcher's activities. His part in the sessions of the Scottish Parliament from 1678 to 1682 and from 1703 to 1707 is well documented in the letters and memoirs of others. Apart from that, we have very little solid information. The family papers of the Fletchers of Saltoun are now in the National Library of Scotland, but there is a conspicuous gap for the member of the family in which we are most interested. This is almost certainly because his papers were sent to Jean Jacques Rousseau. He had promised both George Keith and James Boswell that he would write a life of Fletcher, and Boswell undertook to supply him with information. A family memoir independently confirms that papers were sent to him.

We do not even have definite evidence of where Fletcher continued his education after Burnet left Saltoun for Glasgow in 1669. Such information as we have suggests that he went first to the University of Edinburgh and then to Leyden in Holland. Leyden was popular with Scots in Fletcher's position and it seems to have been a tradition in the family. At about this time he seems to have had military experience, because we find that a few years later he was regarded as an accomplished cavalry officer.

What we do know for certain is that he was back in Scotland in 1678 when he was one of the two Commissioners for the Shire of Haddington or East Lothian in a Convention of the Estates which first met in June of that year. This was an unhappy time in Scotland when the Duke of Lauderdale, as High Commissioner for Charles II, had been given a free hand to rule the country in a high-handed and despotic manner. He used imprisonment, quartering of troops and confiscation of estates as means of intimidation.

The object was to restore royal power over the Church and State as though the Civil War had never happened and as though the Scottish Parliament had not gained the authority which it had asserted in 1641. The key debate in the Convention was on the Test Act which required everyone in public office to take an oath which renounced all resistance to the will of the King. It was deliberately reduced to a hotch potch of nonsense and self-contradiction by some ingenious amendments. Even so, it passed and the official record makes only one admission of dissent: 'The Laird of Saltoun and the Laird of Grant having noted in the Negative desired their dissent might be marked'.

Fletcher kept up his dissent not only in words, but in deeds. He, and other lairds of East Lothian, were in trouble in the courts for refusing to comply with requests for the quartering of troops of the royal militia and the supply of forage to them. This resistance to royal authority was dangerous. The Earl of Argyll, for instance, was sentenced to death for treason merely for taking the test oath only 'as far as it was consistent with itself'. He escaped from Edinburgh Castle in disguise and made his way to Holland. Fletcher and many others joined him there.

For about the next three years, 1682 to 1685, Fletcher was one of a group of political refugees from Scotland and England who had gathered in Holland around William of Orange to work for the removal of James VII and II from the throne. There was a premature attempt in June 1685 when Monmouth, an illegitimate son of Charles II, landed in south-west England in a desperate attempt to seize the kingdom. Fletcher, against his better judgement, went with them and was expected to take charge of the cavalry. His part in the affair lasted only a few hours. He was unfortunate enough, probably by accident, to shoot the Mayor of Taunton in a quarrel over a horse. Since the unfortunate Mayor was an influential man in the locality, it was thought prudent to send Fletcher away in one of the ships from which the expedition had landed. This was just as well, because otherwise he would probably have been either killed in the Battle of Sedgemoor or sentenced to death by the notorious Judge Jeffries. As it was, he was condemned as a traitor *in absentia* by the Court in Edinburgh and his estates were confiscated.

Fletcher was therefore once again a political refugee for another three years. We have very little information about his activities during these periods of exile. He is said to have been imprisoned in Spain and to have fought in the Hungarian Army against the Turks. To some extent, he was on an extended Grand Tour. He certainly collected books. His library was one of the finest in Scotland and it included books from all over Europe. We know this because among his few papers in his own hand which have survived are two manuscript catalogues of his books. The Greek and Latin classics are, of course, strongly represented, but there are also books in Italian, French, Spanish and Dutch as well as English. There are books of poetry, history, theology, law, physics, mathematics, political thought and military science. The country sections on France, Spain and especially Italy are the most numerous. It seems safe to conclude that Fletcher had spent much time in these three countries and had made a particular study of them.

On the evidence of his library catalogues and of his own writings, it is apparent that Fletcher was very well informed indeed on the history, culture and political evolution of virtually the whole of Europe. He obviously read widely and thought deeply about European affairs. He was also, of course, directly involved both in military matters and in the political intrigues of the political exiles in the circles around Monmouth and William of Orange.

When Fletcher came to write about Europe, he knew what he was talking about.

Fletcher returned from his second period of exile in the entourage of William of Orange at the end of 1688. This is the so-called 'Glorious Revolution' because, unlike the Monmouth fiasco, it succeeded in putting William and Mary on the throne and was without bloodshed. The English accepted them as monarchs with the polite evasion that James VII and II had abdicated. The Scots, a little later, also accepted them on the throne of Scotland, but with a more robust Claim of Right in which they roundly proclaimed that James had been deposed because of his arbitrary misuse of power. In both kingdoms the settlement meant a strengthening of parliamentary authority over the royal prerogatives. Even so, substantial personal power still remained with the monarch, including the appointment of state officials, even those in charge of the Government of Scotland. It was this very substantial remnant of royal power which was shortly to provoke a constitutional crisis in Scotland, but it was power exercised from London, on the advice of English Ministers and invariably in the interest of England.

Andrew Fletcher was now back in Scotland, with his conviction for treason annulled, but not yet restored to his estates, and therefore not eligible for election to Parliament. There was a delay of more than a year over this and Fletcher was naturally impatient. 'You can tell King William from me', he said to the Duke of Hamilton, 'that he has not so good a right to his crown as I have to my estate'. 'Devil take me,' Hamilton replied, 'if it be not true.' Fletcher, as this remark illustrates, was not impressed by hereditary Kings. He believed, too, in curbing the power of the nobility; but he never seems to have questioned the right of his own order, the lairds, to the ownership of their estates nor to their important role in the state. On this point, Fletcher accepted the conventional wisdom of his time, although he did suggest that the lairds should accept very wide responsibilities for the welfare of their workers.

It was at this juncture, between his return to Scotland in 1688 and his election to Parliament in 1703, that Fletcher began to write the essays which, along with his speeches in the Parliament of 1703, are the works on which his reputation as a political thinker rests. They were published separately as short pamphlets during his lifetime, but published together as *The Political Works of Andrew Fletcher of Saltoun* only in 1732, sixteen years after his death. There were three subsequent editions in the eighteenth century and no other until David Daiches edited a selection (which was nearly complete) in 1974 for the Association for Scottish Literary Studies.

The *Political Works* make a slender volume, 136 pages in the

Daiches edition, which may seem a frail foundation for the reputation which Fletcher has achieved. Other works have been attributed to him, although few that can be accepted with much confidence. When I edited *State of the Controversy Betwixt United and Separate Parliaments* for the Saltire Society in 1982, I said that I thought we should accept it as Fletcher's on the strong authority of his nephew and of Thomas Rudiman, a great scholar who was a contemporary of Fletcher's and the Librarian of the Advocates' Library. It certainly has some brilliant phrases, 'flashes as quick as lightening', as Sir John Dalrymple called them, which sound like Fletcher. But there are also some other remarks, including sycophantic references to the Queen, which I am sure Fletcher could never have brought himself to utter. So even this pamphlet, I now think, could at best be a collaborative effort in which Fletcher played a part.

One of the distinguishing features of Fletcher's writing, and it is a large part of the explanation why so few pages have been so influential, is its economy. There is no padding and hardly a wasted word. Very often he stated an idea, which may be significant and original, in a sentence or two or even a phrase. There is often more substance in a page of Fletcher's writing than in whole volumes by more laborious but less original thinkers. He writes in an easy, fluent, idiomatic English, remarkable in a Scotsman of his time, when everyone outside the Highland line spoke Scots and educated men were more familiar with written Latin than spoken English.

One of the first of these pamphlets, *A Discourse concerning the Affairs of Spain*, was written, according to its title page, in July 1698. It was not included in the Daiches edition for the reasons, I suppose, that it stands outside the main body of Fletcher's work and is concerned with different subjects. It stood outside most obviously because it was written in Italian and purported to be published in Naples, although with the same paper and type as the other pamphlets published in Edinburgh. Why this mystification? The essay dealt with the European-wide problem of the consequences that were likely to follow from the imminent death of Charles II, King of Spain, who had no issue and no undisputed successor. There was a risk that the vast territories of the Spanish Empire might fall into the hands of the King of France and so create an immense power that could dominate the world. The Italian states were pawns in any possible settlement. Fletcher may therefore have felt that the pamphlet would have more influence if it appeared to come from an Italian source. John Robertson has suggested that Fletcher was reacting to a book, of which he had a copy in his library, *De Monarchia Hispanica* by Tommaso Campanella. This was a plea for a universal empire under the

King of Spain, which was precisely what Fletcher was anxious
to oppose.

He went about this task in a spirit of Swiftian irony, a technique
which is open to misunderstanding. In his essay Fletcher discussed
the various ways in which the succession to Charles II could lead
to a world empire. The unwary reader might easily suppose that
he was advocating it. Fletcher seems to have realised this after the
publication of the first edition, because he added an explanatory
note, or 'advertisement' in the language of the day, to the subsequent
English translation. In this he said that he had written the essay about
the risk of 'progress towards the empire of the world':

> not with a view of favouring the establishment of a government so
> hurtful to good manners, and so destructive of the general happiness
> of mankind, as a universal one is, and as all great ones, whether
> republics or monarchies, in which power and riches are grown to
> an excessive height, cannot fail to be.

In the essay itself, he criticised Spain both because of the ruthless
slaughter of the native populations of South America and because
of their policy in the Low Countries:

> the violation of the ancient privileges of these countries, by attempting
> to introduce an absolute form of government, and the inquisi-
> tion, was an extremely foolish measure, which, together with the
> cruelty of the Duke of Alva, rendered the inhabitants of them
> most obstinate enemies.

Already, then, from this essay, one of his earliest, we see Fletcher
emerging as a man who thought on a European scale and had
strong convictions about Europe. The essay suggests not only wide
reading, but direct observations. When he speaks, for instance, of
the 'most fertile, delightful fields' of Seville or the shelter of the Bay
of Tangier and 'the fruitful country around it', you have a distinct
feeling that he has been to these places. The essay also shows his
distrust of large and powerful states and his regard for what he calls
'ancient privileges', or what we should probably call the distinctive
culture and institutions of the smaller countries. He thought that
human happiness was served better by small countries than by large
and powerful ones. The history of Europe has constantly proved
how right he was.

From the beginning, Fletcher's European ideas and his concern
for 'the general happiness of mankind' are entirely consistent with
his views on the constitution and government of Scotland and his
defence of Scottish independence. It was this defence, even if it
was unsuccessful in his own time, to which most of his thought,

energies and emotions were devoted in the years when his powers were at their height. It was of this period that George Lockhart of Carnwath wrote:

> The thoughts of England's domineering over Scotland, was what his generous soul could not away with. The indignities and oppression Scotland lay under, gaul'd him to the heart; so that in his learned and elaborate discourses he exposed them with undaunted courage and pathetick elegance. He was blessed with a soul that hated and despised whatever was mean and unbecoming a gentleman, as was so stedfast to what he thought right, that no hazard nor advantage, no not the universal empire, nor the gold of America, could tempt him to yield or desert it.

The arena in which Fletcher earned such praise as this was, of course, the Scottish Parliament elected (to the very limited extent to which Parliaments were elected at that time) with Fletcher as a Member in 1703. It continued in being and met annually for several months in each of the four years which followed until it finally approved the Treaty of Union and adjourned on 16 January 1707. It has not yet met again since that day. The long life of this particular Parliament is a point of some relevance, because it was recognised at the time that the longer a Parliament stayed in being, the more opportunity the government had to win over a majority by the arts of 'management'. That meant bribery and persuasion by money, pension, office and promises or threats of various kinds. It was a skill that played a decisive part in the events which led to the Union.

It was against this background that the courage and integrity of Fletcher stood out as clearly as the power and logic of his arguments. These events are not well known. The historian Hume Brown, who was a Unionist, has suggested that this is because people have averted their eyes by an unconscious instinct from such a sordid affair. English historians have not chosen to dwell on the unpleasant spectacle of a larger country acting the bully with bribes and threats against a smaller neighbour. In Scotland we have had even less stomach to face up to the fact that our parliamentarians, especially the heads of ancient noble families, accepted the bribes and yielded to the threats. In the whole of the nineteenth century and most of the twentieth, Sir Walter Scott was almost the only historian who had the courage to admit the facts.

It is true that the Scottish nobility were particularly vulnerable to this sort of pressure. They had titles, vast estates and great houses, but few sources of money except from government appointments. All of these appointments, including the Offices of State in the Scottish Government, were in the gift of a monarch in London who acted on the advice of English Ministers. 'What less can be expected, unless we resolve to expect miracles,' said Fletcher in one of his speeches, 'but that greedy, ambitious, and for the most part necessitious men, involved in great debts, burdened with great families, and having great titles to support, will lay down their places, rather than comply with an English interest in obedience to the prince's commands?'

Fletcher was, of course, by no means alone. It was agreed on all sides, including the Government, that the great majority of the Scottish people were utterly opposed to the Union. In Parliament, many members stood out for the Scottish cause throughout these years of pressure. In the final vote on the Treaty, there was a comfortable majority of the nobles- 42 for and 19 against. With the other estates (for all three sat together in the Scottish Parliament), the division was very close: Shires (that is to say the lairds of whom Fletcher was one) 38 for and 30 against; Burghs, 30 for and 20 against.

The Scottish Parliament of 1703 was faced with a constitutional issue, which continued to occupy most of its time for the next five years. It had become increasingly clear to everyone that the state of semi-independence to which Scotland had been reduced in 1603 was intolerable. Scotland had a Parliament which from 1689 was again free to debate and decide as it wished; but it was subject to a very severe impediment. Scotland and England both had the same monarch and he or she lived in London and inevitably acted under predominantly English influence. The monarch still had very real power, not only over all appointments as I have said, but over the disposal of government revenue, the conduct of foreign policy and the making of peace and war. All Acts of the Scottish Parliament were subject to royal consent. Scotland was obliged to provide men and money for wars fought in the English interest which damaged the traditional foreign trade of Scotland. When peace was made, no regard was paid to Scottish interests. All of this came to a head at the end of the seventeenth century when William, as King of Scotland, consented to the Act establishing the Scottish Company of the Darien Scheme. As King of England he exerted himself at home and abroad to sabotage it as a potential rival to English trading interests.

There was a second set of reasons. All of Queen Anne's children had died and she was unlikely to have any others. The English Parliament, without consulting Scotland, had passed the Act of Succession in 1701 settling the English Crown after the death of Anne on the Electress of Hanover and her descendants. Scotland was in no sense bound by this Act and could therefore now choose a different successor and return to full independence.

This was the situation which faced the Scottish Parliament of 1703. It was dominated by the ideas and personality of Andrew Fletcher. In a series of speeches he analysed the consequences of the shared monarchy with unmistakable clarity and proposed a solution. Either Scotland should choose a separate successor to the Scottish throne or all effective power should be transferred from the monarchy to Parliament. This was to be done by subjecting royal power to twelve limitations, under which the monarchy would have become, as it is now, a mere symbol. Fletcher's ideas were substantially adopted by Parliament and embodied in an Act of Security. The parliamentary session was a triumphant assertion of the spirit of Scottish independence against all that the Government could do to prevent it. George Ridpath, who wrote a book about the 1703 session, said that 'The memory of this Parliament will be precious for the Nation, so long as it has a being'.

Fletcher's speeches in the 1703 Session of Parliament were printed in two editions that year and in George Ridpath's book. They eventually appeared also in the posthumous collection of Fletcher's writings. None of his speeches in the subsequent sessions was printed, as far as we can now discover and we do not know why. Perhaps the Government found some way to prevent it. Daniel Defoe, who came to Scotland in 1706 as an English agent, spy and propagandist, wrote a long *History of the Union* in which he did not mention Fletcher at all, an obvious propagandist device to dispose of his most formidable opponent. These two facts, the absence of printed texts and of any reference in Defoe's *History*, have persuaded some historians that Fletcher took no further part in the debates after 1703. Nothing can be further from the truth. All the other sources, a diary kept by a Member of the Parliament, letters from the Officers of State to their masters in London and the like, show that Fletcher continued his struggle for Scottish independence to the bitter end.

Royal consent was withheld from the Act of Security in 1703, but the Scottish Parliament passed it again in the session of 1704. Faced with this determination, the Queen, on the advice of the English Lord Treasurer, Godolphin, this time assented and the Act became law. The English Parliament now realised that Scotland had served notice that it intended to escape from English indirect control. They reacted swiftly by passing the Aliens Act, which threatened to treat all Scots as aliens and incapable of inheriting property in England, and to ban the import from Scotland of the principal items of trade, if Scotland had not accepted the same successor to the throne by 25 December 1705. The same Act provided for the appointment of Commissioners to treat for a union between the two kingdoms, provided Scotland did the same. The word, union, at that time meant any form of agreement, and the Scots had long been perfectly ready to enter into negotiations to discuss outstanding difficulties between the two countries. It was only later that it became apparent that by union the English now meant the incorporation of the two Parliaments into one with the Scots in a permanent and helpless minority. If they could no longer control Scotland by one means, they would control it by another.

How was it, you might ask, that the Scottish Parliament, which had been so assertive of Scottish independence in 1703 and 1704, was brought to accept so unequal an arrangement by January 1707? Was it because of a desire on the part of the Presbyterians to reduce the chances of a Jacobite restoration of an Episcopalian or Catholic King? On the contrary, the Church of Scotland was deeply anxious over an arrangement which would subject Scotland to an Anglican Parliament, where the Bishops alone in the House of Lords would outnumber the sixteen representative Peers which was all that Scotland was to be allowed. Was it a bargain over trade, as nineteenth–century historians suggested long after the event? On the contrary the Scottish trading interests, as well as burghs and communities all over Scotland, petitioned against the Treaty, among other reasons, because it would greatly damage Scottish trade. They were right. It cost the Scots two generations before they began to recover economically by their own efforts from the effects of a flood of English exports and the imposition of regulations and excise duties designed for English, and not Scottish, conditions.

What then was the explanation? One was the bribery of the Members of the Scottish Parliament, and of this there is ample and undeniable evidence. The most devastating example of this was the Duke of Hamilton, who posed as the leader of the opposition in the Scottish Parliament and as such was cheered whenever he appeared on the Edinburgh streets. On four separate occasions Hamilton sabotaged the oppostion at decisive stages in the debate. The most crucial was in 1705 when he suddenly proposed, after many of his supporters had left the House at the end of a long sitting, that the appointment of the Scottish Commissioners (that is negotiators) should be left to the Queen. The Government seized the opportunity. It meant that the negotiation of the Treaty was a fake negotiation between two sets of Government place-men.

The Treaty so contrived was skilfully designed to appeal to the vested interests of the classes represented in the Scottish Parliament. The hereditary jurisdictions of the nobility and lairds, the courts of the Scots lawyers and the rights of the burghs were all safeguarded. Above all the shareholders in the Darien Company were to be compensated. This was to be done out of a fund known as the Equivalent, which was also simultaneously said to be compensation to the Scots for accepting responsibility for a share of the English national debt. It was also, in any case, to be repaid by an increase in the excise duty on the beer, wine and spirits drunk by the people at large. In other words, as Sir Walter Scott remarked, the Scottish people were bribed with their own money. The English civil servants of the time were ingenious.

Behind all of this was the implied threat that the alternative to the acceptance of the Treaty was an invasion by England and the imposition of worse terms. Scotland had virtually no defence forces. England had at their disposal troops seasoned in the continental wars under the command of Marlborough, the most successful general of his day in Europe. This was probably the most decisive reason of all.

These then were the pressures against which Fletcher fought with resource, passion, intelligence and conviction. There is a story, with the ring of truth about it, that he left at the end of the last debate with the bitter remark that Scotland was now fit only for the slaves who had sold it.

It was at a happier stage in the debate, at the end of the successful session of 1703, that Fletcher wrote his most polished essay and the one in which he made his most significant remarks about European co-operation. The title is *An Account of a Conversation concerning A Right Regulation of Governments for the Common Good of Mankind* and it purports to be a letter from London on 1 December 1703. I say 'purports' because the conversation which it describes was probably largely imaginary, although it may have been based on one which actually took place. The participants were all real people, two Members of the Scottish, and two of the English, Parliaments. Apart from Fletcher himself, the other Scot was the Earl of Cromartie, one of the very few people in Scotland who from the beginning were enthusiastically in favour of an incorporating Union. Of the two Englishmen, Sir Christopher Musgrave was a high Tory of solid reputation and the leader of his party. The other, Sir Edward Seymour, was also a prominent House of Commons man who had been Speaker during the reign of Charles II. He was virulently anti-Scottish. In the dialogue, Fletcher attributes to him a remark which he did in fact make in the Commons: 'What a pother is here about a union with Scotland, of which all the advantage we shall have, will be no more than what a man gets by marrying a beggar, a louse for her portion?'.

The conversation begins with some preliminary pleasantries about London. It soon turns to constitutional matters when Seymour arrives and immediately launches an attack on Fletcher over his proposals for 'limitations'. Cromartie suggests an incorporating Union, although this had not so far been proposed in either Parliament. Fletcher vigorously defends Scotland's independence against any proposal to reduce it to what he calls, 'the miserable and languishing condition of all places that depend upon a remote seat of government'.

In the course of this discussion, Fletcher said that he was opposed to 'great and overgrown powers' which tended to corruption and which caused wars and great effusion of blood, both in their expansion and in their eventual overthrow and destruction. He is challenged by Musgrave to say what he thought would be a right division of territory into several distinct governments (he said of the world, but in practice the discussion is confined to Europe). This brings Fletcher to suggest that Europe falls naturally, because of geography and climate, into ten regions. Each of these would be subdivided in turn into ten or twelve subdivisions, or sovereign cities as he calls them. They would be united on terms of equality for their common defence and none would be strong enough to attempt the conquest of any of the others.

It is typical of Fletcher that he throws out succinct hints like this of new and far-reaching ideas without attempting to develop them in any detail. His suggestion of a European system of small, autonomous but interlocking states is only a vague sketch, but it is recognisably a Europe of the regions. Such an arrangement was, no doubt, visionary and Utopian at the time when Fletcher proposed it and there was no possibility that it could then be achieved. As Neal Ascherson has remarked, it is so no longer. The break-up of the empires and the multi-national states on the one hand, and the movement towards closer co-operation on the other, is now creating a Europe which begins to meet the ideals which Fletcher expressed in 1704.

In the course of his argument, Fletcher stated two principles, which were revolutionary at the beginning of the eighteenth century when it was generally assumed that a country could only flourish at the expense of others. These were: 'I am of opinion that the true interest and good of any nation is the same with that of any other. I do not say that one society ought not to repel the injuries of another; but that no people ever did any injustice to a neighbouring nation, except by mistaking their own interest.'

Secondly, and it is in fact the same point seen from a different perspective: [all governments should] 'consider the general good and interest of mankind, on which that of every distinct society does in a great measure depend'.

These two principles amount to saying that we all share the same planet and that the interests of all of us are interdependent. All international organisations, the United Nations, the European Community and all others, depend on an understanding of that fact which Andrew Fletcher was one of the first people to grasp nearly 300 years ago.

After making the case for European co-operation, Fletcher in the same essay discussed the advantages of the dispersion of power. For him, as for E.F. Schumacher, small is beautiful. He was opposed to large states and large towns which drew excessive power and wealth to themselves. London, which in many ways he admired, was such a case. 'This vast city is like the head of a rickety child' which draws to itself 'the nourishment that should be distibuted in due proportions to the rest of the languishing body. That London should draw the riches and government of the three kingdoms to the south-east corner of this island is in some degree as unnatural as for one city to possess the riches and government of the world.' All governments which imposed their will over distant peoples were 'violent, unjust and unnatural'. On the other hand, a diversity of small governments gave many men the opportunity of doing good to their fellow citizens and 'many different seats of government will highly tend to the improvement of all arts and sciences', as in the cities of ancient Greece.

Fletcher's vision for Scotland and for Europe were in accordance. He saw no inconsistency between his struggle to maintain and extend the independence of Scotland and his advocacy of an all-embracing European system. On the contrary it was the growth of large and multi-national states, such as the absorption of Scotland in an incorporating Union, which he saw as the denial of justice and good government and a threat to peace. The relevance of Fletcher's ideas to our current concerns both in Scotland and in Europe is inescapable.

In his recent book, *Scotland: A New History*, Michael Lynch said that the SNP policy of independence in Europe 're-establishes one of the most important threads of continuity in Scottish history'. He goes on to give many examples of the close involvement of Scotland in the development of other parts of Europe over many centuries. Andrew Fletcher of Saltoun was a great Scottish patriot, all the more so because he was also actively, learnedly and consciously, European.

(Paper for Saltire Society Conference,
'Scotland in Europe: the Cultural Factor', July 1992.)

4

The Secret Services of John Macky

The *Memoirs of the Secret Services of John Macky* is a short and rare book often mentioned in footnotes by historians of the reigns of William and Anne. It is a collection of miscellaneous papers, mostly by John Macky, published by, or at least with the agreement of, his son, Spring Macky, in London in 1733. The Memoir itself, or *Memorial of his Father's Services and Sufferings*, is only fifteen pages long, but it contains most of the little we know about Macky's life. It is followed by an anti-Jacobite pamphlet, *A View of the Court of St Germain from the Year 1690 to 1695*, and the work on which Macky's claim to fame rests, about 200 short character sketches of the leading political figures in England and Scotland at the beginning of the eighteenth century. As a sort of testimonial, there are two letters from Sophia, the Electress of Hanover, for whom the *Characters* were written. Then, incongruously and with very little in the way of explanation, the full text of the Will of Gilbert Burnet, down to the Codicils dividing his furniture, books and silver between his children.

This Gilbert Burnet is, of course, the Scotsman who became Bishop of Salisbury, and, from a remarkably early age, was a kenspeckle figure in the affairs of Church and State in the two kingdoms. 'This pushing, talkative divine', said Macaulay, 'who was always blabbing secrets, putting impertinent questions, obtruding unasked advice, was nevertheless an upright, courageous and able man'. His *History of the Reformation* and his theological writings achieved a European reputation in their day, but the work which has survived is the *History of his own Times*, one of the liveliest of historical memoirs. Horace Walpole wrote of them, 'it seems as if he had just come from the King's closet or from the apartments of the men he describes, and was telling his readers, in plain, honest terms what he had seen and heard'. His Will, by the way, shows that he had not lost his Scottish partiality, although he spent most of the last forty years of his life in England. He remembered the 'College of New Aberdeen', where he was educated, and the Parish of Saltoun, which was his first charge and where he was the tutor of Andrew Fletcher. He left endowments for scholarships in both, as well as funds for the school-house and Minister's library in Saltoun. But what is the Will doing at all in this strange company? What connection is there between Burnet and Macky?

Macky's *Memorial* was not an autobiography but a petition to the Government against harsh treatment for misplaced zeal. It wastes no time on preliminaries unfortunately (for we know nothing about the early part of his life), but goes straight to the heart of the matter. Like Caesar, he writes in the third person and like Caesar achieves a notably direct opening sentence: 'Mr. Macky came early into the Measures of the Revolution; and on King James's return from Ireland to France, was sent to Paris by King William to see what they were doing'. In other words, he was a spy at the Jacobite Court of St Germain shortly after the Battle of the Boyne of July 1690. He had an early success and brought news of the assembly of an invasion force before James himself had joined it at La Hogue. William's ships were able to destroy the French Fleet in time, and the conspirators in England, revealed by Macky, were caught. For these services, William made him Inspector of the Coast from Harwich to Dover. He intercepted several Jacobite agents, including a Mrs Aldrige travelling from France with seventy letters in the false bottom of a box of dirty linen. From such information, he wrote his pamphlet on St Germain in 1696, intended to prove that James favoured only Catholics and excluded Protestants. It sold 30,000 copies.

Altogether, John Macky was prospering. In 1697, he married the only daughter of Sir William Spring, of a wealthy family, long established in Suffolk. When there was peace for a time with France, he was made Director of Packet-boats from Dover to France and Flanders, and spent his wife's dowry on five new boats. He caught more agents and ran a secret courier service for the King. His fortunes began to decline when Anne came to the throne in 1702, partly, Macky seems to think, because she was less enthusiastically anti-Jacobite. In any case, the return of war with France put his packet-boats out of business. He agreed to see to an estate, of which his wife had inherited a share, on the island of Zant in the territory of Venice. On his way, he visited Hanover, and there 'at the Princess Sophia's Desire, gave her the Characters of the great men of England and Scotland'.

On his return to his post at Dover, his intelligence network continued to prosper, giving advance warning, for instance, of the Jacobite attempt of 1708. It came to an abrupt end in 1711 with an episode which was disastrous for poor John Macky, but had elements of high farce. As he tells the story, his suspicions were aroused by a mysterious traveller to France, and he arrested him with two Frenchmen when he came back to England. He was

surprised to discover that the Englishman was his old acquaintance Matthew Prior, the poet who was also a diplomat. He had
been conducting the secret negotiations which led to the Peace
of Utrecht, and his two companions had full powers to sign for
France. Secret agent had frustrated secret agent, but unhappily
they were both on the same side. Macky's blunder infuriated the
ungrateful Government. They threw him into prison, destroyed
his packet-boat business, and even threatened to have him hanged
for illegal correspondence with France. The Hanoverians eventually
came to his rescue, and he was released when George I became King
in 1714. He was given the packet-boat service to Dublin, but the
income failed to meet the cost of the boats. 'Mr. Macky after thirty
years Service,' the *Memorial* ends sadly, 'is now in a worse Condition
than ever'.

But there is a postscript. The *Memorial* persuaded the Government
to send him abroad again as an agent, and 'Sir Robert Walpole
continued to supply him in so generous a manner, as rendered the
close of his life much more easy to him than the former Part had
been'. He died in Rotterdam in 1726.

So much we know from Spring Macky's book. Apart from this,
there are a few chance references in letters and diaries. The Carstares
State Papers (edited by Joseph McCormick, Minister at Prestonpans;
Edinburgh, 1774) even contain some of the reports which he wrote
as a spy for Melville, then Secretary of State for Scotland. At that
time, March and April 1691, Macky was in Scotland, posing as an
emissary from St Germain to persuade Jacobites, and particularly the
Bishop of Glasgow, to reveal their plans. He was not very happy
in this deceitful and precarious work. There are hints in the letters
that he had been persuaded to take it on by a promise that it would
lead to better things. 'I hope your Lordship, when all danger is past,
will, as you promised, provide me in an employment wherein I may
more openly serve the King and your Lordship'. These reports were
sent by Melville to Carstares who was William's closest adviser on
Scottish affairs. 'Few Scotsmen had Access to the King but by him',
says Macky in his *Characters*, 'so that he was properly Viceroy of
that Kingdom, and was called at Court, Cardinal Carstares'. Macky's
descriptions of his two employers in this shady business are among
his least flattering. Melville 'hath neither Learning, Wit nor common
Conversation', and Carstares 'is the cunningest, subtle Dissembler in
the World, with an Air of Sincerity, a dangerous Enemy, because
always hid'.

Another Macky is involved with the Carstares Papers. In his
Preface, McCormick says that they 'came into the hands of Mr
Charles Macky, late Professor of civil history and antiquities in

the university of Edinburgh, as executor to Mrs Carstares. He had lived much in Mr Carstares' family in the early part of his life'. Carstares lost his influence at court on the death of the King. He became Principal of Edinburgh University in 1703 and lived there until his death in 1715; he had the reputation of keeping open house for promising students. Charles Macky was presumably one of them, and it is tempting to suppose that he was a son of Carstares' agent, rescued when his father was imprisoned in 1711. Whether this is so or not, McCormick indulges in some strange mystification over Macky's *Characters*, from which he includes extracts in his book. 'These are', he wrote, 'excerpted from a manuscript in the possession of the Earl of Hyndford, which the editor found to be more complete, and less partial, than the copy from which an anonymous writer published, in 1732, *The Characters of the Court of Great Britain*'. No mention of John Macky. In fact, the 1733 volume (some of the introductory pieces are dated 1732) was anything but anonymous, and McCormick's extracts are not more complete, but shortened and emasculated. Why did he suppress John Macky's name from his perfectly reputable work but not shrink from attaching it to the reports – revealing him as an *agent provocateur*? Perhaps he was trying to justify his bowdlerisation of Macky's unfavourable remarks about some of the characters, particularly about William Carstares himself.

How does the Electress Sophia become involved? The succession of Sophia and her heirs to the English throne (although the Scottish remained an open question) was established by the Act of Settlement in 1701. In Hanover she was remote from the British scene and needed information. Macky with his special knowledge of Jacobite intrigue was a natural source. It meant, of course, that he could serve two paymasters at once, but everything he wrote suggests that he was entirely sincere in his support for the Hanoverian succession. He seems to have earned Sophia's gratitude and even friendship. The two letters from her in the 1733 book are warm and informal and disregard the enormous social gulf between them. In a letter of 16 October 1703 she regrets that she was not at Hanover when he called there, 'for it is better to Talk than Write on all you inform me of'. It is signed 'votres très Affectionée, Sophie, Electrice'. Macky was evidently more than a spy that one could use but not like or trust.

As part of a working brief, of a kind which Governments still use, the *Characters* are admirable. They are short, but tell you as much as you need to know, summing up the personality and appearance of the subject in a few memorable phrases. They are frank but fair. It is because of their pungency, brevity and objectivity that they have been so useful to historians as a source of ready-made character sketches. Many of them have become well known through quotation, although sometimes attributed anonymously to a 'manuscript in Thomas Rawlinson's collection'. Of Queen Anne's Prince George, for example: 'He is very fat, loves News, his Bottle and the Queen'. One of the most often quoted is of Andrew Fletcher of Saltoun: 'Steady in his Principles, of nice Honours, with abundance of learning; true as the sword he wears and bold as a lion . . . would lose his life readily, to serve his Country; and would not do a base Thing to save it . . . a low, thin Man, brown Complexion, full of fire, with a stern, sour Look, and fifty Years old'. Not all of the entries convey such a feeling of direct observation as that, and some of the English ones are no more than a few brief sentences included more to complete the collection than because Macky had much to say about them. The *Characters* hardly ever show personal hostility or descend to mere gossip or tittle-tattle.

The spite and ill-nature from which Macky was free was supplied by Jonathan Swift in marginal comments which he scribbled in his copy of the book. They became notorious in the eighteenth century and many people had them reproduced in their own copies. The British Museum has two such examples. Sometimes Swift agrees that Macky is 'fair enough', but he often adds denunciation, hardly ever praise. Lord Wharton is 'the most universal Villain', Lord Chesterfield, 'the greatest Knave in England', Dr Tenison, the Archbishop of Canterbury, 'the most good for nothing prelate I ever knew', and Mr Methuen, Ambassador to Portugal, 'a profligate Rogue, without Religion or Morals, but cunning enough, yet without abilities of any kind'. In his comments on the Scots, Swift displays his anti-Scottish animosity. Of the Duke of Argyll, 'ambitious, covetous, cunning Scot; has no principle but his own interest and Greatness. A true Scot in his whole conduct'; of Secretary Johnstoun, 'one of the greatest Knaves, even in Scotland'; of the Earl of Weems, 'handsome–for a Scot'. Not even Andrew Fletcher escapes: 'a most arrogant, conceited Pedant in Politics; cannot indure the least Contradiction in any of his Opinions or Paradoxes'.

The 1733 volume, whether edited by Spring Macky or the 'A.R.' who signed the Dedication, was thrown together without much editorial care. The *Characters* had been written before the Union and were divided between the English and the Scots. The book, which appeared years after the Union, preserves the division, but gives the heading of Great Britain to the English alone. Some of the peers, who were listed by their titles only in the manuscript, were given the wrong Christian names in the book. These slips led W. A. Shaw, who published two articles about Macky in the *Times Literary Supplement* in June 1928, to conclude that the *Characters* had been 'deliberately mangled' to give the impression that they had been written shortly before publication and not a generation earlier. He even suggested that Swift had been misled and did not realise that he was commenting on notes that were already thirty years old. As a later article in the T.L.S., 13 and 20 August 1938, by W. F. Trench and K. B. Garrett had no difficulty in showing, this is a theory which does not stand up to examination. The *Characters* can be dated fairly precisely from internal evidence. The Duke of Argyll, for example, who was John, the second Duke, was described as about twenty-five; he had been given command of the Horse Guards, but not yet appointed Commissioner to Parliament. This means that the entry must have been written between September 1703, when the second Duke succeeded to the title, and May 1704, when he became Commissioner. Or take Robert Harley, who is described as Speaker of the House of Commons, but with a note at the end, 'since the writing of these characters, he is made Secretary of State in the Room of my Lord Nottingham'. That happened on 18 May 1704. Everything is consistent with Macky's own story that the *Characters* were written for his visit to Hanover in October 1703. There were more than one other copy of the manuscript, and to these a few postscripts were added later but without any revision of the entries themselves. If this is obvious enough now, it must have been crystal clear to Swift. In fact, his use of the past tense when he is speaking of people who had died in the meantime is sufficient proof that he knew what he was doing. Nor did the editor in 1733 try to pretend that the entries were up to date; on the contrary, he played up the connection with the Electress for all it was worth, and she died in 1714.

William Shaw has another theory, that the *Characters* were not written by Macky but by Gilbert Burnet. He simply could not believe that a man who was 'a spy, a pacquet master and of no reputed birth . . . should have such intimate acquaintanceship in high places to be able to write first-hand characters of the chief of the land, both from England and Scotland'. If you can stomach the snobbery, you have to admit that he has a point. How could Macky have known these people? There is no great problem about the Scots. We have already seen Macky in a close, if secret, relationship with a Secretary of State. Most of the men he describes were members of the Scottish Parliament. We know from the accounts of visitors like Joseph Taylor that it was fairly easy to watch the debates and meet the members in small and crowded Edinburgh, where everyone lived on top of everyone else. London was, no doubt, more difficult, especially for a Scotsman at a time when they had few friends there. Macky's marriage is one sign that he was accepted in English society; but there is more conclusive evidence in the papers of the Duke of Shrewsbury. He was one of the great grandees of his day, described at one time by Swift as 'the finest gentleman we have', and more than once the key figure of the Government. With some reason he was suspected of secret intrigues with St Germain, and it might have been this that brought him and Macky together. Or it may simply have been the opportunity which his control of the packet-boats gave Macky to meet travellers to the Continent. On 2 November 1700, Shrewsbury wrote in his diary: 'I arrived at Dover, went into no house by the way, lay at Macky's'. Three years later, Macky on his journey to Zant arrived in Vienna. The British Envoy, George Stepney, wrote on 3 November 1703 to Shrewsbury, who was then in Rome: 'Mr Wortley-Montague and Mr Macky of Dover arrived here this morning and will shortly wait upon your Grace'. Shrewsbury duly recorded Macky's arrival in Rome two weeks later. Not only was there an easy social relationship between them, which suggests as with the Electress that he had qualities which overcame his disadvantages; but Shrewsbury even helped with the *Characters*. Macky wrote in a letter from Genoa in August 1704: 'I would send the *Characters* but they are too bulky to go by post, and they are most of them corrected by the D of Shr own hand and dare not therefore part with them out of my sight'.

Even if we do not have to look beyond Macky, with Shrewsbury's help, for the author of the *Characters*, there is still the puzzle of the references to Gilbert Burnet in the 1733 volume. What is the meaning of these cryptic remarks in the introductory note?

> Most of these Characters are inserted by Bishop Burnet in the Second and Third Volumes of the History of his own Time, which will not as yet see the Light, for Reasons his Son Thomas could give, if he thought proper . . .
> It is evident from the Bishop's WILL, that his whole History ought to have been published above ten Years ago . . .
> As Truth is generally brought to Light by Time; it is hoped that these PAPERS, of Mr Macky, will occasion the speedy Publication of Bishop Burnet's History.

But nothing of the kind is evident from the Will. Burnet asks his son not to publish the *History* before six years after his death (which came in 1715), 'but as to the printing it after six Years, or delaying it longer, I refer that to such Directions as I may give him by Word of Mouth'. The second (and final) volume eventually appeared in 1734, ten years after the first. It contained nothing resembling Macky's *Characters*, and no reference to these mysterious taunts and accusations.

Once again, there is a clue in the Shrewsbury Papers. In February 1707 Burnet wrote to Shrewsbury to ask if he would help with the revision of his *History*. He proposed to send a man who, to spare the Duke's eyes, would read the draft and 'write whatsoever your Grace will be pleased to dictate to him . . . A Work of this nature is of such importance that it ought either to be quite suppressed, or reviewed with all possible care and caution'. Shrewsbury, therefore, might have been the connecting link between Burnet and Macky. Many of the characters with which he had helped Macky were the personae of the *History*. What would be more natural than to lend Burnet a copy of Macky's manuscript? There is no evidence that Burnet and Macky ever met. In the *History*,[2] there is one allusion to Macky's activities in the description of the affair of La Hogue: 'a Scotchman brought the first discovery to Johnstoun'. Burnet could easily have had the story from Johnstoun, who was a kinsman and protégé. Equally, Macky's description of Burnet in the *Characters* seems to be based more on his performance in the House of Lords than on closer acquaintance: 'one of the greatest Orators of the Age [Swift inserts the word 'Scotch' before orators]; a Man neither of Prudence nor Temper'.

At all events, Spring Macky knew or suspected that a copy of his father's manuscript was in the hands of Burnet's son, who would sooner or later publish the second volume of the *History*. Then in 1732 one of Macky's *Characters* was published without attribution except to 'a MS in the Library of the late Thomas Rawlinson, Esq'. This was the entry about Andrew Fletcher which appeared as part of the introduction to the first edition of his *Political Works*. Spring Macky, who had published a couple of bawdy novels and therefore knew something about the literary market, evidently decided that the time had come to release his father's manuscript before Thomas Burnet or someone else did. Presumably, the elaborate allusions to Burnet and the Will were intended to prevent Burnet's claiming the credit.

In the last few years of his life, John Macky wrote a series of travel books, two volumes on England, one on Scotland and one on the Austrian Netherlands. Because they were anonymous and described on the title-pages only as 'Familiar Letters from a Gentleman here to his Friend Abroad', some people have questioned whether Macky wrote them. None of his contemporaries seems to have doubted it, and in fact his name does appear in a notice by the publisher in the second edition of the volume on Scotland, and in the Dedication of the fifth edition. The books deserved the success of these repeated editions. Macky claimed that he had included nothing that he had not examined personally, and that is the impression they give. They are fresh and direct. Macky must have been in his fifties or sixties by the time he wrote them, but he was still full of curiosity and enjoyment.

Shortly afterwards, Daniel Defoe, imitating the form and even the title, published his *Tour Thro' the Whole Island of Great Britain*. He made a fairly obvious allusion to Macky in the introduction to his section on Scotland. All previous descriptions, he said, had been written by Scotsmen who had been guilty of 'the most scandalous Partiality'; but 'a more modern, and I must acknowledge, more modest Writer' – who was Macky – 'exaggerated only in writing about the seats of the nobility'. It depends on your point of view, but some people might think that Macky was partial enough. 'The Scots have made a greater Figure abroad, than any other Nation in Europe entirely owing to the Fineness of their Education. The High-Street of Edinburgh is doubtless the stateliest Street in the World . . . There is no Nation where a Man hath fairer Play for his Liberty, than in Scotland . . . I never saw in any Nation an Assembly of greater Beauties, than those I have seen at Edinburgh . . . Glasgow is the beautifullest little City I have seen in Britain; it stands deliciously on the Banks of the River Clyde'. Defoe describes Glasgow and the High Street of Edinburgh in almost the same words. In fact, he plagiarised Macky quite shamelessly.

The frank and spontaneous capacity for enjoyment which enlivens the travel books is no one's idea of a spy. Perhaps on the evidence of his letters to Melville, it is fair to think of John Macky as a spy *malgré lui*, who in easier times would have found a more congenial and less objectionable outlet for his talents. His memorial lies in innumerable footnotes, and he has made a real, if minor, contribution to our understanding of his age. He had to live on his wits, but he was free from malice and despair.

(Scottish Literary Journal, vol. 6, No. 1, May 1979.)

NOTES

1. Historical Manuscripts Commission; Shrewsbury Papers; Buccleuch and Queensberry Manuscripts, II i Part 2 (1903), 688, 720, 746, 785, 786, 788.
2. *History*, 1734 edn, II, p. 93.

5

'The Grand Object of Travelling': Adam, Boswell and Smollett in Italy

In a well-known passage in his *Life of Johnson*, Boswell reports that Johnson said this in 1776:

> 'A man who has not been in Italy is always conscious of an inferiority, from his not having seen what it is expected a man should see. The grand object of travelling is to see the shores of the Mediterranean. On those shores were the four great empires of the world; the Assyrian, the Persian, the Grecian, and the Roman. All our religion, almost all our law, almost all our arts, almost all that sets us above savages, has come to us from the shores of the Mediterranean'.

In spite of this, Johnson himself never succeeded in making the journey to Italy. Instead he went north with Boswell to the Highlands and Islands of Scotland. Then, and since, that was a much more unusual thing to do. For hundreds of years there has been a continuous flood of visitors heading south towards Italy. Since they included a very high proportion of our best architects and painters, poets and writers of all kinds, they have left a very rich record of their experiences, and of the effects which Italy had on them. One might think that this continuous rush to the south was a sufficient proof that Johnson was right, and that the obvious attractions of Italy were a sufficient explanation. Still, his remarks sound rather like gush and enthusiasm which was not typical of him; he was more inclined to the debunking and the dismissive. What did he really mean? Why should a man feel inferior because he had not seen Italy? I should like to look for an answer to these questions in the accounts by travellers of the period, of their motives, experiences and reactions.

Although I shall mention others, I should like to concentrate on three men. The architect Robert Adam, the novelist Tobias Smollett, and Johnson's biographer, James Boswell. They were all in Italy within a year or two of one another. Robert Adam arrived in Italy in January 1765 and spent nearly three years there, mostly in

Rome. Smollett came for three or four months towards the end of 1764, and Boswell spent almost the whole of the year 1765 in Italy. I choose these three men (all of them Scottish, as it happens) largely because they have left particularly frank and lively accounts of their experiences in Italy. Robert Adam wrote constantly to his mother and his brothers and sisters in Edinburgh. Although these letters have never been published in full, they are the basis of a delightful book by John Fleming, *Robert Adam and His Circle in Edinburgh and Rome* which is full of quotations from them. Tobias Smollett wrote a book, *Travels Through France and Italy* (of which, by the way, a new edition has just been published) which is also in the form of letters, although in his case this was merely a convenient and conventional way of writing a travel book. Boswell's record of course is found in one of the volumes of his journals, *Boswell on the Grand Tour: Italy, Corsica and France*.

I have chosen the three also because together they illustrate different types of the eighteenth-century traveller. Robert Adam came largely as a serious and devoted student of architecture; James Boswell was a young man on a spree; and Tobias Smollett an older one, who had come to Nice in search of a good climate for his health, and was irresistibly drawn across the border to Italy. You might say that this selection omits one of the typical figures of the age: the aristocrat, the 'Milordo', as the Italians called them, doing the Grand Tour in the grand style; but most of them were too grand and too indolent to leave much of a record. In any case, Robert Adam came with plenty of money and originally in the company of Charles Hope, the brother of the Earl of Hopetoun. Boswell, of course, had aristocratic connections; he was the son of a man who was not only a Scottish law lord, but the laird of an estate given to the family by James IV in the fifteenth century. As he was fond of remarking, this made him at least the equal of a baron on the continent where titles were scattered around with greater liberality. He also travelled for part of the time with a real aristocrat, Lord Mountstuart, the son of the Prime Minister, Lord Bute. Robert Adam's objectives in coming to Italy were the most clear-cut and precise of the three. His father, William Adam, had established himself as the leading architect in the Scotland of his day in a style which combined solid and sturdy Scottish masonry with ideas of classical elegance, symmetry and decoration, derived from ancient Rome through Palladio. But William Adam had never left Scotland and had no opportunity to study this architecture at its source. Robert's ambition aimed at nothing less than making himself the greatest architect of the day in England as well as Scotland, and perhaps indeed in the whole of Europe. It was self-evident to him that the essential training for this was a detailed study of the remains of classical architecture which could still be found in Italy, and in particular in Rome.

But architectural skill was useless without patrons to commission the buildings, and his stay in Italy served this purpose as well. The Grand Tour was a sort of fashionable finishing school. Fashion demanded that the young aristocrat should complete his education by a tour of a year or two though France, Germany and Italy, and it was in Italy that he expected to find pictures and statues to send back to his country house at home and architectural ideas if he had the whim and the means to extend, re-decorate or re-build. It was precisely among men like this that Robert Adam expected to find his future patrons.

There was something of a conflict between the two objectives. If he wanted to meet the patrons he had to move in polite society. This meant living in style, keeping a coach, wearing expensive clothes and spending most of the time in social frivolity. It also meant that he had to conceal his serious work because in the Rome of the day artists and architects were regarded as little better than hired tradesmen, and were simply not acceptable in polite society. It was a curious convention of the day which, I suppose, survived until quite recent times, that only the idle and useless were socially acceptable. Robert Adam had, of course, the advantage in travelling in the company of a brother of an earl, at least until he decided it was better to stand on his own feet, but he was very conscious of this dilemma. 'If I am known in Rome to be an architect', he wrote in one of his letters, 'if I am seen drawing or with a pencil in my hand, I cannot enter into genteel company who will not admit an artist, or if they do admit him, will very probably rub fronts on him in order to prevent him appearing at their card playing, balls and concerts.'

It was not only a dilemma, it was also a temptation. It is quite clear from his letters that he took a naive pleasure in finding himself accepted by princes and cardinals, and he delighted in splendid clothes, 'light gold lace and red Persian lining' and the like. In the end his Edinburgh habits prevailed, as John Fleming calls it, 'that spartan philosophy of thrift, hard work and strenuous self-improvement', or the last two of these at all events. Robert Adam was not too proud to begin again at the beginning, and take lessons from two French artists who were living in Rome, Clérisseau and Pechaux. He went sketching with Piranesi and Allan Ramsay, and employed draughtsmen to help him in a mammoth project of surveying all the remaining classical buildings of Rome. So there was plenty of hard work and strenuous self-improvement, but perhaps rather less thrift. From his architectural work in Scotland, and I suppose also from the money inherited from his father, Robert Adam had arrived in

Italy with £5,000 and he was determined to use it to extract the last ounce of benefit from his stay in Rome. He set himself up in some style in an apartment in the Casa Guarnieri where Clérisseau stayed with him. He described his domestic arrangements in one of his letters:

> We shall have a cook whose honesty has proved good in these 6 years who shall buy our needs and dress our victuals; we shall have our valet Donald for shaving and dressing our hair; we shall have our coach, which in the summertime costs about 4 shillings sterling the whole day, coachman and all, and we shall have our valet-de-place or servant for going errands and behind the coach, whom we will pay at the rate of a shilling a day, for which he feeds, clothes and provides himself in everything. In short, for 12 shillings one day with another we shall defray our whole expense of eating, drinking, equipage, which the Lord knows is not dear.'

Later on he bought his own coach, 'One of the handsomest little chariots I ever saw, painted green and gold, new lined and as good as new, for which I paid £35 sterling nearly.' In other words, Adam was living rather more like an aristocrat than an artist, but it was a sort of level-headed compromise between his compulsion to work and the need to live in the style required to introduce himself to potential patrons. He says that he spent 'betwixt £800 and £900 a year', apart from his expenditure on works of art. At the other end of the scale, two other Scottish architects, the brothers Mylne, walked most of the way across France and Italy to Rome and managed on an allowance of £30 a year from their father.

Of course, most of the travellers were much less serious minded than Adam. They came close to Robert Burns's description in *The Twa Dogs*; which he wrote in about 1784:

> 'Or maybe, in a frolic daft,
> To Hague or Calais taks a waft,
> To mak a tour, an tak a whirl,
> To learn *bon ton*, an see the worl.
> There, at Vienna or Versailles,
> He rives his father's auld entails;
> Or by Madrid he takes the rout,
> To thrum guitars, an fecht wi nowte;
> Or down Italian vista startles,
> Whore-hunting amang groves o' myrtles;
> Then bouses drumly German water,
> To mak himsel look fair and fatter,
> An clear the consequential sorrows,
> Love–gifts of Carnival signoras.'

It shows, by the way, how widespread the idea of European travel was that Burns, tied to the soil in his native Ayrshire, who hardly crossed the Border into England, let alone the Channel, should have had such precise ideas about it. You notice that the amorous part of the escapade was in Italy. That was part of the tradition too. Boswell's journey was an example. He began, like many Scotsmen of his class destined for a career at the Bar, with the study of law in Holland. But his father reluctantly allowed him to escape, in the hope that it would keep him out of worse mischief, for a tour through Germany and Switzerland to Italy. In Holland, Boswell tried hard to abstain from amorous adventures and devote himself to his books. The effort nearly drove him mad, but he blossomed as he went south. As Geoffrey Scott, the first editor of the journals expressed it, 'Boswell was pedantic in Holland, princely in Germany, philosophic in Switzerland and amorous in Italy, which he approached with min-gled feelings of awe and adulterous anticipation.' He told Rousseau in a letter from Italy: 'I ran after girls without restraint . . .I sallied forth of an evening like an imperious lion.' 'Italy', the editors of Boswell's Italian journal tell us decisively, 'was noted for the beauty and reputed availability of its women.' Stendhal, a few years later, with pardonable exaggeration, said: 'The only sensible activity, in all this fair land, is the art of love.' Byron, who came to Italy at the beginning of the next century, said that he had made love to at least 200 women in two years in Venice, but Venice at that time was perhaps a special case. So was Byron.

Boswell was less successful; his achievements in these matters tended to fall short of his expectations. In Turin, he was so eager and impatient that he frightened everybody off; but in Siena a woman, the wife of the Capitano del Popolo, no less, did genuinely fall in love with him. As so often in such cases, he did not know of his success. The poor woman was left behind, pursuing him for some time with letters of increasing longing and desperation. But it is not quite fair to say that Boswell was only on a spree; you could say that he was hard at work all the time on his major creation, his journal. That meant not only writing it, but creating the situations and finding the people that were worth writing about. 'I am not a great man,' he said in his letter to Frederick the Great, 'but I have an enthusiastic love of great men, and I derive a kind of glory from it.' In Switzerland his great scoops had been his conversations with Voltaire and Rousseau. In Italy, it was his pursuit of Paoli in Corsica, then in revolt against the rule of Genoa. This was one of the supreme moments of Boswell's life. He not only found Paoli, a bold enough undertaking at the time, but they became life-long friends. Boswell wrote a book which brought Corsica and Paoli's struggle to the attention of Europe. In the end, it did not do much to help Paoli, but it gave Boswell a taste of literary fame and bolstered his self-confidence which was more fragile than it appeared on the surface.

Robert Adam and James Boswell were both in their twenties when they came to Italy. In this, they were typical of the true type of the Grand Tourists, the young men seeking continental polish and sophistication as the culmination of their education. For this you needed inherited means or a wealthy and indulgent father, unless you were a scholar or artist with such vocation that you were ready to walk the whole way and live from hand-to-mouth. If you were lucky, you might be able to travel as a 'bear-leader' to a young aristocrat, a sort of itinerant tutor, guardian and purse-bearer. This was a job in such demand that many men of great distinction were prepared, for the sake of it, to abandon their university chairs for a few years. In this way, Adam Smith travelled with the Duke of Buccleuch, and Adam Fergusson with a young Lord Chesterfield. Joseph Addison came with Edward Wortley Montague and wrote a long poem and a book about Italy in consequence. Men who came at their own expense after the first vigour and enthusiasm of youth were much rarer, but Tobias Smollett was one of them. Smollett's own writing at the time gives the impression that he was an old man. He was certainly in bad health, with the cantankerousness and sensitivity of the invalid, and within a few years of his death, but he was only forty-three. According to Walter Scott, Smollett was in real life like Matthew Bramble in his novel *Humphrey Clinker*: generous and benevolent, under a disguise of peevishness and irritability. Certainly his letters from France and Italy were peevish enough. They have the vigour and sharpness of observation of his novels, 'breathing a hard, comfortable commonsense at every pore', as Arnold Bennett said; but they are very critical. Everywhere he found dirt, dishonesty and muddle. But we have to remember that at the least of times, his stomach and his nerves were more than normally sensitive. In any case, he came back to Italy to spend the last three years of his life near Livorno.

Even if Smollett exaggerated, the journey to Italy at that time was certainly long and uncomfortable. When Robert Adam was trying to persuade his brother James to hurry out to join him, he told him that the journey from Edinburgh to Rome need not take more than six weeks. There was no road into Italy that would take a wheeled vehicle. Even the one along the coast from Nice to Genoa and beyond was only a rough, rude track. The only practicable way to take that route was by boat from Nice to Lerici, where a road to Florence and Rome began. Otherwise, when the snow was not too deep, the traveller was quite literally carried across the Alps at Mount Cenis, to the west of Turin. Boswell describes the process: 'At six I mounted the Alps machine, which consisted of two trees between which were twisted some cords on which I sat. There was also a kind of back and arms, and a board hung before, on which I put my feet. In this machine did four fellows (six I should say), changing two and two, carry me over the *Saevas Alpes*.' Even inside Italy where there were roads, and even if you had a carriage, the going was rough. 'From Perugia to Florence', Smollett says, 'the road is so bad that we never could travel above eight and twenty miles a day. We were often obliged to quit the carriage, and walk up steep mountains; and the way in general was so unequal and stony, that we were jolted even to the danger of our lives.' He advised travellers to carry with them, 'a hammer and nails, a spare iron-pin or two, a large knife, and a bladder of grease' for repairs to their carriage wheels. David Hume, who was in Italy in 1747, talks about being delayed by the bad roads and the breaking of wheels. Rivers usually had to be forded because there were few bridges. Towns were walled and shut their gates at six at night. In some ways, though, communications were better than you might suppose. From Florence, Robert Adam sent four large Parmesan cheeses home to Scotland as presents, and they seem to have arrived safely.

Except in the larger towns, food and lodging were very primitive. Smollett, of course, is full of this. 'Of Siena I can say nothing from my own observation, but that we were indifferently lodged in a house that stunk like a privy, and fared wretchedly at supper.' Or on the road to Terni: 'The houses are abominably nasty, and generally destitute of provision: when eatables were found, we were almost poisoned by their cookery.' In one of the ports between Genoa and Lerici: 'We had a very bad supper, miserably dressed, passed a very disagreeable night, and payed a very extravagant bill in the morning, without being thanked for our custom. I was very glad to get out of the house with my throat uncut.' Even Robert's brother James, who was not disposed to be critical, talks of being so attacked in bed in an inn by bugs and fleas that he was obliged to spend the night on a chair in the middle of the room.

I cannot think of any eighteenth-century traveller who has any-thing favourable to say about Italian food. Certainly, they enjoyed the fruit and the wine. 'The best wine I ever tasted which in this country does not amount to a shilling a bottle,' Robert Adam remarked. Addison was lyrical about the oranges, the olives and the vines. Not a word anywhere in praise of the cooking. Clearly, this is one of the ways in which Italy has changed, when you think of the excellence now of the admirable restaurants in every village.

Nor was the eighteenth-century traveller enthusiastic about the sun and the heat. Smollett tells us the summer heat makes travelling dangerous in Italy. Adam often complains about it. Already in April he writes from Naples, 'Really, one is so tired going from one place to another in the great heats here that when one comes home one can do nothing. At present the sweat drops from my fingers in a room without a fire at nine o'clock at night.' In May at Rome, 'at midday a dog can hardly endure the sun'. Of course, the clothes that were fashionable were not very suitable for the climate, and it never occurred to anyone at the time to do anything so irrational as grill themselves on a beach in the sun. Sea-bathing was not entirely unknown in Europe at the time, but strictly as a medical régime. Smollett indulged in it at Nice, and regretted that there were no arrangements to allow a lady to go into the sea with due modesty. She had to have the sea-water brought to her in a tub in her house. Fifty years later, Byron swam a great deal in Venice and at Lerici, but it was one of his eccentricities. At a time when the beaches were unspoilt and the sea unpolluted, they were also ignored. If the food was bad and the sun uncomfortable, there were compensations. The country had not yet been devastated by the debris of industrialisation. The motor car, the greatest single cause of the destruction of our environment, lay far in the future. The towns were still more or less confined to their historic centres within the walls, and were peaceful and uncrowded. Rome was said to have more statues than people. Smollett talks of the solitude of Pisa (Gibbon uses the same phrase) which made it a very desirable place to live. The whole country must have been of breathtaking beauty. Indeed, it is often very sad to compare the present reality with the descriptions of these earlier travellers. In 1644 John Evelyn spoke of the 'pleasant villas', the 'fragrant orchards' and the 'ravishing retirements of the Genovese nobility' at San Pietro d'Arena, 'from whence, the wind blowing as it did, might perfectly be smelt the peculiar joys of Italy in the perfumes of orange, citron and jasmine flowers for diverse leagues seaward.' A century later, even the peevish Smollett was charmed by the same coastline. It is now an ugly industrial area which smells of nothing but oil.

The eighteenth-century traveller, although Smollett was something of an exception, was very much a social animal. The Scotsman or the Englishman tended to call first on his own countrymen, unless, like Byron, he had reasons to avoid them. Many were well-established and were able to help. When Robert Adam was about to take a boat from Nice to Genoa he was nervous about the pirates until he discovered that the boats, and indeed the whole province, were commanded by a Scotsman, General James Paterson of the Piedmontese army. The British Consul at Livorno was Sir

John Dick from Edinburgh, a friend of James Boswell. For years, Sir Horace Mann, the British Minister in Florence, entertained and introduced an unending stream of British visitors. In Venice, the British Resident was another Scotsman, John Murray, and the Commander-in-Chief of the Venetian forces yet another, General William Graeme of Buchlyvie. In Rome, there was a whole colony of Scottish artists, connoisseurs and antiquarians. Men like the Abbé Grant, for example, a jovial cleric who combined his duties as Roman agent for the Scottish Catholic Mission with the role of introducing the visitor to everyone from the Pope downwards even if, as one said, he talked so much that the Pope could not get in a word edgeways. 'As good a Jacobite and as good a Catholic, as true a friend and as worthy a man, as e'er a Christian in Europe,' Robert Adam wrote, 'We are two brothers. He is constantly with me, for four or five hours at a time.' Another Jacobite, for of course the Stuart Court in exile was established in Rome, was the Secretary to the Pretender, Andrew Lumsden, who became, in addition, an authority on Roman archaeology.

With such introductions as these, the visitor did not need to be at a loss for an entry into Italian society, which, if he was conscientious, was one of his main objectives. The fathers and others who offered advice to the young men on the Grand Tour are full of admonitions to them to avoid spending all their time with their own countrymen. The object, as Lord Chesterfield wrote to his son, was to seek 'the best company of Rome, observing their manners and forming your own.' He was to shun the 'idle, sauntering, illiterate English living entirely with one another, supping, drinking, and sitting up late at each others' lodgings; commonly in riots and scrapes when drunk; and never in good company when sober.' Or again, 'You have hitherto, I confess, had very few opportunities of keeping polite company. Westminster school is undoubtedly the seat of illiberal manners and brutal behaviour. Leipsig, I suppose, is not the seat of refined and elegant manners. Venice, I believe, has done something; Rome, I hope, will do a great deal more; and Paris will, I dare say, do all that you want; always supposing, that you frequent the best companies, and in the intention of improving and forming yourself; for, without that intention, nothing will do.'

This is perhaps an extreme statement because Lord Chesterfield was the high priest of this religion of 'refined and elegant manners', of which the Grand Tour was supposed to be the seminary. We may think it trivial and absurd enough, but few eighteenth-century travellers were entirely uninfected. Adam, as we saw, flirted with it and had a professional reason for doing so. Boswell was very conscious of it. Smollett was, once again, one of the exceptions.

Even if this attitude was pervaded by snobbery, it had one positive side. It meant that the traveller felt obliged to learn the language and involve himself in the life of the country on one level at least. If he remained on the outside he had failed. He was helped by the astonishing willingness of the Italian aristocracy of the day to accept and entertain the foreigner. If you had the right clothes, the right manners and the right introductions, you were welcome to their balls, their card parties and their box at the opera. Robert Adam says of Princess Borghese: 'the spirit of that woman is immense; for this month past near one hundred people have dined with her every day; she keeps coaches, chaises and horses for every one of them that stay in her house which are not under fifty, with valets and all sorts of people to attend them which pleasure she has purchased at a very dear rate, having sold many of her jewels to raise the ready.' This is perhaps excessive, but hundreds of other people showed the same kind of hospitality on a smaller scale.

I suppose that all of this was a last flicker of the tradition of the royal court, imitated by the aristocracy, because in a way a royal court was like a continuous party, a sort of free hotel, for those who had the ticket of admission. There is a passage in one of Robert Adam's letters which illustrates both the extent to which clothes were part of the price of the ticket and the way in which his Edinburgh common-sense kept breaking through. He had been considering travelling home through Vienna in the hope of presentation at the court of Maria Teresa, but he decided against it, partly because: 'to be received well I must spend £300 or £400 sterling on a suit or two of embroidered and bedaubed clothes which, by the time I am travelling homewards, I will undoubtedly find a little heavy on my pocket.'

But most of the eighteenth–century travellers who have left records describe their purpose as something quite different from Chester-field's pursuit of elegant manners. They all say more or less the same thing. Let me give some examples. At the end of the previous century, John Clerk of Penicuik, a friend and patron of William Adam and his sons, like Boswell, escaped from his legal studies in Holland to Italy. He gave the reason in his memoirs: 'The vast desire I had to see a country so famous for exploits about which all my time had been hitherto spent in reading the classics, likeways a country so replenished with Antiquities of all kinds on so much excelling all other countries in painting and music, I say these things created such a vast desire in me to see it that I am sure nothing in life had ever made happy if I had denied myself this great pleasure and satisfaction.' Robert Adam wrote from Rome, 'Here are amphitheatres, triumphal arches, fragments of temples and other antiquities so grand, so noble and awful that it really fills the mind with a reverential fear and respect.' Smollett explains why, ill as he was, he undertook the journey from Nice: 'I felt an enthusiastic ardour to tread that very classical ground which had been the scene of so many great achievements; and I could not bear the thought of returning to England from the very skirts of Italy, without having penetrated to the capital of that renowned country.' When Boswell arrived in Milan on 15 January 1765, he wrote in his diary: 'This was the first town I saw mentioned by a classic. Often did I repeat, 'Et Mediolani mira omnia, copia rerum.' From Mantova, he sent a letter to John Wilkes, written, as he said, 'on the spot where Virgil lived from this consecrated seat of the Muses which I have come forty miles out of my road to see'. David Hume at Mantova on 11 May 1747 wrote much the same thing: 'We are now in Classic Ground; and I have kist the earth that produc'd Virgil.' Smollett, too, never misses a chance to refer to a place mentioned by Horace or Pliny. Allan Ramsay, the painter and one of Robert Adam's friends in Rome, spent months at Tivoli searching for Horace's Sabine villa. Gibbon, who reached Rome in October 1764, said in his *Autobiography*: 'My temper is not very susceptible of enthusiasm, and the enthusiasm which I do not feel I have ever scorned to affect. But at the distance of twenty-five years I can neither forget nor express the strong emotions which agitated my mind as I first approached and entered the *eternal city*. After a sleepless night, I trod, with a lofty step, the ruins of the Forum; each memorable spot where Romulus stood, or Tully spoke, or Caesar fell, was at once present to my eye; and several days of intoxication were lost or enjoyed before I could descend to a cool and minute investigation. My guide was Mr Byers, a Scotch antiquary of experience and taste.'

Clerk mentions music and painting, but all the emphasis, all the enthusiasm and intoxication are centred on the idea of classical antiquity. This is, in fact, the point of Johnson's observation. Because of their education, men of the eighteenth century had an emotional response to the idea of ancient Rome which it is now difficult for us to recapture. John Fleming says of Robert Adam's education at the High School of Edinburgh that a boy emerged from it 'with a sound knowledge of Latin grammar and literature, especially Cicero, but of nothing else. For nothing, but Latin was taught at the High School.' This is true enough. Lord Cockburn said of Dr Adam, the most famous Rector of the School, that he 'was born to teach Latin, some Greek and all virtue.' But, of course, it was not only the High School of Edinburgh that concentrated on Latin. It was the staple diet of every educated man. Their heads were full of its sonorous music. Quotations from it came easily to their lips. They knew more about the history of Rome than of their own country. All their ideas of historical achievement, power and grandeur, or of nobility of character were associated with it. In going to Rome, they were going to the scene of the events which had occupied their minds, whether they liked it or not, for years during the most impressionable part of their lives. Rome was more than a place, it was the centre of the Universe, the ideal city of the great age of mankind. Perhaps Scotsmen were particularly susceptible to these ideas (although the Englishman, Edward Gibbon, made one of the most eloquent statements of it) because there is a strange affinity between the Roman ideals of *gravitas* and *severitas* and the Presbyterian philosophy of frugality and high endeavour.

Because of this obsession with classical Rome the eighteenth century traveller was generally unenthusiastic, not to say condescending, about Venice. 'The spectacle of Venice', says Gibbon, 'afforded some hours of astonishment'. You might expect Boswell to enjoy it, but all he says is: 'We went to Venice. For the first week I was charmed by the novelty and beauty of so singular a city, but I soon wearied of travelling continually by water, shut up in those lugubrious gondolas.' Robert Adam, though, enjoyed travelling by gondola, 'a pretty slothful way of doing business, and yet I find we Edinburghers easily come into all manner of fashions and laziness is not at all incongruous to our natures'. But his real purpose in coming to Venice was to go to Dalmatia to visit more Roman remains, the Emperor Diocletian's palace at Spalatro. It was the romantics of a later time who, like Byron, found in Venice 'the green island' of their imagination.

With their elevated ideas of the great age of Rome, the eighteenth-century traveller was bound to find that the contemporary reality fell short of his imagination. Benjamin West, who is said to have been the first American painter to study in Italy and who was in Rome at about the same time as Robert Adam, talks about 'the lamentable state into which everything, as well as Art, had fallen in Italy in consequence of the general theocratical despotism'. Robert Adam said that every time he visited the Capitol or the Forum Romanum, 'I am struck with a respectful horror mixt with pity for the total extinction of all that is great and virtuous, nothing but depravity of sentiment, lowness of manners and mercenary aims reigning in their stead.'

So it was in search of ancient Rome, not the contemporary Italy, that these travellers braved the crossing of the Alps, the bad roads and the bad inns. At the same time, I think it is true that they gradually succumbed when they were in Italy–although this is another subject–to the charms of Italian architecture, painting, sculpture, music and the whole way of life. Boswell said in a letter to Rousseau: 'Nine months in this delicious country have done more for me than all the sage lessons which books, or men formed by books, could have taught me. It was my imagination that needed correction, and nothing but travel could have produced this effect.' He summed up his feelings in a phrase: 'O Italy: Land of Felicity! True seat of all elegant delight!'

(Lecture to British Institute, Bologna, 1978.)

6

The Boswell Syndrome

In 1831, T.B. Macaulay, the historian and Victorian sage, published an essay in the *Edinburgh Review* about a new edition of Boswell's *Life of Samuel Johnson*. This was a powerful piece of writing and it established a view of the book and its author which was unchallenged for about a hundred years. He could not have given higher praise to the biography: 'Shakespeare is not more decidedly the first of dramatists than Boswell is the first of biographers'. But for Boswell himself, he had nothing but contempt:

> Servile and impertinent, shallow and pedantic, a bigot and a sot, bloated with family pride, and eternally blustering about the dignity of a born gentleman, yet stooping to be a talebearer, an eavesdropper, a common butt in the taverns of London, curious to know every body who was talked about . . . Everything which another man would have hidden, everything the publication of which would have made another man hang himself, was a matter of gay and clamorous exaltation to his weak and diseased mind . . . All the caprices of his temper, all the illusions of his vanity, all his hypochondriac whimsies, all his castles in the air, he displayed with a cool self-complacency, a perfect unconsciousness that he was making a fool of himself, to which it is impossible to find a parallel in the whole history of mankind.

So Macaulay rages on for several pages. Nowadays, after Freud, most of us are more tolerant of human weakness and would, I think, agree with Lord David Cecil, 'to dislike Boswell is to dislike ourselves'. As far as facts go, Macaulay is right enough, except in one respect. He tells us at length that Boswell was the laughing stock of society, the butt of the taverns and a bore. All the evidence, and there is a great deal of it, shows that, on the contrary, he was very likeable and very popular. He had a wide circle of friends, including some of the best brains of the time. Johnson is recorded, admittedly by Boswell himself, as saying 'Mr. Boswell never was in anybody's company who did not wish to see him again'. Fanny Burney's sister, Charlotte, recorded in her diary after she had met him for the first time, 'He is a charming creature.' Edmund Burke said that he was 'the pleasantest and best-tempered man in the world'. David Hume described him in a letter as a 'young gentleman, very good-humoured, very agreeable and very mad'.

Boswell was an egotist, acutely interested in his own feelings and experiences, but he was also very curious about other people as well. That is why his *Journals*, which he kept for most of his life, reveal not only himself, but the whole of surrounding society. Macaulay was right that he was particularly curious about the great and the famous. As always, Boswell was the first to admit it. In a letter in 1764, he said, 'I am not a great man, but I have an enthusiastic love of great men, and I derive a kind of glory from it.' He was a brilliant chat show presenter born 200 years too soon.

In his *Journal* for 1779, Boswell tells us of another man's diary which came into his hands in the course of his legal practice in Edinburgh: 'Reading this journal made me uneasy to think of my own. It is preserving evidence against oneself; it is filling a mine which may be sprung by accident or intention. Were my journal to be discovered and made public in my own lifetime, how shocking would it be to me. And after my death, would it not hurt my children? I must not be so plain.' Fortunately for us, he did not take his own advice. His journals are among the most frank and honest in any literature. We can learn more about Boswell than any other man who has ever lived.

When Macaulay scorned Boswell's addiction to self-revelation, he knew only a small part of it. He knew only of the one *Journal* which had so far been published, the *Tour to the Hebrides*, covering four months in 1773. The rest have had to wait to this century for publication. It is a double irony not only that Macaulay was right without knowing it, but that it was almost certainly his fierce denunciation which frightened the family into keeping the papers hidden away for generations. It is a near miracle that they survived. How they eventually came to light and into the hands of Yale University is a fascinating story in itself. At all events, general publication of this vast time-bomb began in 1950 with the *London Journal*, 1762–1763. Volume after volume has followed in chronological order and at irregular intervals since then. We have been able to grow older in pace with Boswell almost as though he was a contemporary of our own. The twelfth volume, *The English Experiment*, 1785–1789, edited by Irma S. Lustig and Frederick A. Pottle (Heinemann) has just appeared. This brings us to six years before Boswell's death and only one volume is still to come.

Irma Lustig is right to begin her Introduction to this volume by saying that it is the 'most painful' of the whole saga. This is paradoxical because it deals with the time which should have been the pinnacle of Boswell's career, the years when he was writing his masterpiece, the biography of Johnson. This went on against a background of indecision, misery and humiliation, the direct consequence of Boswell's obsession with London and his love affair with everything English. For years, he had been swithering whether he should cut loose from Scotland and try to make his way at the English bar. As early as 26 July 1781, for instance, he wrote in his *Journal*: 'I was in a most listless state; felt no pleasure in life, nor could imagine any. My fancy roved on London and the English bar, yet I had faint hopes of happiness even in the metropolis, which I dreaded would pall upon me; and I thought it would be wrong to desert Scotland. In short I did not know what to do.'

The new volume opens on 12 November 1785, when Boswell finally took the plunge. As most of his friends had warned him, it was predictably a disaster. He was forty-five and knew almost nothing about English law. He went on circuit and hung about the courts in London, pathetically taking notes of cases like a young beginner. He got virtually no work. Of three briefs he mentions, one was a hoax and for another he arrived at the court when the case was over. Eventually, he had to accept the patronage of Lord Lonsdale, a mean-minded bully who exacted grovelling submission from his dependants. On a summons from Lonsdale, he had to leave his wife as she was dying. It was all a far cry from his dreams of wealth, power and success in the great metropolis.

Why then did Boswell, after long consideration and well aware of the risks, take the decision which made the last ten years of his life such a sordid mess? There were, after all, many things to keep him in Scotland. He had an adequate, if not brilliant, practice at the Scottish bar and every prospect of eventually following in his father's footsteps and becoming one of the law lords. At Auchinleck (or Affleck, as Boswell tells us that it was pronounced) he had a splendid estate and one of the finest Palladian mansion houses in the country. His wife was evidently an admirable woman, intelligent and resourceful and more tolerant and affectionate than Boswell had any right to expect. She and the children were happy where they were and had no wish to leave. In Edinburgh, although he never seems to have realised it, Boswell was surrounded by the greatest figures of the Scottish Enlightenment, many of whom would have made a better subject for a biography than the boorish and pedantic Samuel Johnson. At Auchinleck, Robert Burns was a neighbour and had sought an introduction.

Against all this were Boswell's complicated feelings about Scotland on one side and England on the other. In some moods at least, his Scottish sentiments were strong and he was certainly proud of

being Laird of Auchinleck, holding lands conferred on the family
by James IV. In Holland in 1764 he recorded his regret at the loss of
the Scots language because he had 'the true patriotic soul of an old
Scotsman' and resolved to write a Scots dictionary. He agreed with
Rousseau that Scotland had undone herself at the 'cursed Union',
and told Lord Dunbar in 1765 that he was afraid that most people
in Scotland were reconciled to the Union because 'they have lost
all principle and spirit of patriotism'. But Boswell himself became
reconciled. In a letter to a London newspaper in 1779 he said that
since Scotland had been deprived of 'all national dignity' and 'all the
advantages' of its own parliament, 'London is now the metropolis
of the whole island, the grand emporium of everything valuable, the
strong centre of attraction for all of us'.

Boswell himself felt that attraction overwhelmingly. He thought
he could only be happy in London. For years his *Journals* were full of
discontent with what he called the 'narrow sphere' of Edinburgh and
longing for the 'eminence of London'. It was not only that London
seemed to offer more glittering prizes for his ambition, but that
Edinburgh seemed to him vulgar, ill-bred and over-familiar. He is
always expressing disgust at this Scottish familiarity. In a letter from
Edinburgh in 1784 to his English friend, William Temple, he said,
'How strange, how weak, how unfortunate is it that my *Native city*
and my *countrymen* should affect me with such wretchedness'. And
later in the same letter, 'What of my ambition? What of my love of
England, where I am *absolutely certain* that I *enjoy life*, where as *here*
it is *insipid*, nay, *disgusting*.'

Boswell had some particular reasons for these feelings. London
was associated in his mind with the escapades described in the *London
Journal*, the first escape from the disapproving eye of his father. In
Auchinleck and Edinburgh there was no escape either from the father
or from friends and acquaintances who knew Boswell only too well
and were always ready with outspoken advice or silent disapproval.
Boswell's relationship with his father was not unlike Archie's in
Stevenson's *Weir of Hermiston*. 'You're splairging; you're running
at lairge in life like a wild nowt': Hermiston's words to Archie, but
they catch the very tone of Lord Auchinleck to James Boswell. As
he said in his *Journal* on 8 April 1781 when he was on one of his
visits to London, he hugged himself when he was out of the reach
of Presbyterian prejudices.

But it became something more, or worse, than that. He was
dazzled by the wealth, the power, the fashion, the ostentation of
London. From this it was a short step to begin to be ashamed
of everything Scottish, especially Scottish speech, and to try to
ape the English as convincingly as possible. Even in this latest

volume, towards the end of his life when he is committed to the English experiment, he is still divided. He could see that it was 'unreasonable to be dissatisfied with Edinburgh' and was 'dismal' at the 'idea of making my children *aliens* from Scotland'. But more often he was disgusted with Scottishness. When he had been to the Royal Academy dinner in London, he wrote in his *Journal*: 'I *felt* myself high above anything in Scotland'. He wanted to replace his perfectly trustworthy Scottish servant with an Englishman, if only he could find one that was honest. The saddest note of all is at the end of the book immediately after the death of his wife who had suffered badly from her move to London and had returned to Auchinleck to die. He is wondering if he can agree to the wish of one of his daughters to stay in Edinburgh and writes: 'Were my daughters to be *Edinburgh-mannered girls*, I could have no satisfaction in their company'.

Sad, pathetic, absurd? A curious mixture of snobbery and a sense of inferiority? It is all of these things, but of course, it is not confined to Boswell. It began in 1603 with the courtiers when the King, the fountain of fashion and patronage, flitted to London. It spread gradually down through the aristocracy and the ambitious, the yuppies of the time, to influence the whole of Scottish society. I think that we all recognise this state of mind, which we might call the Boswell syndrome, as by no means uncommon even now. The aristocracy, bearers of ancient Scottish names, long ago succumbed. MPs, beguiled by the charms of Westminster, are often victims. Whether we like it or not, most of us are affected by it directly or indirectly. It is the reason, for instance, why most of us no longer speak Scots, or even English with much of a Scottish accent. In Boswell's *Journals*, and particularly in this latest volume, we have a full case study of the condition. That is why it is a very topical book.

(Talk on BBC Radio Scotland, April 1987.)

7

David Hume, 'Le Bon David'

'There never was any man more fitted, by the general structure of his genius, for seizing and possessing an extensive dominion over Scottish intellect than David Hume. He was very nearly the *beau ideal* of the national understanding.' Thus J. G. Lockhart in *Peter's Letters*. Perhaps at first sight it is a paradoxical judgement, because many of his Scottish contemporaries (including notably James Boswell) were deeply troubled by his religious scepticism. But Lockhart was not alone in thinking of Hume as in some way typical, if also the supreme example, of the Scottish habit of thought. Harold Nicolson, for example, in his *Journey to Java* said: "I read Hume's *Treatise of Human Nature*. It is a relief after all these self-pityers to find oneself in the company of a Scottish mind. It is David Hume whom I now find invigorating, being fortified by his massive Scottish sense and his firm Scottish style.'

Hume deserves to be taken as our national ideal, not only for the power and lucidity of his mind, but for his benevolence, generosity, good nature and general decency. He seems to have been remarkably free from customary human frailty and pettiness. As he was dying, James Edmonstone described him as 'a man of the best Head and Heart, and of the amiable Manners'. Shortly afterwards, Adam Smith said that he considered him as 'approaching as nearly to the idea of a perfectly wise and virtuous man, as perhaps the nature of human frailty will permit'. Both Edmonstone and Smith, it is true, were among his closest friends; but even those offended by his scepticism, or perhaps irritated by his dislike of the English, have never been able then or since to find anything to mar the reputation of 'Le Bon David'.

He also had a genius for friendship, admirably demonstrated in his delightful letters. He found London unsympathetic, 'among the barbarians who dwell on the banks of the Thames,' because of their anti-Scottish prejudice and contempt of the intellect, but he was lionised by both fashionable and intellectual society in Paris. Above all, he was most at his ease in Edinburgh. To quote Lockhart again: 'Perhaps nowhere could have been found a society on so small a scale including more of vigorous intellect, varied information, elegant tastes, and real virtue, affection, and mutual confidence'. His letters still glow, as his life must have done, with the warmth of precisely that affection and mutual confidence. It is the positive side of that Scottish habit of mutual approval and support which irritated Samuel Johnson so much.

Of course, Hume was not entirely free of the prejudices and limitations of his time. Some of them are analysed by Lockhart in *Peter's Letters*. He accuses Hume, Smith and others of their generation of a disembodied intellect which ignored the 'national mode of feeling' which it was left to Walter Scott to restore to literature. Is Hume's attitude to language an example? He was robustly Scottish, devoted to literature and spoke Scots all his life. In spite of this he ignored Robert Fergusson (he died a few years too soon to know about Burns) and patronised and encouraged Blacklock, who wrote in Augustan English. He went to enormous lengths, of which there is ample evidence in his letters, to purge his writing of 'Scotticisms'. Peach is said to have found over 200 of them in Hume's *History*, and Monboddo joked that he died confessing not his sins but his Scotticisms. In spite of all this, he could not have been unconscious of Scottish poetry. Songs in Scots were an essential part of the entertainment in the circles where he moved in Edinburgh. His friend, Gilbert Elliot of Minto, wrote some of them, and his sister, Jane Elliot, one of the best.

Hume, in fact, was in the opposite situation to some of the Scottish poets of today who write in Scots but speak English. How then do we explain his obsession with writing the English of the London which he thought was lapsing into barbarism? There is, I think, a clue in one of his letters to Edward Gibbon in response to Gibbon's first attempt at writing history. He had written this in French because it was a language then 'more generally diffused' than English. Hume advised him to use English; French might be more widespread than English at the moment, but 'our solid and increasing establishments in America promise a superior stability and duration to the English language', a remarkably percipient observation in 1767. Hume preferred English because it was already widely understood and was likely to endure; Scottish words and usages he thought of as an obstacle to understanding anywhere outside Scotland. He was not writing poetry, but history and philosophy, for which English was a ready-made instrument.

Hume is a splendid subject for a biography. For a man who professed to find his keenest pleasure in a book by the fire-side, or in company with a few kindred spirits, he had a very diverse life. He was in France on a minor military raid as well as Embassy Secretary and the Chargé d'Affaires, surely the most enlightened of diplomatic appointments. He was on familiar terms with the leading spirits of the age in Scotland, England and France. He inspired controversy, even if he made it a principle not to respond to it. He was an open and entirely sympathetic character, whose thoughts and actions are well-documented in the writings of himself and his friends.

Mossner rises magnificently to these opportunities.[1] His *Life*, first published in 1954, was twenty years in preparation. He has probably discovered everything that can now be discovered about Hume, and finds a place for it in this rich and delicious book. It is full of incident and character. This is not one of those pedantic American biographies where the scholarship drowns the subject. Mossner writes a plain, workmanlike prose and does not aspire to fine writing, but he reads easily. This is a book which can be read for sheer pleasure as well as the importance of the content.

This 'revised and enlarged' edition, twenty years after the first, is reproduced photographically from the original text, with room for only minor changes in the body of the work and a textual supplement. I notice only two very minor errors of fact. John Macky pretended to be a foreign visitor when he wrote his *Journey through Scotland*, but he was indubitably Scottish.[2] Allan Ramsay's Goose Pie House was not in the Luckenbooths, but (and is still) just outside the Castle. More important than these is the deterioration in publishing standards forced upon us by inflation. The first edition by Thomas Nelson of Edinburgh had fine printing, generous margins, two illustrations in colour and eighteen in black and white, as well as two line drawings. It cost 42s. The new edition has skimped margins, variations in the density of the printing and only one illustration, hazily reproduced. It costs £20. Even so, it is well worth having at the price, and is another reminder how much Scottish letters owe to American scholarship and to the Oxford Press. It also reminds us how much Scottish publishing lost with the disappearance of Nelson's from the Edinburgh scene.

At one point, Mossner quotes the Abbé Dubos, 'Every nation has, 'tis true a particular library of good books.' This *Life of David Hume* takes its place, along with Lockhart's *Life of Walter Scott* and Cockburn's *Memorials*, among the indispensable biographies in the particular Scottish library.

(*Books in Scotland*, No. 7, Spring/Summer, 1980.)

NOTES

1. *The Life of David Hume*, Ernest Campbell Mossner, 2nd edn, Clarendon Press, Oxford.
2. For John Macky see essay no. 4 above.

8

Walter Scott

I am told that this is the first time that anyone has given a lecture in the British Institute in Florence about Sir Walter Scott. I am happy to have the opportunity to make good this omission. An omission it certainly is, but one which is both understandable and astonishing. It is understandable because the existence of this Institute has coincided with a period in which critical and popular esteem for Scott has been at a low ebb, although there are now many signs that the tide has turned again. In 1927 E. M. Forster gave the Clark lectures at Cambridge. He said that he did not care for Scott as a novelist, that he had 'a trivial mind and a heavy style'. That view was not uncommon for a generation or two. But even if we were to accept it, it would still be astonishing for this Institute to ignore Scott, because of his towering reputation in his own day and for long afterwards, and for his profound influence on the literature of Europe and North America, not least in Italy. By any standard, he was a writer of worldwide importance.

Scott was both very Scottish and very European, a combination which is, of course, not uncommon. If I might digress for a little, I should like to say a word or two about his Italian connection. As has often been remarked, the description of Edward Waverley's youthful reading in the third chapter of the novel is not unlike Scott's own. It included 'the numerous romantic poems, which from the days of Pulci, have been a favourite exercise of the wits of Italy'. In a fragment of autobiography prefixed to Lockhart's life, Scott tells us that during his schooldays he came across Tasso and Ariosto in Hoole's translation. He outraged the Greek class at Edinburgh University by arguing in an essay that Ariosto was superior to Homer. (To be honest, he was never much of a Greek scholar.) Some of the first money he earned he spent on Italian lessons to read Dante, Boiardo and Pulci in the original. For the rest of his life, his writing is full of references to Italian literature and to Italian life, music and painting. More than once, he remarks that the discursive style of his novels follows the example of Ariosto. Of course, this was a compliment which the Italian novelists fully repaid. As Manzoni himself said, 'Già se non ci fosse stato Walter

Scott a me non sarebbe venuto in mente di scrivere un romanzo.'
('If Walter Scott had not existed, the idea of writing a novel would
never have entered my head.'

It is not my present purpose to give any account of the critical
response to Scott; but, since I have quoted Forster, let me give one
or two examples of the opposite. Goethe: 'A great genius who does
not have an equal'. Byron: 'He is undoubtedly the Monarch of
Parnassus . . . I have read all Walter Scott's novels at least fifty
times . . . Wonderful man! I long to get drunk with him . . . Scott is
certainly the most wonderful writer of the day. His novels are a new
literature in themselves and his poetry as good as any–if not better.'
Wordsworth called him, 'this wondrous Potentate', and Southey said
that, 'no man ever afforded so much delight'. Then Jane Austen in a
letter to her sister in September 1814, shortly after the publication of
Scott's first novel, *Waverley*, wrote this: 'Walter Scott has no business
to write novels, especially good ones–It is not fair–He has Fame and
Profit enough as a Poet, and should not be taking the bread out of
other people's mouths–I do not like him, and do not mean to like
Waverley if I can help it–but fear I must.' (It is curious, by the way,
that Jane Austen living in the country and far from the literary gossip
of London or Edinburgh should have had no doubt only two months
after the publication of *Waverley* that Scott had written it. That was
supposed to be a closely-guarded secret for years afterwards.)

Again, it is digressive, but I can't help quoting in exchange what
Scott wrote in his *Journal* about Jane Austen in March 1826. It will
serve, at least, to illustrate how alert his literary perception was (for
he was one of the first people to recognise the quality of Jane Austen)
and how generous his attitude to his contemporaries. (He was always
inclined to underestimate his own work and respond enthusiastically
to others):

> Also read again, and for the third time at least, Miss Austen's very
> finely written novel of *Pride and Prejudice*. That young lady had a
> talent for describing the involvements and feelings and characters of
> ordinary life, which is to me the most wonderful I ever met with.
> The Big Bow-wow strain I can do myself like any now going, but
> the exquisite touch, which renders ordinary commonplace things and
> characters interesting, from the truth of the description and sentiment,
> is denied to me. What a pity such a gifted creature died so early.

Since Forster concedes that Scott had a reputation in his day, let me
quote just one or two remarks from critics in this century to show
that, despite him, it has persisted. Lord David Cecil, for example:
'He is a very great novelist indeed – and so far from not being serious,
touched depths and heights often that most English novelists could

never touch at all . . . Scott's grasp on the essentials of character has a Shakespearean firmness that allows him to shift a figure through every vicissitude of mood and circumstance.'

Herbert Grierson: 'The genial, kindly humanity of a Chaucer, a Cervantes, a Scott.'

Virginia Woolf: 'Scott's characters, like Shakespeare's and Jane Austen's, have the seed of life in them.'

Well, that's enough to be going on with.

It was not only critical esteem, and popularity, fame and money that Scott gained by his work, although we might note in passing that the amounts of money he earned were extraordinary. For long he was earning £10,000 a year from his writing alone, and when he was really trying to make money to pay off the debts resulting from the financial collapse of the publishers with whom he was involved, it rose to £20,000 a year. That was at a time when his income as Sheriff of Selkirk, thought to provide a gentlemanly sufficiency, was £300 per year, when a worker on his land thought that he was lucky with £20 a year, when there was no income tax, when the pound was worth very many times what it is worth now. It does not need much calculation to see that this was reward for literary work far beyond anything which is now imaginable. But it was not of these things alone that Lockhart was thinking when he wrote that Scott had won a position which no other man had won by the pen alone. He was courted and esteemed by the great, and the famous, as well as by the people at large, not only in Edinburgh, but in London, Dublin and Paris. In Scotland, he was a sort of uncrowned king, receiving George IV on his visit to Scotland almost as one monarch to another, and doing the honours of his country at Abbotsford for all visitors of any claim to fame or distinction. His fame spread over the whole literate world, but in Scotland, a country usually disinclined to hero-worship, he was regarded with affection, veneration, gratitude. 'Whoever had Scotch blood in him,' wrote Lockhart, 'felt it move more rapidly through his veins when he was in the presence of Scott.' When Sir Robert Peel walked with him in the High Street of Edinburgh in 1822 he said that the reaction of the crowd was the first thing that gave him a notion of 'the electric shock of a nation's gratitude'. The same word occurs again in the speech which Lord Meadowbank made at a dinner in Edinburgh in February 1827, when Scott for the first time admitted publicly that he had written the Waverley Novels: 'We owe to him, as a people, a large and heavy debt of gratitude'. The reason for this feeling will, I hope, appear in the course of these remarks.

Walter Scott was born in Edinburgh in 1771. His father was a douce, God-fearing Writer to the Signet, that is to say a lawyer in a fair way of business; but he was the first member of his family to settle in a town and adopt a learned profession. For on both sides of Scott's ancestry, his antecedents were people deeply involved in the history and tradition of the Scottish Border, a region where centuries of bearing the first brunt of the war with England had bred a society based on kinship, a sturdy, self-reliant people, accustomed to taking the law into their own hands, and a great oral poetic tradition. When Scott was only eighteen months old he lost the use of a leg from some form of infantile paralysis, and was sent into the heart of the Borders in the hope that country life would restore his health. His earliest memories therefore were of growing up on his grandfather's farm of Sandy-Knowe, in the shade of one of the Border keeps, Smailholme. His head was filled with the old songs and tales which, as he wrote in his brief scrap of *Autobiography* 'then formed the amusement of a retired country family'. He tells us that his grandmother in particular, 'in whose youth the old Border depredations were a matter of recent tradition' used to tell him many a tale. The family tradition was also, for the most part, Jacobite, and 1745 was an even more recent memory.

Years afterwards, in a letter of December 1806 to Robert Surtees, Scott described this Jacobite influence: 'My great-grandfather was *out*, as the phrase goes, in Dundee's wars and in 1715, and had nearly the honour to be hanged for his pains . . . But besides this, my father, although a Borderer, transacted business for many Highland lairds, and particularly the one old man called Stuart of Invernanyle, who had been *out* both in 1715 and 1745, and whose tales were the absolute delight of my childhood . . . I become a valiant Jacobite at the age of ten years, and ever since reason and reading came to my assistance I have never quite got rid of the impression which the gallantry of Prince Charles made on my imagination'. He might have added that he met these Highlanders not only in his father's office, but in journeys on legal business into the depths of the Highlands themselves.

What did Jacobitism mean to Scott apart from a romantic attachment to the Stuarts and an admiration for those who in 1715 and 1745 had been willing to risk life and fortune in attempts to restore them to the throne of their ancestors? In his *Tales of a Grandfather*, he remarks that 'the cause of the Stewart family gained a host of new adherents, more from dislike to the Union [that is, of course, the Union of the English and Scottish Parliaments in 1707] than any partiality to the exiled prince . . . "Prosperity to Scotland, and no Union" is the favourite inscription to be found on Scottish sword blades betwixt 1707 and 1746.' Then, there is a studied judgement in the last chapter of *Waverley*, of which the theme is Jacobitism.

He says of the Jacobites that they: 'Averse to intermingle with the English, or adopt their customs, long continued to pride themselves upon maintaining ancient Scottish manners and customs'. 'This race' he adds, 'has now almost entirely vanished from the land, and with it, doubtless, much absurd political prejudice; but also, many living examples of singular and disinterested attachment to the principles of loyalty which they received from their fathers, and of old Scottish faith, hospitality, worth and honour. It was my accidental lot, though not born a Highlander to reside, during my childhood and youth, among persons of the above description.'

To those influences of the Border and the Jacobites, which were romantic, if you like, were added those of Edinburgh. Edinburgh in the great age of the Enlightenment, 'the Capital of Reason and of Humanity', as Stendhal called it. He lived in it as the New Town was growing up around him, the 'Heavenly City of the Edinburgh Philosophers', in the words of David Daiches, 'ordered, elegant, rational, optimistic'. He went to the High School under Dr Adam, 'born to teach Latin, some Greek, and all virtue'. Then on to the University, where William Robertson, the historian and a central figure in the Enlightenment, was still Principal. He studied Moral Philosophy under Dugald Stewart, History under Tytler of Woodhouselee, and Scots Law under David Hume, a nephew of the philosopher. Adam Fergusson, the son of one of the central figures in the Enlightenment, was one of his closest friends. He was surrounded, in other words, by the atmosphere of philosophical Edinburgh.

Scott, having been steeped in the Ballads, was now steeped in Scots Law; for his father, above all things (like Saunders Fairford in *Redgauntlet*) was determined to keep him to his legal studies. He served an apprenticeship in his father's own office before returning to the University and the lectures of David Hume to study for the bar. Of these lectures, Scott writes this:

I can never sufficiently admire the penetration and clearness of conception which were necessary to the arrangement of the fabric of law, formed originally under the strictest influence of feudal principles, and innovated, altered, and broken in upon by the change of times, of habits, and of manners, until it resembles some ancient castle, partly entire, partly ruinous, partly dilapidated, patched and altered during the succession of ages by a thousand additions and combinations, yet still exhibiting, with the marks of its antiquity, symptoms of the skill and wisdom of its founders, and capable of being analysed and made the subject of a methodical plan by an architect who can understand the various style of the different ages in which it was subjected to alteration. Such an architect has Mr Hume been to the law of

Scotland, neither wandering into fanciful and obstruse disquisitions, nor satisfied with presenting to his pupils a dry and undigested detail of the laws in their present state, but combining the past state of our legal enactments with the present, and tracing clearly and judiciously the changes which took place, and the causes which led to them.

Essentially, you will notice, an historical approach; Scott's description of Hume's methods and purposes could in fact be applied to his own novels.

If the influences of Sandy Knowe and Edinburgh were in many ways at variance–the turbulence, lawlessness, passion and the supernatural of the Border Ballads, the classic order, the rationality and the scepticism of Edinburgh–they also had points in common. For one thing, they were both concerned with history, both were conscious of the past, and aware of the forces of change. David Hume, the philosopher this time, said in one of his letters: 'This is the historical Age and this is the historical Nation.' It was not only that he and Robertson and Tytler wrote history, the whole approach of the Scottish Enlightenment was historical. Bagehot described Adam Smith's *The Wealth of Nations* as an illustration of the thesis 'How man, from a savage, rose to be a Scotchman', and indeed the main concern of the Scottish Enlightenment was with the evolution of civil society. Partly this was because the shock of the loss of national independence in 1707 gave a special quality of nostalgia to the past, and partly because the drastic changes brought about by 1707, 1745 and the beginnings of the industrial revolution forced people to think about the ways in which society had, and should, change. 'There is no European nation', wrote Scott in the last chapter of *Waverley*, 'which, within the course of half a century, or little more, has undergone so complete a change as this kingdom of Scotland.'

Then the influence of Scots Law, if opposed to the lawless traditions of the Borders, was, in a different way, also concerned with the defence of a Scottish institution. It is described by a distinguished Scottish lawyer of today, Lord Cameron, as 'the historic law of a proud and ancient kingdom which had been in large measure fused into a coherent, flexible and compendious scheme of jurisprudence by the earlier work of Stair and the later labours of John Erskine, a child of the Enlightenment'. Like the Church and the national system of education, it had been left intact by the Union, although subject now to modification by a Parliament no longer under Scottish control. Scots lawyers therefore tend to think of themselves as the custodians of an important part of the distinctive Scottish contribution to our common civilisation. Scott, in addition to his writing, was a practising Scots lawyer for his whole working life, as apprentice, advocate, Sheriff of Selkirk and Clerk to the Court of Session. 'I determined', Scott wrote, 'that literature should be my staff, but not my crutch.' This also was part of the tradition. The advocates were an intellectual élite: 'the most intellectual class in the country', Cockburn called them and many wrote books, although Scott was the first, but not the last, to write novels.

Of course, the influences were by no means only Scottish. Apart from the Latin and Greek of school and university, he read widely in English as well as Scottish literature. He yielded to no one in his admiration for Shakespeare. I have mentioned his reading in Italian, and he read French, Spanish and German as well. (Indeed his first appearance in print was in a verse translation of a German poem.) He had a remarkable memory, and retained almost everything he read. He could recite pages of verse which he had read only once. But above all, it was his knowledge of Scottish history which was deep, detailed and at instant command. When, towards the end of his life, he was asked to write a History of Scotland, he confided to his *Journal*, 'this would be very easy work. I have the whole stuff in my head, and could write *currente calamo*'.

With this background, it is hardly surprising that his first major literary work in 1802 should have been a collection of the ballads, *The Minstrelsy of the Scottish Border*. I do not propose to go through Scott's work, book by book. That is subject-matter not for one lecture, but for a whole series, for his output was vast: eight long poems, twenty-seven novels, a Life of Napoleon in five volumes, two Histories of Scotland, editions of Dryden and Swift with biographies, Lives of the Novelists, over thirty volumes of miscellaneous prose, twelve volumes of letters which still does not include all of them, the great *Journal*. All this, in addition to his two legal jobs, his life as a country gentleman and his spacious entertaining, membership of committees, boards and the like, and a good deal of trouble with his health. Don't ask me how he did it; but don't be surprised either that his work is uneven and a lot of it hurried and careless. Nor, by the way, do I mean to go into the details of his financial affairs, if only because I am not sure that I understand them completely myself. Briefly, the story is that he was financially involved in the printing and publication of his own books (originally by lending money to a school friend to help him set up as a printer in Edinburgh). He borrowed money against the credit of these firms to finance the building of his country house, Abbotsford, and more and more land around it. When one of the interdependent firms, publishers in London, could not meet its obligations in a run on the money market in 1826, Scott found that in spite of all his earnings, he was now heavily in debt. Instead of accepting bankruptcy, he sat down to earn enough money by his pen to pay off his obligations. He nearly succeeded, but he killed himself in the process.

I mention *the Minstrelsy* for two reasons. First of all because it involved him in travel all over the Borders, speaking to all and sundry, acquiring an intimate knowledge of Scottish life and the Scottish tongue. 'Sir Walter speaks to every man as if they were blood-relations', one of his workers once said. And Shortreed, his companion on many of these Border forays, adds, 'He aye did as the lave did; never made himsel' the great man, or took any airs in the company. He was makin' himself a' the time.'

I mention *The Minstrelsy* also because of a passage in the *Introduction* which, I think, is one of the keys to the motives and emotions which lay behind his work:

'By such efforts, feeble as they are, I may contribute something to the history of my native country; the peculiar features of whose manners and character are daily melting and dissolving into those of her sister and ally. And, trivial as may appear such an offering to the Manes of a Kingdom, once proud and independent, I hand it upon her altar with a mixture of feelings which I shall not attempt to describe.'

Lockhart in his *Life of Scott* describes an episode in 1806 after a meeting of the Faculty of Advocates about some changes which were proposed in traditional Scottish legal practice. Scott had argued against this with great energy. Lockhart describes what happened afterwards:

When the meeting broke up, he walked across the Mound on his way to Castle Street, between Mr Jeffrey and another of his reforming friends, who complimented him on the rhetorical powers he had been displaying, and would willingly have treated the subject-matter of the discussion playfully. But his feelings had been moved to an extent far beyond their apprehension: he exclaimed, 'No, no 'tis no laughing matter; little by little, whatever your wishes may be, you will destroy and undermine, until nothing of what makes Scotland Scotland shall remain.' And so saying, he turned round to conceal his agitation but not until Mr Jeffrey saw tears gushing down his cheek, resting his head until he recovered himself on the wall of the Mound. Seldom, if ever, in his more advanced age, did any feelings obtain such mastery.'

Clearly, then, Scott, like the Jacobites in his description, rejected with deep feeling this process of 'melting and dissolving'. In fact, there are entries in his *Journal* which show this quite specifically. So does his only open intervention in political controversy, the *Letters of Malachi Malagrowther*. But he felt, in a spirit of melancholy resignation, that it was inevitable. In much of Scott's work, and especially in his poetry, a strain of melancholy is very obvious, which is strange in a man whom everyone found eminently sane, convivial and at peace with the world. One of his recent critics, Thomas Crawford, has described this prevailing mood as 'mourning for Scotland's vanished independence' and he quotes:

> Still, as I view each well-known scene,
> Think what is now, and what hath been,
> Seems as, to me, of all bereft,
> Sole friends thy woods and streams were left;
> And thus I love them better still,
> Even in extremity of ill.

This is from one of Scott's long narrative poems, the *Lay of the Last Minstrel*. This with its successors, *Marmion* and the *Lady of the Lake*, was the foundation of Scott's fame and fortune. They were enormously popular in their day and sold as poetry never sold before. There are fine things in them, and I think they can still be read for pleasure by those attuned to them, even if it is an unfashionable and unsophisticated pleasure. Scott as a real poet does as much appear there as in his imitations of the ballads and in the lyrics, again melancholy for the most part, scattered with reckless profusion throughout the novels.

And, of course, it is mainly of the novels that I want to speak, because it is on them that Scott's reputation as a writer of the first rank depends, and not by any means on all of the twenty-seven. There is a very wide measure of agreement on the novels which demand attention. Lord David Cecil puts it like this: 'All Scott's best books, *Waverley, Guy Mannering*, the *Antiquary*, the *Heart of Midlothian, Redgauntlet*, the *Bride of Lammermoor*, take place in Scotland and its borders; and all happen within that hundred or so odd years of his birth covered by the memory of someone he might have known.' There are surprising omissions from this particular list, especially *Old Mortality* which many people would put in the very first place, and *Rob Roy* with two of the greatest characters, Bailie Nicol Jarvie and Andrew Fairservice, the *Legend of Montrose*, if only because of Dugald Dalgetty. I would add, too, the *Fortunes of Nigel*, which is set not in Scotland but in Stuart London, and outside the 100-year period, but most of the characters are Scottish from James VI and I downwards. Some of the other novels set outside Scotland and in an earlier period are not without merit, especially *Quentin Durward*. I am told that *Ivanhoe* is regarded in Italy as 'il capolavoro dello Scott'; but I can only assume that the real quality of the great novels is lost in translation. For the fact is that these other novels, to a large extent, deserve the sort of condemnation that Forster applied to them all.

Why is it that Scott is only at his best on his native heath? There are, I think, many reasons. In the first place, Scotland was the only country which Scott knew well at first hand and he knew it with an intimacy and depth of knowledge that could not be excelled. That is where all the influences of his early life were leading. Remember Shortreed's phrase, 'he was makin' himself a' the time'. For years, he had been studying the history and literature of the country from every written record that was available to him, to the point where he could write a volume for an encyclopaedia, quite literally, straight out of his head. And his knowledge came not only from written records, but from conversations with people of all kinds with his ability to talk to everyone on their terms. Washington Irving said in a letter to him (and perhaps it took an American at that time to be so unembarrassed about saying such a thing): 'Somehow or other there is a genial sunshine about you that warms every creeping thing into heart and confidence.' Scott's head was so full of anecdotes, reminiscences, oral traditions, and popular songs that he could entertain any company with it for days on end. The country, the people, its traditions and institutions engaged his deepest emotions. Lockhart, his son-in-law and biographer, who knew him as well as anyone could, expressed it in these words: 'The love of his country became indeed a passion . . . he would have bled and died to preserve even the airiest surviving nothing of her antique pretensions for Scotland.' When he was writing about Scotland, he was writing both with knowledge and with passion, and passion, as Forster in fact implies, is the stuff of literature.

Then there was a purely linguistic reason, his ability to write dialogue in Scots which far exceeded any ability he had in the handling of English. In case you may think that this is national prejudice, let me quote what an Englishman and a German have to say on the subject. Lord David Cecil: 'Scott's vernacular dialogue is style in its highest sense; every image apt, every cadence exact to follow the undulation of the speaker's mood, yet never unmusical. He has achieved that rarest of literacy triumphs, a form of speech which sounds perfectly natural and which is yet as expressive as poetry.' The German, Kurt Wittig, says much the same, but in more detail: 'The Scots dialogue is the highlight of Walter Scott's style . . . the rich vivid idioms, the pregnant and suggestive simplicities, the apt and pithy force, the subtle humour, the bold comparisons, and above all the rhythm, of Scots speech . . . Scots thus assumes a semi-poetic quality by its undercurrent of rhythm and submerged music. The vernacular, to Scott, is the language of the heart, and his Scots passages are fraught with a higher significance and strike at the very core of feeling; and in moments of deepest feeling, the suggestive terseness of Scots enables him to be more sharply realistic and supremely articulate . . . These key scenes are invariably written in a powerful rhythm and with a command of sound sequences that show Scott as a verbal artist, a poet, of the highest quality. It is here, and in the interspersed lyrics from the mouths of the same people, that Scott rises to sublime height. . . Scott usually is greatest when most Scottish.'

Another of the points on which most of his critics are agreed is that one of his strengths is in the creation of a great variety of entirely convincing, and often very comic, characters. Time and again over the last 150 years or so since the novels were first published, critics have been driven to bring in the name of Shakespeare when they have tried to find a parallel in the whole of literature. I have quoted two examples. It is perhaps the main reason why the novels gave such a shock of astonished pleasure when they first appeared, and is still their chief delight. But the characters are strangely uneven. Edwin Muir says that they are, 'half flesh and blood and half pasteboard, unreal where he dealt with highly civilised people, and real where he dealt with peasants, adventures and beggars.' This is an exaggeration because the living characters are of a much greater variety than this, including kings and barons as well as beggars, and many of them are civilised enough; but it is true that most, not all, of the flesh and blood are people without social pretention and it is the nominal heroes and heroines who are pasteboard. And most of the flesh and blood speak Scots, another reason why the real quality of the *Waverley* novels hardly exists in the novels set outside Scotland.

This mixture of flesh and blood and pasteboard is the major defect in Scott as a novelist and the reason for it is the major critical problem which we have to try to answer. There is a clue in a passage in Lockhart's *Life* where he describes Scott's reaction when Lockhart made a remark to him which suggested an attitude of intellectual superiority. Scott replied:

'I fear you have some very young ideas in your head:—are you not too apt to measure things by some reference to literature—to disbelieve that anybody can be worth much care who has no knowledge of that sort of thing, or taste for it? God help us! What a poor world this would be if that were the true doctrine! I have read books enough, and observed and conversed with enough of eminent and splendidly culti-vated minds, too, in my time; but I assure you, I have heard higher sentiments from the lips of poor *uneducated* men and women, when exerting the spirit of severe yet gentle heroism under difficulties and afflictions . . . than I ever yet met with out of pages of the Bible.

(A spendidly apt rebuke, by the way, not only to Lockhart, but to Edwin Muir as well; Scott might almost have been replying to him in advance.) These remarks of Scott are illustrated constantly in the novels. We find these simple men and women not only providing ironic comment, and comic relief, bringing the romance back to earth, but rising to the great moments of poetry and tragedy.

Of course, these simple men and women spoke Scots, because that is what they did in the Scotland of his time where Walter Scott knew them; and not only the simple people, but people of all kinds including Scott himself. The change, the 'melting and dissolving', the spread of English speech had begun certainly, but it had not yet gone very far. An Englishman, Edward Topham, spent a year in Edinburgh from 1774 to 1775, just three years after Scott was born, and wrote a book about it. This is what he says about the conversation of the *literati*, David Hume, Adam Smith and the like: 'I shall only say, that they appear to me, from their conversation, to write English as a foreign tongue; their mode of talking, phrase, and expression but little resembling the language of their works.' That is the point, the Scots were learning English as a foreign language, and inevitably spoke it in a stiff and stilted manner, like those pasteboard figures, losing much of the pith, warmth and humour of their native speech in the process. Alexander Carlyle, who died in 1805, wrote in his *Autobiography*: 'Since we began to affect speaking a foreign language, which the English dialect is to us, humour, it must be confessed, is less apparent in conversation.' But it was not only humour that was lost. D. D. Derlin in his book on Scott says this: 'It is often remarked that Scott's strength lies in his handling of the vernacular. What, perhaps, needs saying is that his strength lies here not simply because he had an ear for Lowland speech, but because he endorsed those qualities of mind and character which the vernacular so accurately conveyed.' If that is true, as I think it is, it suggests that with the erosion of a language, the character expressed by it is eroded as well. There is a very intimate relationship between language and personality, which is why people from Belgium to Quebec, let us say, feel so emotionally about it. It helps, I think, to explain why Scott felt so strongly about the 'melting and dissolving'.

Now, we must turn to history, for these are historical novels, and the historical approach, you will remember, was the essence of the intellectual atmosphere of the Edinburgh of the Enlightenment which Scott breathed in his youth. The novels are historical in several senses, apart from the obvious one that they were set in the past. Firstly, in most of them there are brilliant succinct accounts of the political, economic and sometimes military situation in which the events take place. They are admirably fair and objective, so that you could hardly guess from them where Scott's own sympathies lay. In these passages, taken in isolation, Scott is behaving like a conventional historian of his time, although it was new to place a novel so firmly in its historical context, instead of taking it for granted. Historical analysis of this kind was however only ancillary to Scott's principal method which is to express the history through the attitudes and experiences of his characters. He invests some of them, although again it is only a subsidiary method, with a remarkable gift to sum up a whole historical situation in a sentence or two of dialogue. Bailie Nicol Jarvie in *Rob Roy* for example says this:

> 'Whisht, Sil! Whisht! it's ill-scraped tongues like yours, that make mischief atween neighbourhoods and nations. There's nothing sae gude on this side o' time but it might hae been better, and that may be said o' the Union. Nane were keener against it than the Glasgow folk, wi' their rabblings and their risings, and their mobs, as they ca' them now-a-days. But it's an ill wind blows naebody gude. Let ilka ane roose the Lord as they find it. I say, Let Glasgow flourish! Whilk is judiciously and elegantly putten round the toun's arms, by way of by-word. Now, since St Mungo catched herrings in the Clyde, what was ever like to gar us flourish like the sugar and tobacco trade? Will anybody tell me that, and grumble at the treaty that opened us a road west-awa' yonder?'

Well that's the argument for the Union in a nutshell. And the argument against? Here in another nutshell is a scrap of dialogue from *The Heart of Midlothian*:

> 'I dinna ken muckle about the law,' answered Mrs Howden, 'but I ken, when we had a King, and a Chancellor, and parliament men o' our ain, we could aye peeble them wi' stanes when they werna gude bairns. But naebody's nails can reach the length o' Lunnon.'

But even when his characters are not referring like that to great historical events, Scott makes us see that they are part of them, that history is the sum-total of the lives of the people of the time who were once as alive as we are now, if not more so. This may now seem commonplace enough; but when the Waverley Novels first appeared, it was a sensational novelty. The point was made by Thomas Carlyle in 1838:

> These Historical Novels have taught all men this truth, which looks like a truism, and yet was as good as unknown to writers of history and others, till so taught: that the bygone ages of the world were actually filled by living men not by protocols, state-papers,

controversies and abstractions of men . . . History will henceforth
have to take thought of it.

Well, history has taken thought. Scott's influence on historians even
more than on novelists has transformed historical writing. It is one
of the ways in which his influence continues to affect indirectly even
people who have never read one of his novels in their lives.

There is yet another sense in which the novels are historical. The
theme of nearly all of them is change, the conflict between one way of
life and another, one set of values and another, one old and decaying,
one new and forceful, one replacing the other, not necessarily because
it is better, but because it is stronger. Scott, usually through the eyes
of one of his pasteboard heroes, who have their purpose, looks
at both sides with a clear-sighted realism which is anything but
romantic. The hero is for a time tempted by the attractions of the
weaker side, but avoids total commitment and escapes in time the
full consequences of the inevitable defeat. But our sympathies have
been engaged like the hero's and we feel the pathos of the defeat, but,
again like him, are made to see, as Flora MacIvor says in *Waverley*:
'it was impossible it could end otherwise than thus'. The resolution
is not compromise or optimism, but resignation, with a tinge of
melancholy. And we have seen why Scott felt like this.

This theme of conflict, change and the human response to it is
universal because it is something which is experienced in every
country and in every age. Walter Scott was firmly rooted in his
Scottish background. 'No Scotchman of his time was more entirely
Scotch than Walter Scott', wrote Thomas Carlyle, 'the good and the
not so good, which all Scotchmen inherit, ran through every fibre
of him'. But the appeal of his writing was universal as was evident
from his enormous popularity and influence in the whole literate
world of his day. It was universal for many reasons and perhaps
not least because of this theme. Heine thought so and so I end with
a quotation from him:

'Their theme is the mighty sorrow for the loss of national peculiar-
ities, swallowed up in the universality of the newer culture, a sorrow
which is throbbing in the hearts of all peoples.'

(Lecture to the British Institute, Florence, 1977.)

9

The Politics of Sir Walter Scott

The earliest of the biographies of Walter Scott, the *Life* published by George Allan in Edinburgh in 1834, drew attention to one of the paradoxes about him which is, I think, still puzzling, and which leads directly to the question of his political attitude. There was, wrote George Allan, 'an extraordinary inconsistency in his character. In his habits, his demeanour and his desires, he was decidedly aristocratic. On the other hand, if we examine his prose writings, it will be found that a spirit of what is termed "Liberalism" predominates throughout; it will be found that almost all his best, that is to say, his most virtuous and amiable specimens of human character, are taken from the lower classes. Scott's heart was evidently with the great mass of society'.[1] Allan refers, of course, to Scott's novels. He is making the same point as John Buchan made when he said that the plain folk are the 'true heroes and heroines of the novels'.[2] There is also the frequent ridicule of the pretensions of rank, as with such characters as Lady Bellenden or Sir Arthur Wardour, and the outspoken social criticism by the sexton in the *Bride of Lammermoor*, for instance, or by Christie Steele in *The Chronicles of the Canongate*.

George Allan, as you may suspect from the quotation with which I began, was evidently no Tory himself. Nor did he have any illusions about Scott's party allegiance. 'Scott', he wrote, 'had thrown himself, with the blind vehemence of youth, into the ranks of the British Tories, the most narrow minded politicians of the age. Dogged adherence to what was established, be it right or wrong, deep, bitter and enduring hatred of every opponent, was what they required'.[3]

Whether or not that is a fair description of the Tory party of Scott's time, there is no doubt that he always thought of himself, and always described himself, as a Tory. In a letter to Anna Seward in January 1807, for example, he wrote:

'I was not only very early disposed to what have been called Tory principles by the opinions of those whom I respected and was brought up to respect, and was bound to respect, but the favours I received, the intimacy in which I lived with many of Lord Melville's family, his nephew and son in particular, was founded as much upon attachment to their measures in 1792-3, as to gratitude for favours received at a time when they were truly valuable.'4

You notice in that passage that Scott gives equal weight to 'favours received' as to 'attachment to their measures'. Scott was consistent throughout his life in a frank acceptance of the patronage system as one of the bonds which held society, and the Tory party in particular, together. It is easy for us to disapprove today, when patronage is more subtle and discreet, and when there are other avenues open for advancement in politics, the law, the universities or government service. In Scott's time it was otherwise. Patronage was part of the political machinery of the time and Scott evidently saw no reason to be ashamed of it. He used it, with due restraint and modesty, in the service of himself and his family and generously in support of innumerable friends and acquaintances. As Graham McMaster said in his recent book, 'At one time or another he seems to have tried to find jobs for half of the unemployable gentry of the borders'.5 When he wrote in this way to Lord Melville in January 1825 to further the career of J.G. Lockhart, he was quite plain in his language: 'Make him your own, my dear Lord, by your countenance and patronage, as your father made me his many years ago'.6

It was, of course, not only in operating the patronage system that Scott was an active, if usually discreet, Tory. He played his part in the wheeling and dealing that went on to arrange parliamentary elections among the handful of voters then entitled to vote. Much of the correspondence that Grierson did not print is taken up with it,7 but there is enough in his edition of the letters to show the process at work.8 We find Scott buying a feudal superiority to secure an extra vote.9 He was even asked, at least once, to stand as a candidate himself.10 In the politics of the universities, he helped to organise the campaign to secure the chair of Moral Philosophy in Edinburgh for John Wilson, the 'Christopher North' of Blackwoods. Wilson knew nothing about philosophy but his politics were reliable, and he was therefore thought preferable to Sir William Hamilton, who was the opposite in both respects.

Scott, too, was at times, directly or indirectly, a propagandist for the Tory cause. He helped to launch the Quarterly as a Tory riposte to the Whig Edinburgh Review. Especially when Lockhart became editor, Scott was profuse with his political advice. He pirated Constable's idea of an Edinburgh Annual Register, at least partly to prevent him publishing one under Whig influence. He wrote two series of political articles, The Visionary in 1819 and The Letters of Malachi Malagrowther in 1826. There are the well-known episodes of his frustrated attempt to publish a fourth *Malachi* letter and his address to the electors of Jedburgh. He was ready to take up arms in defence of the Government and the established order. In 1791 he instigated the formation of the Royal Edinburgh Volunteer Light Dragoons, and in 1819 he took the lead again in forming a corps of yeomanry in the Borders.

From all these points of view then, Scott was what would now be called (although I am not sure that the Tories themselves use the term) a party activist. This fact alone, no doubt, tells us a good deal about his feelings and opinions, but, at the best, only vaguely. Party labels at any time cover a multitude of diversity. The party system of Scott's day bears only a very remote resemblance to its present counterpart. Obviously, we have to try to look beyond the label. In attempting this, I shall rely partly on Scott's published writing, including the *Journal*, and partly on his letters. I am mindful of David Hewitt's recent warning about the unreliability of letters as a record of views and opinions. He quotes Scott himself: 'letters at least those of a general and miscellaneous kind very rarely contain the real opinions of the writer.'[12] However, there are some points in Scott's letters which he repeats so often to diverse correspondents, that I think that it is reasonable to conclude that they represent strongly held convictions. They are consistent, too, with the views which he expressed in works which gave him an opportunity to express his political opinions directly: *The Life of Napoleon, The Visionary* and the *Letters of Malachi Malagrowther*.

Let me begin with the two charges which George Allan made against the Tory party of his time – 'dogged adherence to what was established' and 'enduring hatred of every opponent'. Scott has often been accused of the first of these, most notably by Hazlitt: 'The author of *Waverley* might just as well get up and make a speech at a dinner at Edinburgh, abusing Mr MacAdam for his improvement in the roads, on the grounds that they were nearly *impassable* in many places 'sixty-year since'.[13] Certainly Scott was resistant to what he called 'rash innovation' and I shall look at this in more detail later. At the same time he was not opposed in theory or practice to cautious and necessary change. He was even an enthusiast for technological innovation. Abbotsford, you will remember, was equipped with gas-lighting as well as auld nick-nackets. In his account of the origins of the French Revolution in the *Life of Napoleon*, he suggested that a major cause was the suppression of criticism of the practice, as distinct from the theory, of government[14] and its consequent failure to make 'such alterations as the lapse of time and change of manners may render necessary.'[15] He advocated a balance between reckless experiment and necessary improvement and change, as in this passage: 'If there were no Whigs, our constitution would fall to pieces for want of repair; if there were no Tories, it would be broken in the course of a succession of rash and venturous experiments'.[16]

Allan's second accusation, enduring hatred of every opponent, is not one that can be applied to Scott at all. Certainly, he was capable at times of strong language about Whigs and Radicals. In a letter to William Laidlaw in 1818, he said: 'I am very jealous of Whiggery, under all modifications; and, I must say, my acquaintance with the total want of principle in some of its warmest professors does not tend to recommend it'.[17] He wrote to his brother, Thomas Scott, in 1819: 'Radical is a word in a very bad odour here, being used to denote a set of blackguards a hundred times more mischievous and absurd than our old friends in 1794 and 1795'.[18] Normally his tone was much more conciliatory. In the letter to Anna Seward in which he declared his Tory principles he went on to say: "I am candid enough to esteem the principles and cherish the friendship of many whose political opinions are different from my own, because I know they are adopted by those who hold them from an internal conviction of their rectitude'.[19] In the Preface to *The Visionary*, he wrote: 'Thinking a competition of parties for power and popularity makes, in fact, one of the vivifying principles of our constitution, I cannot look with angry feelings on those arranged opposite to me in this war of opinion'.[20]

Scott's instincts were conciliatory and not confrontational. He was fond of referring with approval to the judge who always wanted when faced with two conflicting parties to 'gar them gree'. He was often impatient of party conflict and anxious for a truce between them in the interests of Scotland. 'The Tories and Whigs may go be damned together, as names that have disturbed old Scotland, and torn asunder the most kindly feelings since the first day they were invented'[21] he wrote in his *Journal* on 20 January 1826. He even had at least a tentative idea of forming an all-embracing party in the Scottish interest. 'I would fain have a society formed for extending mutual understanding,' he wrote to Henry Francis Scott in January 1831. 'Why should not old Scotland have a party among her own children?'[22] There is a similar thought in the second *Malachi* letter: 'The Scottish Members of Parliament should therefore lose no time – not an instant . . . in uniting together in their national character of the Representatives of Scotland. Do not let us, like our ancestors at Falkirk, fall to jealousies among ourselves, when heart, and voice, and hand, should be united against the foreign enemy.'[23]

Scott, of course, often described himself as a Jacobite. He writes in the Ashesteil *Memoir* of:

a very strong prejudice in favour of the Stuart family, which I had originally imbibed from the songs and tales of the Jacobites. The latter political propensity was deeply confirmed by the stories told in my hearing of the cruelties exercised in the executions at Carlisle, and in the Highlands, after the battle of Culloden. One or two of our distant relations had fallen on that occasion, and I remember detesting the name of Cumberland with more than infant hatred'.[24]

Scott never entirely lost this 'prejudice', although he described it in later years as belonging to 'the fancy rather than the feelings'[25] (in a letter to Lockhart in August 1828). He told George Ellis in October 1801: 'I believe a tincture of Jacobitism which tho' rather an Instinct than a principle adopted from reason, forms a frequent feature in the character of the animal called a thorough bred Scotsman'.[26]

The question is what did he mean by this 'political propensity', Jacobitism? He certainly did not mean that he was in favour of anything so wildly unrealistic as a new attempt to restore the Stuarts. In a letter of July 1813 to Marianne Clephane, he said: "Seriously, I am very glad I did not live in 1745, for though as a lawyer I could not have pleaded Charles's right, and as a clergyman I could not have prayed for him, yet as a soldier I would, I am sure, against the convictions of my better reason, have fought for him, even to the bottom of the gallows'. But then he goes on to say: 'But I am not the least afraid nowadays of making my feelings walk hand in hand with my judgement, though the former are Jacobitical, the latter inclined for public weal to the present succession'.[27]

Even so, I do not think that Scott's Jacobitism can be dismissed as no more than a childish prejudice which had no effect on his adult political judgements. There is a remark which seems to me significant in his letter of January 1831 to Henry Francis Scott:

> I am old enough to remember well a similar crisis. About 1792, when I was entering life, the admiration of the godlike system of the French Revolution was so rife, that only a few old-fashioned Jacobites and the like ventured to hint a preference for the land they lived in; or pretended to doubt that the new principles must be infused into our own worn-out Constitution.[28]

This seems to me to imply that by Jacobitism, Scott meant not so much devotion to the Stuarts as devotion to his idea of the character, structure and values of the old Scottish Kingdom. He makes this explicit, I think, in the last chapter of *Waverley*, where he says that the Jacobite party, 'averse to intermingle with the English, or adopt their customs, long continued to pride themselves upon maintaining ancient Scottish manners and customs'. And he adds, 'This race has now almost entirely vanished from the land, and with it, doubtless, much absurd political prejudice; but also, many living examples of singular and disinterested attachment to the principles of loyalty which they received from their fathers, and of old Scottish faith, hospitality, worth, and honour.'

There are two elements then in Scott's view of Jacobitism, resistance to the erosion of the Scottish identity and to the loss of sense of community based on traditional social relationships and social values. Both of these preoccupations are central to his political thought.

The extent to which Scott's views on the importance of the community echo those of Adam Ferguson is very striking. Of all the 'giants' (to use his own words) of the Enlightenment who influenced Scott, Ferguson was, I think, the most important. Scott had a close personal relationship with him through his friendship with his son. Scott was a constant visitor in his house, where, you remember, he had an encounter with Robert Burns in 1786. Ferguson lived to 1816, when Scott said in a letter[29] that he had known and looked up to him for upwards of thirty years. As far as I know, Scott never specifically mentions Ferguson's *An Essay on the History of Civil Society*. Perhaps he had absorbed it so completely that he took it for granted, and no doubt the influence of Ferguson's views came from conversation with him as much as from reading. I venture to suggest, even so, that the *Essay* had more influence than any other book on Scott's political thought.

For Ferguson, human happiness depended largely on the community. He expressed it as follows in the *Essay*:

> The interests of society, however, and of its members, are easily reconciled. If the individual owes every degree of consideration to the public, he receives, in paying that very consideration, the greatest happiness of which his nature is capable; and the greatest blessing that the public can bestow on its members, is to keep them attached to itself. That is the most happy state, which is most beloved by its subjects; and they are the most happy men, whose hearts are engaged to a community, in which they find every object of generosity and zeal, and a scope to the exercise of every talent, and of every virtuous disposition.[30]

Throughout his life, Scott was moved by precisely this vision of community. He sought to create a microcosm of it at Abbotsford with his concern for the well-being of his tenants and dependants. In 1819, when he was in a mood of particular alarm over what he saw as a revolutionary threat from the Radicals, he wrote many letters to enlist support for his proposal for a force of yeomanry. He saw this as a means not only of armed defence of the establishment, but as helping to create a spirit of community. He wrote to Lord Melville, for instance:

In a general point of view the maintaining such corps, even though tranquil times should return, would be a great advantage to the common people. It would keep them united amongst each other and combined with those on whom they have a natural dependence and prevent that division of the country into rich and poor taken as two classes which have different and contradictory interests.[31]

Ferguson saw industrialisation as a threat to his ideal community. Of the commercial state, he wrote in the *Essay*:

It is here indeed, if ever, that man is sometimes found a detached and solitary being: he has found an object which sets him in competition with his fellow-creatures, and he deals with them as he does with his cattle and his soil, for the sake of the profits they bring. The mighty engine which we suppose to have formed society, only tends to set its members at variance, or to continue their intercourse after the bonds of affection are broken.[32]

Scott often expresses the same thought. In letters to Lord Montague and John Morritt, he regrets the effects of the invention of the steam engine. When industry depended on water power, it was scattered over the country in small villages where the manufacturer knew his workmen and felt concern for their needs and morals. 'This is now quite changed', Scott continues:

The manufacturers are transferred to great towns where a man may assemble 500 workmen one week and dismiss the next without having any further connection with them than to receive a week's work for a week's wages nor any further solicitude about their future fate than if they were so many old shuttles. A superintendence of the workers considered as moral and rational beings is thus a matter totally unconnected with the Employer's usual thought and cares.[33]

Ferguson also saw industry as degrading the mechanic 'whose art requires no exertion of genius'.[34] 'Many mechanical arts, indeed, require no capacity; they succeed best under a total suppression of sentiment and reason; and ignorance is the mother of industry as well as of superstition.'[35] 'In every commercial state, notwithstanding any pretension to equal rights, the exaltation of the few must depress the many'.[36] Scott again follows Ferguson. In a letter to Maria Edgeworth in February 1829 he wrote: 'The state of high civilisation to which we have arrived is scarcely a national blessing, since while the *few* are improved to the highest point, the *many* are in proportion brutalized and degraded, and the same nation displays at the same time the very highest and the very lowest state in which the human race can exist in point of intellect'.[37]

For both Ferguson and Scott, community depended on the division of society into classes determined by property. 'It must appear very evident', wrote Ferguson, 'that property is a matter of progress.'[38] 'In the progress of arts and of policy, the members of every state are divided into classes'.[39] 'It is obvious, that some mode of subordination is as necessary to men as society itself; and this, not only to attain the ends of government, but to comply with an order established by nature'.[40] Time and again, Scott makes the same points. In the *Life of Napoleon*, for instance, he writes: 'But to erect a levelling system designed to place the whole mass of the people on the same footing as to habits, manners, tastes and sentiments is a gross and ridiculous contradiction of the necessary progress of society. It is a fruitless attempt to wage war with the laws of Nature'.[41] Or again, 'In every state far advanced in the progress of civilisation, the inequality of ranks is a natural and necessary attribute'.[42] Or, 'the doctrine of equality is absurd in theory and impossible in practice'.[43] One of the three papers of *The Visionary* was devoted to the same point. For both Ferguson and Scott, the division of society into classes was both a consequence and a precondition of social progress and, at the same time, a reflection of the natural graduation of human accomplishment. Ferguson's reference to the 'order established by nature' is reflected in Scott's use of such phrases as 'natural dependence' (in the letter of December 1819 to Lord Melville)[44] and 'natural superiors' (in the letter of January 1820 to Lord Montague).[45]

Scott saw men of property as exercising a special role of responsibility in the State. In a letter to Lady Louisa Stuart in January 1817 he compared them to the children's toys which always come upright because of the weight of the lead in their feet: 'The mass of property has the same effect on our Constitution, and is a sort of ballast which will always right the vessel, to use a sailor's phrase, and bring it to due equipoise'.[46] In the *Life of Napoleon*, he describes property as a conservative force in politics: 'Property, cautious, doubtful, jealous of innovation, acts as a regulator rather than impulse on the machine, by preventing its moving either rapidly, or changing too suddenly'.[47]

For Scott also the ownership of property involved obligations towards dependants. As he expressed it in the *Life of Napoleon*:

> the plain country gentleman living on his own means, and amongst his own people becomes the natural protector and referee of the farmer and the peasant, and in case of need, either the firmest assertor of their rights and his own against the aggressions of the crown, or the independent and undaunted defender of the crown's rights against the innovations of political fanaticism.[48]

That is exactly as he saw himself as Laird of Abbotsford. In the *Life of Napoleon* he said, in the well-known passage about La Vendée, that 'there alone was any stand made in behalf of the ancient proprietors, constitution, or religion of France; for there alone the nobles and the cultivators of the soil held towards each other their natural and proper relations of patron and client, faithful dependants, and generous and affectionate superiors'.49 Notice the use of the words 'natural' and 'affectionate' in precisely the sense used by Adam Ferguson. When Christie Steele in *The Chronicles of the Canongate* and the Sexton in *The Bride of Lammermoor* criticised the Croftangrys and the Ravenswoods, they were not objecting to their status as lairds but to their failure to honour the obligations of lairdship. Anyone who failed in this way, he said in the *Life of Napoleon*, was 'guilty of little less than high treason, both to his own rank, and to the community in general'.50

When Scott spoke in this way of property, he was, of course, talking about the ownership of land, and the web of relationships between the land-owner and his tenants and workers. This can be a dominant social force only in a mainly agricultural country. Already in Scott's own time, industrialisation was beginning to take over in Scotland. As we have seen, he was well aware of that and was out of sympathy with it. This was partly because of its social effects, which had been foreseen by Ferguson and other writers of the Enlightenment. It was partly also for what we should now call ecological reasons. He wrote in his *Journal* on 20 February 1828:

> Nature intended that population should be diffused over the soil in proportion to its extent. We have accumulated in huge cities and smothering manufactories the numbers which should be spread over the face of a country; and what wonder that they should be corrupted? We have turned healthful and pleasant brooks into morasses and pestiferous lakes. What wonder the soil should be unhealthy?.51

We might say that if Scott's view of society was in many ways backward-looking, then in other ways his thought was in advance of his time.

The Ferguson and indeed the Enlightenment view of the development of the advanced forms of society was that it was a sort of organic growth which was too complex to be planned or intended by individual human will. Ferguson said in his *Essay*: 'Every step and every movement of the multitude, even in what are termed enlightened ages, are made with equal blindness to the future; and nations stumble upon establishments, which are indeed the result of human action, but not the execution of any human design'.52

It follows logically from this view that it was unwise to tamper recklessly with such a complex and painfully evolved organism. It was safer to trust to what Ferguson called the 'mighty machine' and Adam Smith the 'invisible hand'. There is a passage in the Preface to the first and second editions of John Millar's *Observation concerning the Distinction of Ranks in Society*, first published in 1771, which expresses this view succinctly:

> When these enquiries are properly conducted, they have likewise a tendency to restrain that wanton spirit of innovation which men are too apt to indulge in their political reasonings. To know the laws already established, to discern the causes from which they have arisen, and the means by which they were introduced; this preliminary step is essentially requisite, in order to determine upon what occasions they ought to be altered or abolished. The institutions of a country, how imperfect soever and defective they may seem, are commonly suited to the state of the people by whom they have been embraced; and therefore, in most cases, they are susceptible of those gentle improvements, which proceed from a gradual reformation of the manners, and are accompanied with a correspondent change in the condition of society. In every system of law or government, the different parts have an intimate connection with each other. As it is dangerous to tamper with the machine, unless we are previously acquainted with the several wheels and springs of which it is composed; so there is reason to fear, that the violent alteration of any single part may destroy the regularity of its movements, and produce the utmost disorder and confusion.[53]

I have quoted that in full because it could have been written not by the Whig, John Millar, but by Walter Scott. It expresses precisely what Scott himself said over and over again throughout his life. Scott expresses the same thought, employs the same metaphors and even uses the same phrases. In an earlier passage in the Preface, by the way, Millar says something else which also became part of Scott's credo: 'The manners and customs [the phrase which Scott used in the last chapter of *Waverley*] of a people may be regarded as the most authentic record of their opinions, concerning what is right or wrong, what is praiseworthy or blameable, what is expedient or hurtful'.[54] Obviously Scott had absorbed and accepted the writings of John Millar in the same way that those of Ferguson had become part of the pattern of his mind. There is a close parallel between these ideas of Millar and the passage which I quoted from Scott's *Life of Napoleon* about cautious innovation in response to a change of manners. There are many other echoes of this kind. In the first of the *Malachi* letters, for example, he argues against 'hasty and

experimental innovations' and goes on: 'it is surely better that existing evils should be endured for some time longer, than that violent
remedies should be hastily adopted, the unforeseen and unprovided
– for consequences of which are often so much more extensive than
those which had been foreseen and reckoned upon'.[55] The *Malachi*
letters are a sustained argument in support of Millar's point that the
institutions of a country are likely to be best suited to its needs. In
The Visionary Scott argued for a policy of 'Let weel bide',[56] or, as
he expressed it in a letter to James Ballantyne in December 1819:
'Let the country alone – have patience – and things will come round
– attempt any short turn and you will overthrow the machine . . .
Believe me, dear James, there is nothing which can be proposed of
a sweeping or dashing nature in religion, politics or public economy
which is not therefore radically wrong. Of *every* political measure
in *every* country the unforeseen and collateral consequences have
been much more important than those which human foresight could
calculate'.[57] Again in a letter to Lockhart in April 1830, reflecting
also the ideas of Adam Smith: 'I am far more afraid of the country
suffering from being practised upon by quack remedies than from
her natural constitution failing her. Leave commerce time to shake
itself clear of the thousand bonds which hamper her and she will find
much better ways of disposing her own wealth than any statesman
can point out for her'.[58]

Consistently with this organic view of society, and also perhaps
because he drew his conclusions largely from a study of Roman
history, Adam Ferguson distrusted democracy. It tended, in his
opinion, to lead to anarchy and to be replaced by military despotism.
He says in the *Essay*: 'In the disorder of corrupted societies, the scene
has been frequently changed from democracy to despotism, and from
the last too, in its turn, to the first. From amidst the democracy
of corrupt men, and from a scene of lawless confusion, the tyrant
ascends a throne with arms reeking in blood . . . Democracy seems
to revive in a scene of wild disorder and tumult: but both the
extremes are but the transient fits of paroxysm or languor in a
distempered state'.[59] For Scott, this theoretical argument appeared
to be powerfully demonstrated and reinforced by the history of the
Revolution in France. In *The Visionary*, he spoke of the 'military
despotism to which we have fled in all ages and countries, as an
evil whose terrors were incalculably less than those of a factious and
furious democracy'.[60]

In considering the political views of anyone, even one's own,
it is always difficult to determine the part played by instinct or
temperament and the part played by conscious theory. At least one
can say in Scott's case that he adhered consciously and consistently

to a coherent view of society derived, virtually intact, from the speculations of the Scottish Enlightenment and particularly from the work of Adam Ferguson, Adam Smith and John Millar. No doubt, the tendencies which this involved were strengthened by the nostalgia for the Scottish past in which he was steeped from his boyhood in Sandyknowe onwards. Scott took the abstractions and generalities of Enlightenment thought, developed them in detail and applied them to his own place and time. Where the Enlightenment had drawn their examples from classical Greece and Rome, the Americas, or almost anywhere but Scotland, Scott planted their conclusions firmly in his native soil. Millar, for example, talked about 'the institutions of a country'; Scott applied the same argument in detail to the particular case of Scotland.

He admitted to certain prejudices and has been accused of others. His Jacobitism was of a kind which accorded with his general philosophy. So too, generally, did the Scottish feelings which were so strong a part of his composition and the impulse behind the best part of his writing. In a letter to Robert Dundas in March 1826 he spoke of them: 'so much for my Scottish feelings – prejudices, if you will; but [which] were born, and will die with me'.[61] He has often been accused, too, by James Hogg and J.S. Mill onwards, of a prejudice in favour of the old aristocracy. He expressed his view of this very clearly in a passage in the Life of Napoleon: 'The estimation set upon birth or rank, supposing its foundation illusory, has still the advantage of counterbalancing that which is attracted by wealth only; the prejudice has something generous and noble in it, it is connected with historical recollections and patriotic feelings, and if it sometimes gives rise to extravagances, they are such as society can restrain and punish by the mere effect of ridicule'.[62] There are many examples of that ridicule in the Waverley novels. He had, too, that opposite, or in his view of society complementary, prejudice in favour of the ordinary people to which George Allan drew attention. No matter how much he admired them, his political theory firmly excluded any move towards according them political power. He saw the Reform Bill as the first step that would lead to tumbrils on the street.

With such views as these, Scott inevitably tended to pessimism. There were so many pressures at the time at variance with everything he believed. He saw the traditional structure and values of society being undermined by industrialism. The distinctive 'manners and character' of Scotland were 'daily melting and dissolving' under the attack of 'hasty and experimental innovations from England'. Radical agitation and the Whig policy of parliamentary reform threatened, as Scott saw it, the bloody process of democracy, anarchy and military despotism which had engulfed France. These two fears reinforced each other because Scott saw the traditional values and structure of Scottish society as a barrier against the contagion of revolution. 'Scotland, completely liberalized, as she is in a fair way of being', he said in his letter to J. W. Croker in March 1826, 'will be the most dangerous neighbour to England that she has had since 1639. If you *unscotch* us, you will find us damned mischievous Englishmen'.[63] No wonder that he saw, as he said in the same letter 'a black, gloomy, and most ominous aspect'. No wonder too, that he had moments of political panic, as in December 1819 when he imagined '50,000 blackguards ready to rise between Tyne and Wear'.[64] It is easy to ridicule Scott for this but we should remember the influence of both Adam Ferguson's theories and his close knowledge of the realities of civil war in 1745 in Scotland and of the revolution in France in his own lifetime.

In writing of Scott's politics, John Buchan said that they had 'positive substance' of which 'the first element was nationalism. He believed firmly in the virtue of local patriotism and the idiomatic life of the smaller social unit. Whenever Scotland was concerned he was prepared to break with his party, with his leaders, and with the whole nobility, gentry and intellectuality of Britain'.[65] Buchan is thinking, of course, of the *Letters of Malachi Malagrowther*. This is a much more important book than is generally realised. Too often it has been described by those who cannot have read it as concerned only with the comparatively trivial question of Scottish bank-notes, not that the question was merely symbolic in 1826 as it might be now. As Scott himself said, he 'desired to make a strong impression and speak out, not on the Currency Question, alone but on the treatment of Scotland generally'.[66] He told James Ballantyne: 'I will sleep quieter in my grave for having so fair an opportunity of speaking my mind'.[67] It is both Scott's political testament and the first manifesto of modern Scottish nationalism. He makes a powerful case for the ideas that diversity is preferable to uniformity and centralisation; that Scottish characteristics are valuable for their own sake and should not be abandoned without good reason; that government should be responsive to local needs and wishes; that the overburdened government machine in London should refrain from interfering in Scottish affairs. Even here, you might say that Scott remained true to the doctrines of Adam Ferguson. In the *Essay*, Ferguson argued that it was not necessary to enlarge communities in order to obtain their advantages. He continued: 'We frequently obtain them in the most remarkable degree, where nations remain independent, and are of a small extent.'[68] In this respect, as in their concern over the effects of industrialisation, the political ideas of Ferguson and Scott may still have something relevant to say to us.

(Paper for Scott Conference, Aberdeen, August 1992.)

NOTES

Letters: *The Letters of Sir Walter Scott*, edited by Sir H. J. C. Grierson (London, 1932–37).

Life of Napoleon: Sir Walter Scott: *The Life of Napoleon Buonaparte* (Edinburgh, 1827).

Essay: Adam Ferguson, *An Essay on the History of Civil Society*, edited by Duncan Forbes (Edinburgh, edn of 1978).

1. George Allan *Life of Sir Walter Scott* (Edinburgh, 1834), pp. 314–15.
2. John Buchan *The Life of Sir Walter Scott* (8th edn, London, 1961), p. 368.
3. George Allan *op. cit.*, p. 159.
4. *Letters*, vol. I, p. 345.
5. Graham McMaster *Scott and Society* (Cambridge, 1981), p. 80.
6. *Letters*, vol. VIII, p. 480.
7. Graham McMaster *op. cit.*, p. 80.
8. See, for example, *Letters*, vol. VI, pp. 133–6.
9. *Letters*, vol. VII, p.460.
10. *Ibid.*, vol. VI, p. 147.
11. *Ibid.*, vol. VI, pp. 162–5.
12. David Hewitt *Scottish Literary Journal*, vol. 7 no. 1, May 1980, p. 12 and pp. 17–18.
13. William Hazlitt 'The Spirit of the Age' (1825) in Scotti, *The Critical Heritage*, edited by John O. Hayden (London, 1970), p. 288.
14. *Life of Napoleon*, vol. I, pp. 70–1.
15. *Ibid.*, vol. I, p. 68.
16. *Ibid.*, vol. I, p. 278.
17. *Letters*, vol. V, p. 71.
18. *Ibid.*, vol. VI, p. 2.
19. *Ibid.*, vol. I, p. 345.
20. Somnambulus (Sir Walter Scott), *The Visionary* (Edinburgh, 1819), Preface, p. 6.
21. Sir Walter Scott *Journal*, edited by David Douglas (Edinburgh, 1891), p. 87.
22. *Letters*, vol. XI, pp. 455–6.
23. Sir Walter Scott *The Letters of Malachi Malagrowther*, edited by P. H. Scott (Edinburgh, 1981), pp. 72 and 74.
24. In J. G. Lockhart *Memoirs of Sir Walter Scott* (edition of 1900, London) vol. I, p. 14.
25. *Letters*, vol. X, p. 482.
26. *Ibid.*, vol. XII, p. 197.
27. *Ibid.*, vol. III, pp. 302–3.
28. *Ibid.*, vol. XI, pp. 455–6.

29. *Ibid.*, vol. IV, p. 181.
30. *Essay*, p. 58.
31. *Letters*, vol. VI, p. 82.
32. *Essay*, p. 19.
33. *Letters*, vol. VI, pp. 103–4 and p. 190.
34. *Essay*, p. 184.
35. *Ibid*, p. 182.
36. *Ibid.*, p.186.
37. *Letters*, vol. XI, p. 128.
38. *Essay*, p. 82.
39. *Ibid.*, p. 150.
40. *Ibid.*, p. 36.
41. *Life of Napoleon*, vol. I, p. 213.
42. *Ibid.*, vol. I, p. 215.
43. *Ibid.*, vol. I, p. 219.
44. *Letters*, vol: VI, p. 82.
45. *Ibid.*, vol. VI, p. 103.
46. *Ibid.*, vol. IV, p. 382.
47. *Life of Napoleon*, vol. I, p. 121.
48. *Ibid.*, vol. I, p. 30.
49. *Ibid.*, vol. I, p. 31.
50. *Ibid.*, vol. I, p. 34.
51. *Op. cit.*, p. 541.
52. *Essay*, p. 122.
53. John Millar *Observations concerning the Distinction of Ranks in Society* (2nd edn, Edinburgh, 1773), Preface, p.v.
54. *Ibid.*, Preface, p. iii.
55. *Op. cit.*, p. 8.
56. *Op. cit.*, p. 23.
57. *Letters*, vol. VI, pp. 34–5.
58. *Letters*, vol. XI, p. 315.
59. *Essay*, p. 73.
60. *Op. cit.*, p. 14.
61. *Letters*, vol. IX, p. 470.
62. *Life of Napoleon*, vol. I, p. 218.
63. *Letters*, vol. IX, p. 471.
64. *Ibid.*, vol., VI, p. 76.
65. John Buchan, *op. cit.*, pp. 364–5.
66. *Letters*, vol. IX, p. 470.
67. *Ibid.*, vol. IX, p. 437.
68. *Essay*, p. 68.

10

Peter's Letters

Many Scottish books of the last century, now appearing in scholarly new editions from various publishers, were first printed in the pages of this magazine or published as books under the Blackwood imprint. We have had work from Galt and Hogg, for instance. Now we have a selection from J. G. Lockhart's *Peter's Letters to His Kinsfolk*, edited by William Ruddick (Scottish Academic Press, £3.95). It is a key book for the understanding of the early history of *Maga* and indeed of the literary and intellectual history of Scotland at one of its peaks, the period of Walter Scott.

The previous fifty years, the age of the Enlightenment, of Hume, Robertson, Ferguson and Adam Smith, had placed Scotland in the forefront of European thought. In Scotland itself an intellectual atmosphere had developed which was rational and sceptical, Whig in politics and moderate in religion, distrustful of feelings of all kinds, aspiring to the universal and therefore repudiating national traditions and characteristics. This was the spirit transmitted by *The Edinburgh Review*, founded in 1801 and for years the undisputed arbiter of literary taste and intellectual fashion in the whole of the English-speaking world.

Lockhart, a son of the manse and educated partly in Oxford, returned to Scotland and became an advocate in 1816. He was a bright young man of twenty-two, and a member of the profession who were the intellectual élite of Edinburgh. He might have been expected to join the Whig ascendancy and try his hand at contributions to *The Edinburgh Review*. Instead he found himself in revolt against it, for reasons which seem to have become clearer to himself as he wrote *Peter's Letters*. The ostensible purpose of the book was to describe the social and intellectual life of Edinburgh, and the people involved in it, in a light-hearted, satirical and even flippant spirit. It developed as it was written into a systematic criticism of the inadequacies of the Enlightenment. Lockhart had felt instinctively that something was missing. In the *Letters* his exploration of the Scottish scene gradually enabled him to see why. It is one of those rare books which achieve more than they set out to do; and it gives a direct insight into the working of a man's mind.

It was William Blackwood who gave Lockhart his opportunity. In October 1817 Blackwood took the editorship of his magazine into his own hands; he made Lockhart and his friend and collaborator, John Wilson, the chief contributors. In *Peter's Letters*, Lockhart describes a meeting with Blackwood when he was persuaded to join the team.

> 'Have you seen our last Number? Is it not perfectly glorious? We are beating the Reviews all to nothing and, as to the other magazines, they are such utter trash. You must really be a contributor. We've a set of wild fellows about us; we are much in want of a few sensible, intelligent writers, like you, sir, to counterbalance them But anything you like, sir only do contribute. It is a shame for any man that dislikes whiggery and infidelity not to assist us.'

'Whiggery and infidelity', that phrase is one of the clues to Lockhart's, and Blackwood's, dislike of *The Edinburgh Review*; but it does not tell the whole story.

Lockhart had in fact been one of the 'wild fellows' himself before he wrote the *Letters*. He almost certainly had a hand, with Wilson and James Hogg, in the notorious '*Chaldee Manuscript*' in the issue for October 1817, which satirised the Edinburgh Reviewers with gusto and caused an enormous sensation. In subsequent issues of *Blackwood's*, he attacked with an animus that he afterwards regretted other Edinburgh men, as well as the 'Cockney School' of poets. Walter Scott, partly it seems to persuade Lockhart to turn his pen to less destructive use, encouraged him to follow up his idea of a longer and less abusive study of the Scottish scene. In proposing the idea of the *Letters* to Blackwood, Lockhart said that they were to be 'graphically done but with kindly feeling'. The basic idea was simple and one quite common at the time, a series of letters written in the name of an imaginary character, in this case a scholarly Welshman, Peter Morris. The general format was to be similar to Smollett's novel *Humphrey Clinker*; but Lockhart had a closer model, from which he even borrowed the title, in Scott's *Paul's Letters to His Kinsfolk*, published only three years earlier in 1816. By writing in his Welsh disguise, Lockhart could assume an air of detachment, and the form of personal letters allowed him to choose his subjects with flexibility and freedom. There were to be two volumes mainly on Edinburgh, and a third on Glasgow, the Highlands and the Borders. Wilson was to help with the third volume, but Lockhart apparently wrote most of the book himself. A selection was published with great success in the Magazine in February and March 1819, and the three volumes appeared a few months later.

At their most obvious level, the *Letters* are invaluable as a first-hand account of literary and intellectual life in Edinburgh. We have lively descriptions of Hogg at a Burns dinner, Jeffrey and Cockburn in court or in the drawing-room, Dr Chalmers in the pulpit, and Scott at Abbotsford. It is a pity that we do not have books like this for other periods. In one of his letters, Scott said:

> What an acquisition it would have been to our general information to have had such work written, I do not say fifty but even five and twenty years ago, and how much of grave and gay might then have been preserved, as it were in amber, which have now mouldered away.

We might say the same today. Will no one give us an account of the Edinburgh of Sydney Goodsir Smith and Douglas Young?

The development of Lockhart's analysis of *The Edinburgh Review* School is, however, the chief fascination of the book. At the beginning he seems to be accusing the Reviewers of nothing worse than inadequate classical scholarship. He more or less says: these men know no Greek, therefore they are not competent to pass judgement on literature. We are reminded how young Lockhart was when he wrote the book, because it radiates the air of a man straight from university, confident of Oxford superiority. But remembering Edward Gibbon's description of eighteenth-century Oxford, 'steeped in port and prejudice', one wonders how sound the scholarship was. Lockhart scatters Greek tags around (and his present editor continues the élitism by not condescending to translate, although he gives the sources).

Lockhart seems to be indulging no more than an instinctive dislike and distrust of Jeffrey and his Reviewers. But then, in his description of the Burns dinner, he remarks, almost incidentally, that Jeffrey is deficient in both 'nationality of feeling' and 'humanity of feeling'. In his description of his meeting with Scott at Abbotsford, he expands the theme. Scott had restored 'whatever is Scottish in thought, in feeling or in recollection' to literature. The writers of the Enlightenment had shown 'merely the force of intellect, as applied to matters of reasoning'. They had displayed only 'speculative acuteness'; it had been left to Scott 'to grapple boldly with the feelings of his countrymen'. He was 'the sole saviour of all the richer and warmer spirit of literature in Scotland'. The Enlightenment and *The Edinburgh Review* were not enough in themselves. This was not to deny that the Enlightenment was a great achievement. Lockhart does not do that, but he detected in it the same lack of nationality and humanity which he found in Jeffrey.

Throughout the book, Lockhart identifies Wordsworth with this distrust of the disembodied intellect; it could be described as an

apologia for the Romantic revolt against eighteenth-century rationalism. It is also a protest against the suppression by the men of the
Enlightenment of Scottish traditions and characteristics, symbolised
by their strenuous efforts to purge their writing (but not their speech)
of Scotticisms. Of course, the division is not clear-cut. Scott was in
many ways a product of the Enlightenment. David Hume and his
friends (as one may easily discover from their letters) were happy,
as Scotsmen, to be beating the English at their own game.

We tend to think of Lockhart as the author of one great book,
his *Life of Scott*. William Ruddick and the Scottish Academic Press
have done a valuable service in making this other work more widely
available. Ruddick contributes an admirable introduction and notes
which are helpful (even if he does not translate the Greek!).

(*Blackwood's Magazine*, April 1978, No. 1950, Vol. 323.)

II

Byron and Scott

At first glance, you might suppose that it would be hard to find two men more different and incompatible in character than Sir Walter Scott and Lord Byron. Scott, outwardly at least, was a prudent, douce, respectable Edinburgh lawyer, devoted to the Roman, and Scottish, virtues of effort, stoical endurance and self-control. *Agere atque pati Romanum est*, as he remarked in his *Journal*.[1] What would such a man, one might ask, have in common with the reckless, outrageous, passionate, self-indulgent, convention-defying Byron? Of course, the truth is the opposite from what one might expect. Each liked and admired the other to a degree which must be rare between two writers who were clear rivals for public favour.

Each expressed his feelings about the other as a man and a writer frequently and consistently. Scott of Byron, in a letter of 10 January 1817 to John Murray: 'No one can honour Lord Byron's poems more than I do and no one has so great a wish to love him personally'.[2] Byron of Scott in his *Journal* on 17 November 1813: 'I like the man and admire his works to what Mr Braham calls *Entusymusy*'.[3] In his *Journal* a few days later, he said that Scott was 'undoubtedly the Monarch of Parnassus' and placed him on the top of his 'Gradus ad Parnassum'.[4] Again in 1821, 'Scott is certainly the most wonderful writer of the day. His novels are a new literature in themselves, and his poetry is as good as any – if not better . . . I like him, too, for his manliness of character, for the extreme pleasantness of his conversation, and his good nature towards myself, personally. May he prosper for he deserves it. I know no reading to which I fall with such alacrity as a work of W. Scott's'.[5] Equally Scott gives pride of place to Byron. He spoke of Byron's 'boundless Genius',[6] and said that he gave up writing poetry because Byron beat him.[7] 'It is well for us', he remarked in a letter to his publisher Cadell, 'that he has not turned himself to tale telling, for he would have endangered our supremacy in that department'.[8]

This relationship, 'warm and cordial on both sides', as Leslie Marchand describes it,[9] began rather inauspiciously. Byron published his *English Bards and Scotch Reviewers* in March 1809 anonymously, but it was no secret that he had written it. The poem makes some mocking references to Scott's *Lay of the Last Minstrel* and *Marmion* and accuses him of writing for money:

And thinkst thou, Scott! by vain conceit perchance,
On public taste to foist thy stale romance,
Though Murray with his Miller may combine
To yield thy muse just half-a-crown per line? No! when the sons of song
   descend to trade,
Their bays are sear, their former laurels fade.'

Scott seems to have come across the poem in August when he mentions it in the course of a letter to Robert Southey:

> In the meantime, it is funny enough to see a whelp of a young Lord Byron abusing me, of whose circumstances he knows nothing, for endeavouring to scratch out a living with my pen. God help the bear, if, having little else to eat, he must not even suck his own paws. I can assure the noble imp of fame it is not my fault that I was not born to a park and £5,000 a-year, as it is not his lordship's merit, although it may be his great good fortune, that he was not born to live by his literary talents or success.[10]

Scott evidently did not nurse a grievance, as many people attacked like this would have done. Little more than a month after the publication of Cantos I and II of Byron's *Childe Harold's Pilgrimage* in February 1812, he was praising the poem in letters to Joanna Baillie and J.B.S. Morritt. 'It is, I think, a very clever poem', he wrote to the former, 'but gives no good symptom of the writer's heart or morals . . . I wish you would read it.'[11] To Morritt his praise was even stronger, although he still had reservations about the morality of the piece: 'Though there is something provoking and insulting both to morality and to feeling in his misanthropical ennui it gives nevertheless an odd poignancy to his descriptions and reflections and upon the whole it is a poem of most extraordinary power and may rank its author with our first poets.'[12]

So far Scott and Byron had not met or even exchanged letters. They knew each other only by reputation and from their published works. As it happens, they were brought together very shortly after Scott had been writing these letters to his friends about *Childe Harold*. Byron took the initiative, perhaps regretting his attack in *English Bards and Scotch Reviewers* or because of a generous impulse to tell Scott something which he knew would please him. In June 1812, Byron had met the Prince Regent at an evening party where the Prince had talked about poetry at some length. He had displayed 'an intimacy and critical taste which at once surprised and delighted

Lord Byron'. In particular, he spoke about Scott, whom he preferred 'far beyond every other poet of his time'. These phrases
come from a letter from the publisher, John Murray, whom Byron
had asked to pass on the report to Scott.[13] Scott responded by
asking Murray to convey his thanks for this 'very handsome and
gratifying communication', and took the opportunity to clear his
name 'from any tinge of mercenary or sordid feeling in the eyes
of a contemporary of genius'. He had *not* written *Marmion* under
contract for a sum of money.[14] Thus encouraged, Byron replied by
apologising for the satire, 'written when I was very young & very
angry, & fully bent on displaying my wrath and my wit'.[15] In his
reply, Scott invited Byron to visit Abbotsford, then a new and far
from complete house.[16] From its beginning, their correspondence
was friendly, warm and relaxed. Byron sent Scott a copy of his
poem *The Giaour* inscribed 'To the Monarch of Parnassus from one
of his subjects'.[17]

In the event, Byron never visited Abbotsford (although Lady
Byron did so in 1817). Eight years and much turmoil after the
first invitation, Byron wrote from Ravenna to John Murray on 23
April 1820: 'My love to Scott . . . I hope to see him at Abbotsford
before very long, and I will sweat his Claret for him'.[18] It was, of
course, not to be. Their only meetings were in London in 1815 when
Scott was passing through to and from Paris. Scott described them
in a letter which he wrote in response to a request from Tom Moore
for facts and recollections which would help him with his *Life* of
Byron. I think that it is worth quoting at length because it says so
much about Scott and Byron:

> It was in the spring of 1815, that, chancing to be in London, I had
> the advantage of a personal introduction to Lord Byron. Report had
> prepared me to meet a man of peculiar habits and a quick temper,
> and I had some doubts whether we were likely to suit each other
> in society. I was most agreeably disappointed in this respect. I found
> Lord Byron in the highest degree courteous, and even kind. We met
> for an hour or two almost daily, in Mr. Murray's drawing-room,
> and found a great deal to say to each other. We also met frequently
> in parties and evening society, so that for about two months I had
> the advantage of a considerable intimacy with this distinguished
> individual. Our sentiments agreed a good deal, except upon the
> subjects of religion and politics, upon neither of which I was inclined
> to believe that Lord Byron entertained very fixed opinions . . .
>
> On politics, he used sometimes to express a high strain of what
> is now called Liberalism; but it appeared to me that the pleasure it
> afforded him, as a vehicle for displaying his wit and satire against
> individuals in office, was at the bottom of this habit of thinking,

rather than any real conviction of the political principles on which he talked. He was certainly proud of his rank and ancient family, and, in that respect, as much an aristocrat as was consistent with good sense and good breeding. Some disgusts, how adopted I know not, seemed to me to have given this peculiar and (as it appeared to me) contradictory cast of mind; but, at heart, I would have termed Byron a patrician on principle.

Lord Byron's reading did not seem to me to have been very extensive, either in poetry or history. Having the advantage of him in that respect, and possessing a good competent share of such reading as is little read, I was sometimes able to put under his eye objects which had for him the interest of novelty. I remember particularly repeating to him the fine poem of Hardyknute, an imitation of the old Scottish ballad, with which he was so much affected, that some one who was in the same apartment asked me what I could possibly have been telling Byron by which he was so much agitated.

I saw Byron for the last time in 1815, after I returned from France. He dined, or lunched, with me at Long's in Bond Street. I never saw him so full of gayety and good-humor . . .

Several letters passed between us – one perhaps every half-year. Like the old heroes in Homer, we exchanged gifts. I gave Byron a beautiful dagger mounted with gold, which had been the property of the redoubted Elfi Bey. But I was to play the part of Diomed in the Iliad, for Byron sent me, some time after, a large sepulchral vase of silver. It was full of dead men's bones . . .

I think I also remarked in Byron's temper starts of suspicion, when he seemed to pause and consider whether there had not been a secret, and perhaps offensive, meaning in something casually said to him. In this case, I also judged it best to let his mind, like a troubled spring, work itself clear, which it did in a minute or two. I was considerably older, you will recollect, than my noble friend, and had no reason to fear his misconstruing my sentiments towards him, nor had I ever the slightest reason to doubt that they were kindly returned on his part. If I had occasion to be mortified by the display of genius which threw into the shade such pretensions as I was then supposed to possess, I might console myself that, in my own case, the materials of mental happiness had been mingled in a greater proportion.[19]

Scott retained warm memories of his last meeting with Byron, which was on 14 September 1815.[20] Ten years later he referred to it in his *Journal*: 'I never saw Byron so full of fun, frolic, wit and whim: he was as playful as a kitten'.[21] But playful or not, Byron was then in the middle of his disastrous marriage. During the scandal of the separation which followed, almost all of Scott's correspondents took the side of Lady Byron.[22] Joanna Baillie even tried to persuade him to intervene over the financial settlement, since there was nobody, she said, whose good opinion Byron was more anxious to preserve.[23] Scott regretted the breakdown of the marriage, but he refused to be stampeded into the general mood of condemnation. 'I was in great hopes', he told Morritt in February 1816, 'that the comfort of domestic society might tame the wayward irregularity of mind which is unfortunately for its owner connected with such splendid talent. I have known Lord Byron to do very great and generous things and I would have been most happy to find that he had adopted other and more settled habits.'[24] In another letter to Morritt in May: 'Lord Byron with high genius and many points of a noble and generous feeling has Child Harolded himself and Outlawd himself into too great a resemblance with the picture of his imagination'.[25]

Byron left Britain to escape both the bailiffs and the weight of public disapproval in April 1816. By the end of June he had written the third canto of *Childe Harold* and it was published by John Murray in November. Scott responded by writing a review for the *Quarterly* (published in February 1817) of the generous length that was accepted at the time of some thirty pages. He know that he was taking a risk. The poem was so autobiographical in content that it was impossible to comment on it without saying something about Byron's personal situation, and, as he told Murray, he did not want to cause him pain.[26] The review praised Byron for his 'wild, powerful and original view of poetry' and suggested that his 'family misfortunes' were the consequences of 'a powerful and unbridled imagination . . . the author and architect of its own disappointments'. Scott concluded with the 'anxious wish and eager hope' that Byron would recover peace of mind for the exercise of his 'splendid talents'.[27] At any time, this would have been a kind and understanding review. In the circumstances of the time, the writing of it was not only delicate and tactful, but courageous.

Byron was deeply touched. 'He must be a gallant as well as a good man', he wrote to Murray in March, 'who has ventured in that place – and at this time – to write such an article even anonymously . . . It is not the mere praise, but there is a *tact* & a *delicacy* throughout not only with regard to me but to *others*.'[28] A week later he had heard that Scott was the author and wrote to Thomas Moore, 'you will agree with me that such an article is still more honourable to him than to myself'.[29] Byron never forgot this example of Scott's courage and generosity. He mentioned it in a letter to Scott for the first time in January 1822: 'You went out of your way in 1817 to do me a service when it required not merely kindness – but courage to do so . . . The very *tardiness* of this acknowledgment will at least show that I have not forgotten the obligation.'[30] On 29 May 1823, when Byron was preparing to leave Italy for his final journey to Greece, he took time to write to Henri Beyle (who was Stendhal). Beyle had praised Scott's writing in a pamphlet but said that 'his character is little worthy of enthusiasm'. Byron rose to his defence: 'I have known Walter Scott long and well, and in occasional situations which call forth the *real* character – and I can assure you that his character *is* worthy of admiration – that of all men he is the most *open*, the most *honourable*, the most *amiable*. With his politics I have nothing to do: they differ from mine, which renders it difficult for me to speak of them. But he is *perfectly sincere* in them . . . *Believe* the *truth*. I say that Walter Scott is as nearly a thorough good man as man can be, because I *know* it by experience to be the case.'[31] There cannot be much doubt that when he wrote these words the *Quarterly* article was in his mind.

Scott proved his robust support for Byron once again by accepting in December 1821 the dedication of one of his boldest works, *Cain*. In his letter of acceptance to Murray, Scott said that 'Byron matched Milton on his own ground. Some part of the language [is] bold, and may shock one class of readers . . . But they must condemn the Paradise Lost, if they have a mind to be consistent.'[32]

Byron's admiration for Scott as a writer was based at first on his poetry, but he became a great enthusiast for the novels as soon as he discovered them. The first of them, *Waverley*, was published on 7 July 1814. As soon as the 24th of the same month Byron wrote to Murray: 'Waverley is the best and most interesting novel since – I don't know when . . . besides it is all easy to me – because I have been in Scotland so much – (though then young enough too) and feel at home with the people lowland and Gael.'[33] From then onwards Byron read all of Scott's novels as they appeared and, by his own repeated account, many times over. He said that he liked no reading so well.[34] Although they were still anonymous, 'by the author of Waverley', Byron seems never to have had any doubts that Scott was the 'great unknown'. In a letter of February 1820, for instance: 'I have more of Scott's novels (for surely they are Scott's) since we met, and am more and more delighted. I think I even prefer them to his poetry.'[35] Or in his *Journal* on 5 January 1821: Read the conclusion, for the fiftieth time (I have read all W. Scott's novels at least fifty times) of the third series of "Tales of my Landlord", – grand work – Scotch Fielding, as well as great English poet – wonderful man I long to get drunk with him.'[36]

From 1814 to the end of his life Byron's letters are full of allusions to the novels, praise of them, requests to Murray to be sure to send new ones as they were published. There are also frequent quotations from them, usually phrases of the dialogue in Scots, which show how familiar he was with them and how much at home with Scots vocabulary. He wrote to Scott himself about them from Pisa on 12 January 1822:

> I don't like to bore you about the Scotch novels (as they call them though two of them are wholly English and the rest half so) but nothing can or could ever persuade me since I was the first ten minutes in your company that you are *not* the Man . . . To me those novels have so much of 'Auld lang syne'. (I was bred a canny Scot till ten years old) that I never move without them – and when I removed from Ravenna to Pisa the other day – and sent on my library before – they were the only books that I kept by me – although I already knew them by heart . . . I need not add that I would be delighted to see you again – which is far more than I shall ever feel or say for England or (with a few exceptions 'of kith – kin – and allies') any thing that it contains . . . But my 'heart warms to the Tartan' or to any thing of Scotland.37

Byron's response to the Waverley novels helps to explain, I think, the evident affinity between him and Scott. In his *Journal*, Scott describes himself as 'tolerably national'.38 This was a calculated understatement, because Scott's passion for Scotland was a dominant force in his composition.39 I think that there is strong evidence that Byron too was 'tolerably national', if not to the same overwhelming degree as Scott. In his essay on Byron, T.S. Eliot said that Byron was a Scottish poet, and in comparing him with Scott remarked: 'Possibly Byron, who must have thought of himself as an English poet, was the more Scotch of the two because of being unconscious of his true nationality'.40 On the contrary, I think that Byron makes it very clear, as in the letters which I have just quoted, that he was perfectly conscious of his Scottishness.

Indeed when Byron said in Canto X of *Don Juan* that he was himself half a Scot by birth, and bred a whole one,41 he was speaking the literal truth. He was 'half a Scot' because his mother was Scottish; he was 'bred a whole one' because he spent the first ten years of his life in Aberdeen and was educated at the Grammar School. (In the same stanza, incidentally, Byron, addressing Francis Jeffrey of the *Edinburgh Review*, said: 'I would rather take my wine/ With you, than aught (save Scott) in your proud city.'). I think it is generally agreed that the first few years of life are the most influential in determining character and attitudes. Many people, including Eliot and Grierson, have noted the influence on him of Scottish Calvinism.42 It is also quite certain that he heard all around him in Aberdeen, and learned to speak, good Buchan Scots. His frequent quotation in his letters of phrases in Scots shows how he responded to it. No doubt he acquired an English veneer at Harrow and Cambridge; but, as Eliot says, he 'remained oddly alien' in

English society.43 I think that is because he was fundamentally Scottish.

There is a significant episode in Byron's correspondence with his half-sister, Augusta Leigh. She wrote in February 1817 to congratulate him on the assumption that he was 'P.P.'. By this she meant Peter Pattieson, the fictitious character to whom Scott attributed *Tales of My Landlord*, the four volumes published in December 1816 which contained *The Black Dwarf* and *Old Mortality*. The books had not yet reached Byron in Venice and he had no idea what Augusta was talking about. 'I am not P.P.', he replied, – and I assure you upon my honour & do not understand to what book you allude – so that all your compliments are quite thrown away'.44 However, after he had read the *Tales*, he wrote to John Murray in May: 'The *Tales of My Landlord* I have read with great pleasure & perfectly understand why my sister & aunt are so very positive in the very erroneous persuasion that they must have been written by me – if you knew me as well as they do – you would perhaps have fallen into the same mistake.'45

In his footnote to the first of these two letters, Leslie Marchand suggests that Augusta was misled by the character of David Ritchie in *The Black Dwarf* who was 'haunted by a consciousness of his own deformity'. Certainly, it is quite possible that this resemblance to Byron himself triggered off her conclusion. (Incidentally, another bond between Scott and Byron was, of course, that they were both lame and both compensated for their handicap by vigorous physical activity, Byron by his swimming and Scott on horseback.) But this point alone could hardly have led anyone to imagine that Byron was the author, unless they could also suppose that he was capable of writing anything so essentially Scottish as these two novels and of writing superb dialogue in Scots. Although the *Tales* were not attributed on the title page to the 'author of Waverley', it was very clear to everyone that they were by the same writer. The implication of Augusta's conclusion, and of Byron's understanding of it, was that he was Scottish enough to be conceivable as the author of the first six, and some of the most Scottish, of the Waverley novels.

Yet another quality which Byron and Scott shared, and which they recognised and appreciated in each other, was a general approach to life which might seem inconsistent with their reputation as leaders of European romanticism. In a letter to Murray in March 1817, Byron said of Scott: 'He & Gifford & Moore are the only *regulars* I ever knew who had nothing of the *Garrison* about their manner – no nonsense – nor affectations look you'.46 Elsewhere, he refers to Scott as a man of the world.47 Scott said very much the same of Byron: 'What I liked about Byron, besides his boundless genius, was his generosity of spirit as well as purse, and his utter contempt of all affectations of literature'.[48] Scott was delighted by a story which Moore told him about Byron: 'While they stood at the window of Byron's Palazzo in Venice looking at a beautiful sunset, Moore was naturally led to say something of its beauty, when Byron answered in a tone that I can easily conceive, "Ah come, d-n me, Tom, don't be poetical".'[49]

This feet on the ground, no-nonsense attitude is remote from the Byronic hero, but it is entirely consistent with the realistic, and sceptical attitude, the eighteenth-century rationalism, which formed one aspect of both Byron and Scott. Both had been educated in cities, Aberdeen and Edinburgh, where the atmosphere of the Scottish Enlightenment prevailed and it left its influence on both of them. Its co-existence with romanticism of diverse kinds might perhaps be an example of what Gregory Smith called 'the Caledonian antisyzygy' and identified as the 'combination of opposites', or 'the contrasts which the Scot shows at every turn'.[50]

Another obvious link between the two men is, of course, that they both wrote long narrative poems. There are many similarities in metre, style and manner, even if the setting and content is very different and if Byron eventually added a new dimension to this kind of writing. Byron probably got the idea of writing poems of this kind because of Scott's example. Lockhart had no doubt that this was so: 'indeed in all his early serious narratives, Byron owed at least half his success to clever though perhaps unconscious imitation of Scott'.[51] Lockhart has another anecdote which shows how closely the minds of the two poets sometimes resembled one another. In London in 1828, he was with Scott listening to Mrs Arkwright singing some of her own settings. After one of them, Scott whispered to him 'Capital words – whose are they? – Byron's I suppose, but I don't remember them.' Lockhart continues, 'He was astonished when I told him that they were his own in *The Pirate*. He seemed pleased at the moment, but said next minute – "You have distressed me: – if memory goes, all is up with me, for that was always my strong point".'[52]

Before Byron decided in 1823 to go to Greece to help in their revolution, he had considered other possibilities. In 1819 he had thought in particular of South America where states were struggling for their independence.[53] In May 1822, he asked John Murray to send him the *Lockhart Papers*, 'a publication upon Scotch affairs of some time since'.[54] These papers were the *Memoirs* of John Lockhart of Carnwath, a member of the Scottish Parliament from 1703 to 1707 and a strong opponent of the Union with England. Byron did not say why he wanted the books, but since they contain the best contemporary exposure of the sordid transaction of the Union, it might be that he thought also of Scotland as a country where an independence movement might be stimulated or encouraged.

But, of course, it was Greece that he chose, and there he died on 19 April 1823. When the news reached Edinburgh, Scott wrote an obituary for the *Edinburgh Weekly Journal*, calling Byron, 'That mighty genius, which walked among men as something superior to ordinary mortality, and whose powers we beheld with wonder, and something approaching to terror'.[55] So ended a relationship which did credit to both men and gave much pleasure and satisfaction to both of them. During the rest of his life, Scott's thoughts often turned to Byron: 'I very often think of him almost with tears', he told Moore in August 1825.[56] Once shortly after Byron's death, he imagined for a moment that he saw him 'with wonderful accuracy' standing in the hall at Abbotsford.[57] He summed up his view of Byron in his *Journal*: 'This was the man – quaint, capricious, and playful, with all his immense genius. He wrote from impulse never from effort and therefore I have always reckoned Burns and Byron the most genuine poetical geniuses of my time and half a century before me'.[58] In 1832, as Scott was himself close to death and was hurrying home to Abbotsford from Italy, he visited Venice and went to see the balcony on which Byron had said to Moore, 'Damn me, Tom, don't be poetical'.[59]

(Contributed to *Byron and Scotland*, edited by Angus Calder, Edinburgh, 1989.)

NOTES

Abbreviations

J.   Sir Walter Scott, *Journal* (Edinburgh, 1950)
G.   *The Letters of Sir Walter Scott*, edited by Sir H.J.C. Grierson, 12 vols (London, 1932–7)
M.   *Byron's Letters and Journals*, edited by Leslie A. Marchand, 12 vols (London 1973–82)
L.   J.G. Lockhart, *Memoirs of Sir Walter Scott*, 5 vols (London, 1900)

1. J. 22 June 1826, p. 188.
2. G. IV/365.
3. M. III/209.
4. M. III/219–20.
5. M. VIII/23.
6. J. 23 Nov. 1825, p. 11.
7. L. V/391.
8. Edgar Johnson, *Sir Walter Scott, The Great Unknown* (New York, 1970), 2 vols, vol II, p. 219 (quoting a letter from Scott to Cadell).
9. M. IV/358.
10. G. II/214.
11. G. III/98–9.

12. G. III/114–15.
13. G. III/135 f.n. 1.
14. G. III/135–9.
15. M. II/182.
16. G. III/140–1.
17. L. II/508.
18. M. VII/83.
19. L. II/514–17.
20. L. III/24.
21. J. 21 Dec. 1825, p. 52.
22. Wilfred Partington, *Sir Walter's Post-Bag* (London, 1932) p. 114.
23. *Ibid.*, p. 116.
24. G. IV/184.
25. G. IV/234.
26. G. IV/364–5.
27. *Quarterly Review*, vol. XVI, dated October 1816 (but published in Feb. 1817), pp. 189, 207, 208.
28. M. V/178.
29. M. V/185.
30. M. IX/85–6.
31. M. X/189–90.
32. G. VII/37.
33. M. IV/146.
34. M. VII/48.
35. M. VII/45.
36. M. VIII/13.
37. M. IX/86–7.
38. J. 22. Nov. 1825, p. 7.
39. See Chapter 7 of my *Walter Scott and Scotland* (Edinburgh, 1981).
40. T.S. Eliot on Byron, in *From Anne to Victoria Essays by Various Hands* (London, 1937), p. 602.
41. Stanza XVII.
42. T.S. Eliot, *op. cit.*, p. 604 and Herbert Grierson, *The Background of English Literature* (Harmondsworth, 1962), p. 152.
43. T.S. Eliot, *op. cit.*, p. 617.
44. M. V/171.
45. V/220.
46. M. V/192.
47. M. IX/30.
48. J. 23 Nov. 1825, p. 11.
49. J. 9 Feb. 1826, p. 95.
50. G. Gregory Smith, *Scottish Literature: Character and Influence* (London. 1919), p.40
51. L. II/509.
52. L. V/195–6 f.n.

53. M. VI/123 f.n. 1; 212.
54. M. IX/156.
55. Sir Walter Scott, *Miscellaneous Prose* (Edinburgh, 1834), vol II, p. 343.
56. G. IX/199.
57. L. V/131–2 and f.n. 57; J. 9 Feb. 1826, p. 96.
58. J. 9 Feb. 1826, p. 96.
59. Edgar Johnson, *op.cit.*, vol. II, p. 1248.

12

A New Dimension: The Edinburgh Edition of the Waverley Novels

In *Memorials of his Time*, that indispensable book, Henry Cockburn described the 'instant and universal impression' made by the first publication in 1814 of the first of Scott's novels, *Waverley*: 'The unexpected newness of the thing, the profusion of original characters, the Scotch language, Scotch scenery, Scotch men and women, the simplicity of the writing, and the graphic force of the descriptions, all struck us with an electric shock of delight.'

I have long felt that a rediscovery of the best of Scott's novels (which for good reasons means those set in Scotland) could produce the same shock of delight for a new generation of readers. Serious criticism has been at variance with the general attitude of readers at large for about forty years, which is an astonishing state of affairs. After a century of triumphant popularity over the whole of Europe and North America, Scott fell out of fashion in the 1920s. E.M. Forster endorsed this attitude with some notorious and absurd observations in his Clark lectures in Cambridge in 1927. Among other things, he accused Scott of a trivial mind and that is about as far from the truth that it is possible to go. Modern criticism from the '50s onwards, in which David Daiches has played a distinguished part, has found new pleasures, depths and subtleties in Scott. In fact, as Daiches has remarked, it is only since about that time that we have really understood what the novels are about.

Of course, Scott has not been entirely neglected. The more popular of his novels have never been out of print. A writer of Scott's stature and international influence, however, needs something more than uncritical and spasmodic reprints of a few of the *Magnum Opus* texts. That was a collected edition of the novels on which Scott began work in the 1820s as part of his stalwart efforts to pay off his debts. It included some changes to the novels themselves, but the most important additions were new introductions and notes. The latter were short essays, mainly on the historical background. A reader looking for a novel alone may well be put off by this apparatus and it is possible, as is often said, that it accounts for the notion that Scott is unbearably long-winded. However, any one who wants to get on with the story can easily ignore the notes, and there have been many reprints of the novels without them. Personally, I am not persuaded that the notes are an obstacle to the enjoyment of Scott. On the contrary, I find them full of interest and of value for themselves.

There are other problems about the text of the novels. Both the writing and printing were carried out at great speed. Scott began to write *The Tale of Old Mortality* (the new edition insists on the full form of the title) in early September 1816. He had finished it by early November and the printing was completed by the 20th. Scott's writing was not easy to read and he did not bother much with punctuation. To protect the mystery of his identity, his manuscript was transcribed before it went to the type-setter. His friend, partner and publisher, James Ballantyne, supervised the printing with a somewhat prudish and pedantic eye. Even the early editions, therefore, did not always reflect exactly what Scott had actually written. He had a chance to correct mistakes when he was working on the *Magnum Opus*, but then he was concerned more with the addition of new material than with corrections. Perhaps, too, under the pressure of the financial crisis, his imagination had lost something of the freshness and force of a decade before.

For all these reasons, Edinburgh University Press decided in 1982, on the basis of the best available advice, that a reliable edition of the Waverley Novels was the 'main unfinished task facing Scottish letters'. They took the brave decision to do the job thoroughly. Since then, a team of scholars, with David Hewitt as editor-in-chief, has been sifting all the surviving evidence to re-establish Scott's original intentions as fully as possible. They have had the financial support of the Bank of Scotland and the co-operation of the National Library of Scotland and of the Pierpont Morgan Library of New York, which both hold Scott manuscripts. The first results of this major campaign of scholarship have now been published, *The Tale of Old Mortality, Kenilworth* and *The Black Dwarf*. Twenty-seven further volumes (including finally two with the Introductions and notes from the *Magnum Opus*) are to follow at the rate of two or three each year for the next ten years. There are presumably good practical reasons why they are not following the original order, but it is a pity that a new generation of readers cannot recapture in this respect also the experience of Scott's first readers.

The *Old Mortality* volume (I have not yet seen the others) is a model of painstaking and precise scholarship. The editor, Douglas Mack, gives us an excellent essay on the text which illuminates the working methods of Scott and his publishers. He provides notes and a glossary, with references to page and line, which explain every allusion and obscurity. There is also a note on the historical background to the story and a list of variant readings. This last takes thirty-four pages, but nearly all are of single words or a letter or two and make very little difference to the general sense. All of this supporting material takes 267 pages in addition to sixteen of introduction. This is very nearly as much as the novel itself, which takes 353, and the ratio of notes to text is much greater then in the *Magnum Opus*.

A devil's advocate then might argue that if the impact of the novel is impaired by the mass of scholarly apparatus, then the new edition has made things worse instead of better. He might also question if all the enormous labour of comparing manuscripts, proofs and editions is worthwhile when the final result is a text that does not differ very much in overall effect from the one which has been reprinted so many times.

I think that there are good answers to these points. Scott's notes were not explanations of obscurities but tangential essays. Douglas Mack gives the modern reader all the information which he might need for a full appreciation of the text. Most readers will probably prefer to race on with the pace of the novel, which is compelling, but Mack is there to help, if he is needed. On the other point, there is a real satisfaction in having at last a text which is as free from accidental error as modern scholarship can achieve, and there may be cases (perhaps in other novels more than in this one) where the amendments are of significance. One thing is certain, you could not wish for a more accomplished and thorough work of editing, although I regret the removal of Scott's own notes to another volume ten years hence. Still, this does not really matter because they are readily available elsewhere.

With the publication of this edition, scholarship on Scott, and indeed on Scottish literature as a whole, enters a new dimension. This is reinforced by the fact that Edinburgh University Press have already announced similarly complete and scholarly editions of Hogg and Stevenson and a republication of the Yale edition of the Boswell papers. For too long both the academic study and the general appreciation of our literature, which is of infinite value and interest, has been hampered by the lack of adequate editions or even the lack of any editions in print at all. We have often complained that our universities, until very recently at least, have carried a large share of the responsibility for the comparative neglect of our literature. Edinburgh University Press therefore deserves warm congratulation for these ventures which will not only make good editions available, but encourage a complete change of attitude.

It is also good to hear that paperback reprints of the Waverley novels are planned with much less supporting material. This is what is needed if the rediscovery of the pleasures and illuminations of the novels are to reach a wider public. They might begin with *Old Mortality*. It is a splendid and provocative novel, full of character, rich and witty dialogue in Scots, and with a painfully topical relevance in its study of extremism and moderation.

(*Books in Scotland*, No. 48, Winter 1993.)

13

John Leyden: Polymath and Border Reiver

I. SCOTLAND

Who exactly was John Leyden, and what happened to him? These are questions which puzzled me for years. I seemed always to be coming across references to him and remarks and anecdotes that invited further inquiry. There is, for instance, the well-known story that he could speak thirty or forty languages, but refused to learn English on the grounds that it would spoil his Scots. There is the episode in Lockhart's *Life of Sir Walter Scott*, when Richard Heber, the most assiduous of book collectors, found him perched on top of a ladder in Constable's bookshop in Edinburgh and discovered that he was a prodigy of learning and the ideal ally for Scott in his search for Border ballads. 'This extraordinary man,' said Lockhart, 'confounded the doctors of Edinburgh by the portentous mass of his acquisitions in almost every department of learning, perplexing those about him by manners and habits in which it was hard to say whether the mosstrooper or the schoolman of former days most prevailed, he was at heart a poet.' The judicious Cockburn has a similar description in his *Memorials*: 'Ever in a state of excitement, ever ardent, ever panting for things unattainable by ordinary mortals he was a wild-looking, thin, Roxburghshire man, with sandy hair, a screech voice, and staring eyes. His physical energy was as vigorous as his mental; so that it would not be easy to say whether he would have engaged with a new-found eastern manuscript, or in battle, with the more cordial alacrity. His love of Scotland was delightful. It breathes through all his writings and all his proceedings, and imports to his poetry its most attractive charm.' John Buchan summed him up as 'a curious blend of the polymath and the Border reiver'.

But passages like these leave a lot of questions unanswered. What did Leyden do with all this prodigious learning? If he was a poet, why do we find nothing in the anthologies? What were the results of all his energy and enthusiasm? I had to try to find the answers.

It was not difficult to discover the facts, even if some of them only raise new mysteries. There is a biographical essay by Walter

Scott, who also often mentioned Leyden in his letters and in the *Journal*, and always with affection. There are two rather pedestrian biographies, including one by a cousin, James Morton. In the library of Edinburgh University there is a very thorough Ph.D. thesis by Isobel Brown. Observations by an unsympathetic contemporary of Leyden eventually found their way into that great compendium of unexpected information, *Blackwood's Magazine*. This is the story.

John Leyden was born on 8 September 1775 at Denholm, a pleasant little village near Hawick, which, strangely enough, was also the birthplace sixty-two years later of another hero of learning, linguistic study and high endeavour, James Murray, editor of the *Oxford English Dictionary*. Leyden was typical of the lad o' pairts, reading everything he could lay his hands on, walking six miles to school every day, setting poverty at defiance. He absorbed the Border ballads and with them an admiration for bold deeds and a contempt for soft and easy living.

In 1790, when he was fifteen, he walked to Edinburgh to study for the ministry with almost no money but plenty of determination. Scott, in his essay, described the effect of Leyden's first appearance in the Greek class in almost the same words that he used later about Dominic Sampson in his novel, *Guy Mannering*. His outlandish appearance, wild gestures and harsh voice 'discomposing', Scott said, 'the gravity of the professor and totally routing that of the students'; but it was not long before they realised that the strange exterior concealed a formidable scholar. He mastered Latin, Greek, French, Spanish, Italian, German, Icelandic, Hebrew, Arabic and Persian, and it was only a beginning. His studies were not only linguistic. I think that Boswell said of Johnson that he was born to grapple with whole libraries; Leyden grappled with the whole university, with almost every class of every faculty. He spent ten years at Edinburgh, taking full advantage of the tradition which allowed students for the ministry to attend lectures without payment. He supported himself by earning a pittance from writing and teaching. 'Bread and water, and access to books and lectures' were, Lockhart wrote, all that he needed, and thus sustained, 'he toiled and battled at the gates of science after science'.

In 1797, Leyden was a founder-member of a student club with the unusual name of the Academy of Physics. It was one of those self-improving endeavours which are, or used to be, quite common in Edinburgh. The members met to read papers to one another on scientific and philosophical subjects, including assessments of new books; but this was a club which had important consequences. Among the members were a group of friends from the High School of Edinburgh, Jeffrey, Brougham and Horner, who were joined later by Sydney Smith. They were, in fact, the original team of the *Edinburgh Review*, which, Cockburn wrote, 'elevated the public and the literary position of Edinburgh to an extent which no-one not living intelligently then can be made to comprehend'. Years later, Smith claimed that he had suggested the launching of the *Review*; but there is a letter from John Leyden dated March 1798, two years before Smith came to Edinburgh, in which he made exactly that proposal.

Meanwhile, John Leyden's own literary career had begun. From 1793 he contributed poems to the *Edinburgh Magazine*, signed only with his initials, which Scott had noticed long before they met. Then in 1799 Leyden published his first book, an account of African exploration, for which he had acquired an enthusiasm, fired by the expeditions of another Scottish Borderer, Mungo Park. It is a book full of radical opinions, condemning slavery, the treatment of women by Islam and the African tribes, and even the bigotry of Protestant missionaries, which was scarcely tactful in a young candidate for the ministry. In fact, when Leyden completed his trials for his licence for the ministry he had some difficulty in explaining away allegations of atheism.

His next work was an edition of *The Complaynt of Scotland*, commissioned by Archibald Constable, then at the beginning of his reign as the Tsar of Scottish publishing. This remarkable book, written in 1548 and one of the earliest examples of Scots prose, covers a vast range of subjects from political controversy to music, poetry and the dance. It was a perfect field for Leyden to display his immense knowledge of early literature. To the alarm of Constable, the introduction grew to about 300 pages, almost as long as the text itself. Constable, thinking of his printing costs, asked Leyden to drop the idea of an additional essay on the Scots language. This is a pity because it deprived us of the unique contribution which Leyden could have made to the subject. It is an odd coincidence that the next editor of the *Complaynt* was none other than James Murray of the *O.E.D.* He was astonished at the range and accuracy of Leyden's scholarship and found it impossible to improve on his version of the text. Constable, too, was evidently impressed by Leyden; in 1802 he made him editor of his *Scots Magazine*.

It was at about this time that Leyden was introduced to Scott after the encounter with Heber in Constable's bookshop. He responded eagerly, of course, to Scott's idea of a collection of Border ballads, and more or less took over the project. He derided the idea of a single volume. 'I have more than that in my head, myself,' he told Scott. 'We shall turn out three or four volumes at least.' He thought nothing of working sixteen hours a day in the Advocates Library or walking scores of miles in search of an old ballad. Scott described an evening when his dinner guests were disturbed by a 'sound at a distance like the whistling of a tempest through the torn rigging of a vessel'. It was Leyden chanting the recovered fragment of a ballad, for which he had walked forty or fifty miles and back.

Among all these activities, Leyden was putting the final touches to his most ambitious poem, *Scenes of Infancy*. He was also in love with Janet Brown, the sister of his friend Thomas Brown, who later succeeded Dugald Stewart as Professor of Moral Philosophy at Edinburgh. He addressed her in many of his verses as Aurelia, but his letters were more passionate: 'I shall not lose you tamely. You are mine, soul and body, and there exists not a living being that could draw you from me.'

Here I must digress to say a word about Leyden's verse. I should like to be able to claim that he is a great neglected poet, ripe for rediscovery. The sad truth is that the anthologists are right to forget him. His verse is trite and sentimental. To modern taste, it is unreadable, even if it was admired in its day by such men as Scott and Lockhart. It was written in English, in a poetic diction of the most tired and hackneyed kind, and this by a man who insisted on speaking Scots, and who lived and breathed the atmosphere of the ballads and early Scottish literature. He was, of course, fully conscious of the linguistic dilemma of the Scottish poet. In his introduction to an edition of two Scottish poets, he complained that when a Scotsman was obliged to write in English he used 'a species of translation, which checks the versatility of fancy and restrains the genuine and spontaneous flow of his conceptions'. So why did he use this 'species of translation' himself? From his letters, he does seem to have written poetry in Scots, but little has survived. Perhaps the publishers were reluctant to accept it; but we are talking of a time only a few years after Burns had proved that the thing was possible. It is difficult to imagine that Leyden, with his Scottish patriotism, energy and force of character, could easily be diverted into a false course. I find it sad and mysterious.

There is an even greater mystery. Leyden suddenly decided that he must go abroad. Then as now, it was so common for Scotsmen to feel compelled to leave the country to seek their fortunes elsewhere that one might think that it calls for no comment. Leyden's case was different. If he had left in the early days of his struggle that would have been commonplace enough; but here he was, established with the leading publisher of the day, engaged in a joint undertaking with Scott, to which all their literary and Scottish enthusiasm responded, finishing his major poem which was also rooted in the Borders, on familiar terms with the men who were about to launch the most influential periodical of the time; all this and in love. A man of his strong Scottish feeling would be reluctant to leave Scotland at any time; but the moment when Leyden insisted on doing it, urgently and against all influence and advice, is very curious. Perhaps there is a relationship between this and the choice of English for his poetry. Perhaps it reflects impatience with the trauma, uncertainty and ambiguous status inflicted on Scotland by the Union. He may suddenly have lost all tolerance for a country that was incomplete. His abrupt decision had all the marks of an emotional revulsion. He was impulsive and impetuous: the sort of man who wanted all or nothing.

Leyden's first idea was an expedition to Africa in emulation of Mungo Park, and he mentioned this to Scott about three months after they first met. Scott was dismayed. He would risk, he said, 'getting himself literally broiled'. Scott wrote to his friend George Ellis: 'Will you have the goodness to beg Heber to write to him seriously on so ridiculous a plan, which can promise nothing either pleasant or profitable? I am certain he would get a church in Scotland with a little patience and prudence, and it gives me great pain to see a valuable young man of uncommon genius and acquirements fairly throw himself away.'

Scott assumed that it was Leyden's failure to find acceptance by a church and the absence therefore of a steady income which was driving him to desperate courses. 'The various kinds of distress under which literary men, I mean such as have no other profession than letters, must labour, in a commercial country, is a great disgrace to society,' he said in another letter to Ellis. Some years later, the New Scots Magazine said much the same, that he had 'wearied of bookseller's hackwork which took sweat from the aching brow, but did not give bread in return'. On the other hand, there is plenty of evidence that Leyden cared little about money. He was proposing to leave Scotland just at the time when Constable was transforming the rewards of literature by his payments to his writers. Even after more than 170 years of inflation, they still sound substantial: 'Ten, even twenty guineas a sheet for a review, £2,000 or £3,000 for a single poem, and £1,000 each for two philosophical dissertations.' In this atmosphere, and Leyden was in the thick of it, it does not seem likely that he, of all people, was driven away by financial anxiety or the need for a steady job.

The best that Scott could do was to divert Leyden from Africa to India. With the help of influential friends, which was the only way to manage such things in those days, he sought a place for him in the Indian establishment. Leyden was offered an appointment as a physician and surgeon, provided he could qualify within six months. To anyone else this would have seemed an impossible condition; but

Leyden, building on his diverse studies in Edinburgh, took it in his stride. In January 1803, he left Scotland in such a rush that his friends had to correct the proofs of *Scenes of Infancy* and see it through the press. He was not pleased with the result; they had 'curtailed what I liked, and left what I did not care sixpence about'.

Of course, there may be yet another explanation. Leyden may simply have felt an irresistible urge to conquer new worlds. We know that he was determined to surpass Sir William Jones, a member of Samuel Johnson's Club, who had won fame by his translations from the Persian. 'India,' wrote Leyden in a letter to Heber, 'was the finest literary field in the world.' India was rich in languages unknown to the European. For Leyden this was a tempting challenge.

Or was he running away from something? In a letter he wrote to Heber a few days before he sailed there is a curious, incoherent sentence: 'I do not regret my confidence for since that night when you became acquainted with the *dreadful secret* which I believe but for your society would have overturned my mind.' That is all we know about it. There is no explanation; no further reference of any kind. The outspoken, natural, confident, courageous Leyden is the last man you would expect to find trying to escape from guilt on the other side of the world. So his abrupt and final departure from Scotland remains mysterious. One of his friends in Scotland, R.P. Gillies, said that 'probably no-one ever left his own country with more acute emotion of regret'. Almost all the poetry which Leyden wrote afterwards is heavy with melancholy and foreboding of early death.

2. INDIA

Men who made fortunes in India and came home to buy estates and parade their wealth, the nabobs, are familiar in the literature of the early nineteenth century. They were the survivors. Many never got to India at all because the voyage under sail was long and dangerous. Others arrived but succumbed quite quickly to disease, the heat and the unfamiliar conditions. Leyden survived the voyage, with one or two narrow escapes; but his notorious powers of endurance were no match for the climate. For much of his time in India he was miserably ill and within eight years he was dead. In fact, he might easily have got no farther than the Margate Roads, because the ship on which he was at first supposed to sail was wrecked there with the loss of twenty-four lives. His voyage in another ship took 134 days. There were two attempts at mutiny, which Leyden helped to subdue, and twenty duels. War with France had started again, and for three months they were under threat of attack by enemy ships. On 18 August 1803, invigorated no doubt by his adventures, Leyden eventually arrived in Madras.

His first job, and it is a little startling considering his six months' training and no medical experience at all, was physician-in-charge of the Madras General Hospital. There is a glimpse of him in this capacity in the private papers of Thomas Taylor, who afterwards worked with Leyden on the staff of Lord Minto and later fought as a general at Waterloo: 'Leyden is a curious mixture of apothecary, poet and scholar. He bled me for a fever, though goodness knows, I was bloodless enough already. Having done so, he solaced me with porter and poetry.' It sounds as though he had an agreeable and distinctive bedside manner, at least. Before long, Leyden was ill himself, with prickly heat, fever and dysentery. He was lucky enough to be rescued by a Dr James Anderson, the first of several Scots he met in India who had literary and scientific tastes similar to his own.

Aided by introductions which Scott had made for him, Leyden did not have to wait long for a job suitable for his talents. He was to assist Colin Mackenzie in a survey of the virtually unknown territory of Mysore, which had recently been acquired by the defeat of Tipu Sultan. Everything from the geology and botany to the social structure and the languages and literature was to be discovered and recorded. Once again he was fortunate in his colleague. Mackenzie, eventually the first Surveyor-General of India, was, his biographer wrote, 'a Lewis man with a thirst for knowledge almost as great as Leyden's own'.

For months, Leyden ignored the prickly heat and the fever. Once he crossed a swollen river in a 'great brass kettle'. Once he was 'dogged by a monstrous tiger for nearly three miles'. By the end of the year, he had to collapse into bed in Seringapatam and stay there for six weeks in, as he wrote, 'a pestilential state of health – liver, spleen, bloody flux and fever of the jungles'. He had boils on his back, 'like mushrooms after rain'. Anderson warned him that he would die if he did not relax the pressure of his studies, but he refused. He was resolved, he said, to be the greatest Oriental scholar of the age or die in the attempt. Soon he had learned seven or eight Indian languages, the beginning of a process which Lord Minto described as 'more the ancient gift of tongues, or some peculiar privilege of his own, than the slow acquisitions of ordinary men'. This was even more astonishing because he was breaking new ground, working from the raw material of the spoken and written language, without dictionaries or grammars except for the notes he made for himself. One of his early triumphs was to translate an inscription in Cochin, where no one before had been able to identify the language or the alphabet.

While Leyden was lying in his misery in Seringapatam, but still working ten hours a day, another Borderer arrived on the scene. This was John Malcolm, who had been appointed Resident in Mysore. When he later became a general, he had the reputation of 'a careless, good-humoured fellow, illiterate but with pregnant ability'. In battle, he was said to wave his hat and lead the files at a run 'more like a subaltern than a general'. But appearances were deceptive. He learned Persian to prepare himself to lead a diplomatic mission there and wrote a history of the country that was long a standard work. His response to reading Leyden's *Scenes of Infancy* was to write at once a set of more than adequate complimentary verses. Evidently he, too, was yet another mixture of the Border reiver and the scholar. Perhaps the type is not so rare as one might suppose.

Leyden's friends bent their efforts to persuade him to take a sea-voyage to restore his health. He agreed eventually to go to Penang, where the climate was said to be healthy; but the voyage does not sound like a health cruise. The crew, Leyden wrote, were 'as black as demons, as impertinent as monkeys, as lazy as lizards, as nasty as polecats, and as ignorant of navigation as Cockneys. This cursed ship is now become completely detestable. The tainted odour of spoiled rice, and rotten salt-fish, spoiled by the salt-water which washes over us from day to day, has quite filled the cabin, and legions of small scorpions begin to make their appearance amid myriads of cockroaches and ants, by which we are constantly infested. The ship smells all over like an open sepulchre, and the water is putrid and nauseous'. Strangely enough, Leyden survived. He arrived in George Town, the capital of Penang, in October 1805.

For most of the next three months, Leyden lived in the house of Stamford Raffles, who became one of the great colonial administrators and the founder of Singapore. They were kindred spirits. Raffles was delighted to find that Leyden was ready to throw himself into the study of the Malayan language and traditions. Both had an insatiable appetite for work. Perhaps even Leyden was for once outclassed. Raffles is said to have had the inhuman habit of working from four a.m. to eleven p.m. Almost immediately, they became close friends and collaborators, and it was Raffles who eventually completed the translation of a fifteenth-century Malayan chronicle, *Sejarah Malayu*, which Leyden left unfinished at his death. They exchanged ideas on more practical matters as well. 'Most of the principal measures of my administration,' Raffles wrote afterwards, 'were suggested by his all-powerful genius.'

Raffles's wife, Olivia, took charge of Leyden and nursed him back to health. She was described by Minto as a 'great lady, with dark eyes, lively manner, accomplished and clever', and she is said to have been one of the beauties addressed by Thomas Moore in his love poetry. Leyden, too, wrote sad and tender verse to her. It all sounds a little like the sort of situation that a hundred years later might have made a plot for Somerset Maugham; but as far as we know, all three lived happily together without a discordant note.

From Penang, Leyden sailed to Calcutta. He spent the next two years there, still formally on the staff of the hospital in Madras, but in fact devoting all his time to studying the languages. He drew up a plan for the Government on the systematic investigation of the languages and literatures of the whole Indo-Chinese area, and proceeded to carry it out. He learned language after language, and translated the scriptures into seven of them. The old accusation of atheism appeared again when a local missionary regretted that such a work should be undertaken by 'so confirmed and hardened an infidel'. Leyden began a translation from the Jaghatai Turki, the language of Ghengis Khan, of the memoirs of Baber, a sixteenth-century Emperor of Hindustan, which was completed after his death by his student friend from Edinburgh, William Erskine. It was not merely that Leyden had a phenomenal capacity for learning languages, but, in the words of Sir James Mackenzie, an 'unparalleled ability' to grasp their general features, relationships and evolution. As Erskine put it: 'In the course of 8 years, he nearly effected for Asia that which after centuries has been only imperfectly accomplished for Europe: a classification of the languages and their kindred dialects.'

The fortunes of Leyden changed dramatically when Gilbert Elliot, Lord Minto, arrived in Calcutta as Governor-General of India in July 1807. Each had been recommended to the other by Scott, and both were Borderers. This alone was enough to give Leyden a favourable reception, but Minto soon recognised his talents. His learning was 'stupendous', Minto wrote, and all within instant recall. He was 'excursive' in conversation, but his pen was 'sober, steady, concise, [and] lucid'. 'His reasoning [was] just, his judgement extremely sound, and his principles always admirable. His mind, upright and independent, his character spirited and generous, with a strong leaning to the chivalrous.'

In 1807 Leyden was appointed Professor of Hindustani and Persian at Fort William College in Calcutta, but within a few months Minto had evidently decided that Leyden was too useful a man to leave in academic seclusion. He was made a magistrate with the special task of suppressing the dacoits and succeeded in bringing 300 to justice. In 1809 he became Commissioner of the Court of Requests and in 1810 Assay Master of the Calcutta Mint. The news reached Scott in Edinburgh. He wrote to George Ellis: 'Leyden, by the by, is triumphant at Calcutta – A *Judge*, of all things! and making money! He has flourished like a green bay tree under the auspices of Lord Minto, his countryman.' Scott seems to have regarded this as perfectly satisfactory, natural and proper; but was it not an example of the sort of Scottish clannishness which Samuel Johnson detested?

The English, of course, did not fail to notice the number of Scots in high places in India. William Cobbett remarked that 'the Navy will, like India, soon be a Scotch thing altogether'. In *Vanity Fair*, Thackeray described Joseph Sedley as 'very witty, regarding the number of Scotchmen whom Lord Minto, the Governor-General, patronised. How [Becky Sharp] laughed at the stories of the Scotch aides-de-camp!' This was before the age of competitive examinations. All appointments to government jobs were made on the basis of personal recommendations. Both the Minister in the Government responsible for India, Henry Dundas, and the Governor-General in India itself were Scottish. It was natural enough that Scotsmen would tend to know and trust more of their own countrymen than other people. An unjust system, no doubt, but not one that failed to pay attention to qualification and merit. It is obvious enough that people like Colin Mackenzie, John Malcolm and Leyden were civilised and agreeable men, with active and well-stocked minds, courageous and ready to accept danger and hardship. A system which could produce administrators of this quality was not doing badly. Perhaps it was not merely national partiality. Probably more men of this type were available from Scotland than England because in Scotland education was more widespread, although the country was poorer. From Scotland's point of view, there is little doubt that the most important effect of the Union was precisely the way in which it opened up opportunuties for careers in the Empire. Whether this was a good thing for Scotland itself is another matter. Leyden is only one example among many thousands of brilliant people, including a high proportion of the most active and enterprising part of the population, who were lost to Scotland for ever.

Leyden's brief career in India moved into its last phase in 1811. Raffles had involved him in a proposal for the annexation of Java, which had become enemy territory after the French occupation of Holland. There was a risk, which carried conviction with Minto, that the French might use it as a base for an attack on India. Raffles viewed Java as a step towards trade with Japan. Whitehall was less enthusiastic, first opposing the whole idea and then giving reluctant approval to the overthrow of the French-Dutch authorities on the island, but not to its annexation. Minto was not the man to take his instructions too literally. Thomas Taylor, who had been one of Leyden's first patients in Madras, was now Minto's Military Secretary. He had a ringside view of these events and left an account of them in his private papers. 'The pundits considered that it was the duty of the Governor-General to stay put, and obey orders rather than issue them. His Lordship gave the big-wigs at the seat of Government a terrible shock. They threw up their hands in horror at the Governor-General demeaning himself over a paltry place like Java.' In spite of them, Minto took personal charge of the political conduct of the expedition. He sailed from Calcutta on 9 March 1811 with Taylor and Leyden on his staff. If Raffles became Governor of Java, as he expected, it was understood that Leyden would be Secretary.

Taylor gives us a description of life on board during the peaceful interlude of the approach voyage: 'Leyden and Lord Minto get on pretty well; Leyden is a sort of clansman of the Elliot family, coming as he does from Teviotdale, and having helped Walter Scott write it, keeps Lord Minto happy by constant recitals of the *Minstrelsy of the Scottish Border*. Stewart being a Scot has to feign interest, but I suspect he prefers the Captain's sherry; I being a mere Sassenach have to grin and bear it.' The truth is that Taylor did not like Leyden very much, and found it hard to tolerate his loud voice and incessant talk about Oriental languages and Scottish poetry.

The expedition of 10,000 men and eighty-one ships reached the coast of Java on 4 August. Their landing was unopposed, but Leyden was determined to make the most of it. Dressed like a pirate in a red-tasselled cap, with a cutlass in one hand and a pistol in the other, he was the first man ashore. The more serious fighting came later. Java, and in particular, the capital, Batavia (the present-day Djakarta), had the reputation of being 'the most destructive place in the world for Europeans' because of its 'pestilential atmosphere'. The Dutch withdrew to a strongly fortified position in the centre, expecting the climate to do their work for them. The British troops under Auchmuty and Rollo Gillespie decided on an immediate assault and destroyed resistance at the point of the bayonet.

While this battle was going on, Leyden was engaged in peaceful, but no less lethal, work. He had rushed to examine books and manuscripts stored in an unventilated cellar. He came out shivering, took to his bed with a fever, and died three days later on 28 August, in the arms of Raffles. He was not yet thirty-six. 'We have lost in him a host of men,' Raffles wrote, 'and Eastern literature its firmest support.' Minto duly set up an Administration and made Raffles Lieutenant-Governor; but Taylor tells us that a celebration of this on 17 October was a lugubrious affair because Minto and Raffles were still feeling the loss of their friend.

When the news reached London, Robert Southey commented: 'So Batavia has cost us John Leyden's life, which was worth more than ten Batavias.' Walter Scott's thoughts, for the rest of his life, often turned to Leyden, as in the *Lord of the Isles*:

> His bright and brief career is o'er,
> And mute his tuneful strains.
> Quench'd is his lamp of varied lore,
> That loved the light of song to pour.
> A distant and a deadly shore
> Has Leyden's cold remains.

(*Blackwood's Magazine*, October and November 1978; nos 1956 and 1957; vol. 3240.)

14

Henry Dundas

Henry Dundas and his son, Robert, the 1st and 2nd Viscount Melville, were virtually the personal rulers of Scotland from the 1770s to the 1830s. This period has been called the 'Dundas Despotism' and this is the title which Michael Fry uses for his new book[1] on the subject, although he argues that it is a misnomer. The Dundases have certainly had a bad press. Carlyle, for instance, said that they were 'noisome in the nostrils of all men'. But the history has mostly been written by their political opponents, the Whigs, who replaced them after the Reform Act of 1832.

Michael Fry shares the Conservatism of the Dundases and has a natural sympathy for them, but that does not mean that his book is a party tract. It is a serious work of scholarship which required the mastery of a mountain of manuscript sources. Also Fry is an unusual Conservative; he has an independent mind and fresh ideas. He has often been penetrating in his analysis of the failings of the present Conservative Party in Scotland. It is, he has said, the only conservative party in the world which is unpatriotic in resisting the national aspirations of its own people. They want to conserve the Union with all its disadvantages, but are ready to go along with all the radical proposals for change that come from their masters in London, even when they are entirely inappropriate and unwelcome in Scotland. Fry argues that the Dundas policy was the precise opposite of this. They regarded the Union, not as an excuse for the assimilation of Scotland, but as a means of defending Scottish interests, ideas and institutions.

Michael Fry is a neighbour of mine and I have had the opportunity of a long and illuminating discussion with him about this impressive book. He told me that he had three purposes in writing it. Firstly and obviously, he wanted to do justice to the Dundases and show that they were not the ogres of the myth; secondly to show that they were part of the Scottish Enlightenment and wanted to give practical expression to its ideas; thirdly to show that they thought that the Union could be made to work in the sense that it had left all Scottish institutions, except Parliament, intact and that they could be used to give Scotland self-government of a kind. To the objection that the absence of Parliament was an important exception, Fry replies that it was not a democratic age. It is certainly true that at that time such institutions as the Church, the legal system, the burghs, the universities and the banks had far more influence on daily life than any Parliament.

It is part of Fry's thesis that these Scottish institutions were destroyed or seriously weakened, not by the Dundases and the Conservatives, but by the Whigs, and he hints that this might be the subject of another book. He accuses them of ruthless anglicisation which resulted from an uncritical enthusiasm for the British, or rather English, Parliament (which, in spite of its antiquated inadequacy, is still true of many unionists). In their view, everything English was right, and anything Scottish was therefore wrong. 'The law degenerated. The Church suffered the catastrophic Disruption. The universities were forced into conformity with their inferior English counterparts.'

Fry makes the point that the Scots were faced with a dilemma. They were obliged to be conservative to guard a nationality for which the State offers few guarantees. 'Yet so much of the finest in the spirit of their nationality, its self-improving energy, its intellectual rigour, its idealism and its democracy, drives them into being progressives'. This last sentence is as good a statement of the best Scottish qualities that I have seen anywhere; but the process of anglicisation has continued under both Labour and the present Conservative Governments and we have already lost so much that it is restoration and not conservation that we now need.

Fry makes a strong case to justify the conclusion of Henry Cockburn, even if he was a Whig, that Henry Dundas 'was the very man for Scotland at that time, and is a Scotchman of whom his country may be proud, skilful in Parliament, wise and liberal in council and with an almost unrivalled power of administration'. He also sustains the judgement of Castlereagh, who was surprised to discover that Dundas 'felt for Scotland all that partiality that has been remarked as a characteristic of the people of that country'. Horace Walpole records an episode when Dundas in his cups broke out into an invective against the English and said that he would move the repeal of the Union.

It remains true, of course, that the Dundas style of government had nothing to do with democracy. The Union and the indifference of London to Scottish affairs had left Scotland like a rudderless ship. Henry Dundas did his best for Scotland in the circumstances and somehow found time to run India and the war with France as well. It is largely due to him that the Empire, for good or ill, was not English, but British. While it lasted, it provided the Scots with some compensation for their lost independence.

It may look like a quibble to mention one slip in so substantial a book, but it is on a point on which a misleading myth is growing up. Some years ago both Nicholas Phillipson and Hugh Trevor Roper misquoted Walter Scott's *Malachi* Letters to suggest that he had said that he would rather Scotland became 'a subordinate species of Northumberland' than see the Union dissolved. Fry follows them on this point. In fact, it is very clear from the context that Scott was referring not to the dissolution of the Union, but to a resumption of war between the two Kingdoms, which is a very different matter on which no one would disagree.

Michael Fry has written a book which is not only a very considerable contribution to Scottish historiography, but which has important contemporary implications, not least for his own political party.

(*The Herald*, 12 December, 1992.)

NOTE

1. *The Dundas Despotism*, Edinburgh University Press.

15

Burns and Stevenson

These pillars of Scottish literature, with whom along with Walter Scott every Scot is assumed to have at least a nodding acquaintance, are the subjects of impressive new biographies[1] and both from Mainstream publishing. They are in good time for the first centenary of Stevenson's death in 1994 and the second of Burns in 1996.

At first glance, Burns and Stevenson might seem to have little in common: Burns close to the land and harassed by poverty; Stevenson a privileged son of professional Edinburgh. Stevenson travelled across the world; Burns crossed the Border only once for a few days. But Stevenson felt a close affinity with Robert Fergusson and Burns too looked to him as mentor and inspiration. Both suffered from poor health and both died young, Burns at thirty-seven and Stevenson at forty-four. Both were largely self-educated. Stevenson, it is true, was in theory educated at Edinburgh Academy and Edinburgh University; but, Ian Bell tells us, his appearances in either were very rare. Still, when his future wife, Fanny Osborne, first met him in France, she thought that he was 'overeducated'. The reason, of course, was his constant reading and conscious effort to teach himself to write. Burns's father did his best to see that his sons had a sound basic education. Henry Mackenzie started the idea that he was a 'Heaven-taught ploughman' and Burns often played the role. In fact, he too was widely read. He evidently had a fair knowledge of French, at least some slight acquaintance with Latin, and an unrivalled familiarity with traditional Scottish song.

There were similarities also in their attitude to Scotland. Bell says of Stevenson that he had 'a Scottish sense of himself' and so, of course, had Burns. Both felt for Scotland as an extension of themselves, thought constantly about her history and literature and were consciously part of a Scottish tradition. Neither can be understood in any other terms.

In spite of this, as James Mackay remarks, Burns's early education in the hands of John Murdoch was entirely based on English books. The same is no doubt true of Stevenson at the Edinburgh Academy. Nothing can demonstrate the English domination of Scottish education more convincingly than the fact that Burns himself seems to

have carried on the practice. At least, Mackay quotes from a letter from James Gray of the Dumfries Academy and later of the
High School of Edinburgh in which he describes Burns instructing
his eldest son in the 'English poets' and heroic examples from
the pages of 'our most celebrated English historians'. Of course,
Gray may have used the word, 'English', loosely, which was common at the time, as Burns complained in one of his letters to
Mrs Dunlop. The fact remains that Burns and Stevenson, like
many people in Scotland still, were left to discover Scottish books
by accident and by themselves. I say 'books' deliberately, because
Scottish song, poetry, story and language came to them orally.
That was the basis of Burns's concern for Scottish song, 'a sacred
trust', as Mackay calls it, and of most of his own best work.
Stevenson was exposed to it as well, both in his stravaigings about
Edinburgh and the Pentlands and in the tales of his nurse, Cummy,
although Bell thinks that her influence was more disturbing than
stimulating.

If then there is much in common between Burns and Stevenson,
the approaches of their latest biographers is very different. James
Mackay says in his Introduction that more than 2,000 editions of
Burns and more than 900 biographical works have appeared. You
might ask, what remains to be said? Mackay would reply that much
that has been written about Burns is false and that much previously
undiscovered detail lies in records that previous biographers have
not consulted. Since he has edited the works and the letters (which
makes cross-reference convenient) and has edited the *Burns Chronicle*
for fourteen years, his knowledge of Burns is formidable and so
is his energy and persistence in research. He has taken the major
biographies of Burns and subjected their accounts to the test of a
minute examination of the surviving records.

The result is a book of more than 700 pages which is packed with
detailed information, not only about Burns, but about everyone with
whom he comes in contact. At first I was afraid that this was likely
to result in a deluge of tedious and superfluous fact. On the contrary,
it gradually builds up into a very solid and convincing picture of
irresistible fascination. It is compulsive reading (ideal for a holiday
of ten days or so), particularly as there is constant reference to
the poems which arise out of the circumstances of Burns's daily
experience.

This must now, I think, be regarded as the standard life of Burns
and the one which gives the most substantial and reliable account,
although you will still have to go to Daiches and Crawford for the
literary criticism. Mackay's life, though fuller and more scrupulous
with the evidence, does not differ fundamentally from the other

major biographies of this century. Burns was unfortunate in his first two biographers, Heron and Currie, who started the legend, which has been slow to die, that Burns was a habitual drunkard. Mackay rightly says that anyone who got through the amount of work that Burns did was a 'workaholic, not an alcoholic'. He is tolerant too of Burns's fathering of bastard bairns, another not unusual circumstance which has been too much discussed.

This is not to say that the book is a work of whitewash or hagiography. Mackay is frank as well as balanced and does not conceal Burns's failings, as in his wire-pulling over his Excise postings or his tendency to write satirical epigrams which probably hurt more than he intended. If the picture which emerges is of an immensely likeable, intelligent and warm-hearted man, that is what he was. There is only one judgement in the book which seems wildly exaggerated. That is when Mackay suggests (on page 169) that Burns deserves to be regarded as a religious reformer because of his satires against the Auld Lichts 'just as much as John Knox'.

Ian Bell's subject is much less overlaid with accumulated legend, even if some of the early biographies of Stevenson inclined to the romantic. Bell's method could not be more different from Mackay's, although he also is more concerned with the man than the work. I have no doubt that he has made an exhaustive study of the sources and could give detailed evidence to support his every statement, but that is not his style. He gives us his conclusions, but does not necessarily argue the case. The result is a book which suggests the omniscience of the novelist and reads with the fluency of a good novel. It is a sensitive and intelligent interpretation, not a painstaking account of every fact which can be discovered. In this account, Stevenson appears rather more as the indulged son of a generous and long-suffering father than as the reckless rebel against convention. Even so, Bell brings out the real courage which, in his state of health, Stevenson displayed in his uncomfortable dash across the Atlantic to marry Fanny. Bell is fair about the strength of her character, but finds her difficult to like.

Bell is right, I think, when he says: 'Stevenson's attitude to history had much to do with Scotland; his feeling for the historical forces affecting vulnerable cultures was utterly Scottish. Small nations feel such tides most acutely'. That is why Stevenson was so responsive to the problems of the native peoples of the South Seas. It is also why from Samoa his thoughts turned irresistibly to Scotland. He died leaving unfinished *Weir of Hermiston*, which had the makings of one of the two greatest Edinburgh novels. He said of it: 'I never felt so sure before in anything I ever wrote. It will be my best work; I feel myself so sure of every word'.

These in their different styles are excellent biographies of two of our most interesting writers. I recommend them both very warmly indeed.

(*Books in Scotland*, No. 45, Spring 1993.)

NOTE

James Mackay, *Burns, A Biography of Robert Burns* and Ian Bell, *Dreams of Exile, A Biography of R.L. Stevenson* (Edinburgh, Mainstream, 1992).

16

Linmill Stories

Robert McLellan, who died in 1985, is best known for his plays. They are subtle, witty and intelligent and illuminated by sharp observation of character. They form a very impressive body of work in Scots and include several of the best plays ever written for the Scottish stage. They are mostly set in the past, when Scots was spoken naturally by the whole population, but they are not without topical and universal relevance.

It is less well known that McLellan also wrote some fine verse and some very remarkable short stories. These *Linmill Stories* were written for the radio in the '60s but not published at the time. Many of them have since appeared in *Lallans*, the magazine of the Scots Language Society, and six in a booklet published by Duncan Glen's *Akros*. This new volume[1] in the Canongate Classics series is, however, the first time that the whole series of twenty-four stories has been printed in its entirety, and the publication is therefore an important literary event. The distinguished poet, J.K. Annand, who was also responsible as editor for the publication of fourteen of the stories in *Lallans*, contributes a lucid, informative and justly enthusiastic introduction.

As Annand points out, it is very rare indeed to find Scots used for the whole narrative as well as the dialogue. McLellan, in fact, reverses the usual practice and, at least once, breaks into dialogue in English: '"Will one of you sit on its head?" askit Fred. He was an Englishman.' For the rest the stories are told in a beautifully expressive, fluent and natural Scots, so natural that it is hard to imagine them in any other language.

Presumably they are largely autobiographical. When he was very young, McLellan spent his holidays at his grandfather's fruit farm at Linmill on the Clyde, near Lesmahago. The stories are told in the first person by a small boy, called Rab, doing precisely that. We see the life of the countryside through his eyes and are given a vivid account of what it felt and looked like, of all his ploys and scrapes and of the work of the farm. The description of the place and the people is cumulative and gradually becomes very full and concrete. Rab, like the adult McLellan, had a sharp eye:

The ferms on the ither side of Clyde frae Kirkfieldbank, richt doun the watter to the end o the Stanebyres Wuids, near Hazelbank, were in an estate caaed Sunnyside. They werena like oor ferms, for the bank was steeper on the ither side o the watter, and the parks abune it lay up oot o the bield, and wadna growe fruit. If they werna in gress they were in hey or corn or neeps, and the fermers keepit kye.'

As a social document of the Scottish countryside early in the century the book is full of interest. More than that, it must be one of the most wholly credible and substantial evocations of childhood ever written. One reviewer has said that it has touches of sentimentality. Perhaps, but they are entirely natural in the relationship between a small boy and his grandparents. Harsher reality keeps coming through, especially in the references to the conditions of the Irish immigrant workers and the mentally handicapped people who were also used as cheap labour.

Canongate and Jim Annand have done a great service in making this delightful book available. It fully deserves the accolade of a 'classic', because it is bound to become a fast favourite and a permanent addition to the range of indispensable Scottish books. What we need now is a complete edition of the plays.

(*The Scotsman*, 28 July 1990.)

NOTE

1. *Linmill Stories* by Robert McLellan (Canongate, Edinburgh, 1990).

17

Scotland and Eng. Lit.

The point of departure of Robert Crawford's impressive and stimulating book[1] is the introduction to the university curriculum of the
study of English Literature, for the first time anywhere, in the
Scottish universities in the second half of the eighteenth century.
In this sense, English Literature was, as Robert Crawford says, a
Scottish invention, but it was anti-Scottish in intent. Crawford has
no difficulty in demonstrating how Adam Smith in Glasgow, Hugh
Blair in Edinburgh and William Barron in St Andrews systematically
used their lectures to dismiss all Scottish language and most Scottish
literature and to extol the English example as the model on which
ambitious young men should model themselves. The Chairs, signifi-
cantly, were not of Literature, but of Rhetoric and Belles Letters,
because the object was to help the students to write, and if possible
speak, like the English. Otherwise, they could not expect to make
careers among the English, who were intolerant in such matters.
The pattern so established has persisted to this day with incalculable
harm to the power of self-expression of generations of Scots.

There is no doubt that Crawford is right about the facts, but
he does not say very much about the reasons which lay behind
this extraordinary phenomenon. Perhaps the men of the eighteenth
century were perceptive in realising that events in America were
about to make English useful as an international *lingua franca*, the
modern equivalent of Latin. Hume certainly understood this and he
urged Gibbon to write in English, and not French, for this reason.
Fair enough, but it does not explain why they should denigrate our
own languages and literature and virtually wish to see them forgotten
as something shameful. Why did we not, as the Swiss do, keep our
own and add on the English as a useful extra? Were we possessed by
a massive inferiority complex and, if so, why?

Perhaps I am suggesting that Crawford should write another
book, but I certainly think that this is a subject which badly needs
examination. If we understood the reasons, we should be in a better
position to understand some of the consequences which are still with
us. It is easy to see the motives of the socially ambitious, but the
intellectual effort and commitment of sincere and intelligent men,

like Smith and the rest, suggests that they thought that they were engaged in something much more important than a charm school for the aspiring young executives of the day.

Crawford does offer one clue when he says: 'Particularly after the Jacobite Rebellions many influential Scots believed that common British norms which meant, generally, Anglocentric norms were needed if Scotland were to prosper and win English approval.' No doubt, the brutal suppression of the '45 was intimidating; but the usual consequence of terrorism of this kind is to stiffen resistance. We had many previous examples in our history from Edward I onwards, and that had always been the consequence in the past. Perhaps it was the shame of the way in which the Union came about that destroyed our morale, as William Wolfe has recently suggested. The remark, attributed to Andrew Fletcher, that Scotland was now fit only for the slaves who had sold it, perhaps explains a great deal. Another line of explanation lies in the eighteenth-century notion of refinement as the highest of aspirations. The Scots had persuaded themselves that the English model represented a higher degree of refinement (which is odd when you think of their barbarous criminal laws at the time); but I suppose that this merely brings us back to the inferiority complex.

Even if the Scottish universities started the academic study of English Literature, and for this very particular purpose, it took a very different direction in England itself. Here the key document, which Crawford mentions only briefly, is the Newbolt Report of 1921. According to this, 'for *English* children no form of knowledge can take precedence over a knowledge of English, no form of literature can take precedence over *English* literature'. In spite of this heavy emphasis on the needs of the English, the curious thing is that for many years afterwards the same recipe was applied all over the English-speaking world. There was, of course, confusion (as there still is) between English as a language and as an adjective applying to a nation and its literature. Gradually, most of the other countries where English is spoken have realised that if English literature should have precedence for English children, then the same applied to their own literature in their own country. Scotland is perhaps now the only exception.

Crawford's second main thesis is that Scottish writers, in response to the political situation in which they found themselves, evolved a form of British literature. Even Burns he sees as 'a model of Britishness precisely because of the language which he deployed'. This seems to me a highly dubious proposition. It is, of course, true that Burns wrote in both Scots and English and in his poetry usually used a mélange of both. But Scots and English are closely related in any case and share a great deal of common vocabulary. The poems of Burns very often look more English than they are because of the way they are printed on the page, but in the head of Burns and of the reader they sound very different. The point which Crawford is making is not a purely linguistic one because he also applies Britishness to Thomson and Smollett, for example, because they introduced Scottish characters, scenes or concerns to works written in English. Is British the right word? If it were, it should apply to something found all over Britain; but it would be hard to find an English writer who deliberately introduced an element of Scottishness into his work. It is open to Scottish writers, as it is to American or Irish, to look to England or anywhere else that pleases them. That does not necessarily mean that they are any less Scottish, Irish or American. I think that the concept of a British literature is more confusing than helpful.

Crawford quotes, with apparent approval, Carlyle's remark that 'No Scotchman of his time was more entirely Scottish than Walter Scott'; but he also describes Scott as 'the devoted advocate of full Britishness'. I think that this view of Scott, although conventional enough, is profoundly mistaken. About ten years ago I wrote a book, *Walter Scott and Scotland*, precisely to show that Scott had serious misgivings about the Union and its effects on the Scottish identity. If anyone doubts this, they should read Scott's *Letters of Malachi Malagrowther*.

If I have these reservations, I have no doubt that this book is a major contribution to Scottish literary criticism and a great pleasure to read. Crawford has many illuminating things to say about the concern of Scottish writers from Boswell and Smollett to Scott and beyond with multi-culturalism and the crossing of borders, with the influence of the Scottish example on American thought and litera-ture, with the pervasive influence of Scott and on J.G. Fraser as the missing link between Scott and modernism. Having demonstrated the extraordinary pervasiveness of the Scottish literary influence, he is in a strong position to end with a plea for liberation from the anglocentricity of the so-called English Literature. I suspect that an essential first step is to find a new name for the subject which corresponds more closely with the reality.

(*Books in Scotland*, No. 43, Autumn 1992.)

NOTE

Robert Crawford, *Developing English Literature* (Oxford, 1992).

18

Muir and Scotland

In 1984 the Open University in Scotland published a Study Guide to Scottish Literature. It opens with the remark that 'one book is essential reading', Edwin Muir's *Scott and Scotland*.[1] They are therefore beginning a course in Scottish literature by recommending a book which, in effect, denies that any such thing exists or has much hope of existing. In the Introduction to his book Muir says of a writer who 'wishes to add to an indigenous Scottish literature, and roots himself deliberately in Scotland': 'He will find there, no matter how long he may search, neither an organic community to round off his conceptions, nor a major literary tradition to support him, nor even a faith among the people that a Scottish literature is possible or desirable, nor any opportunity, finally, of making a livelihood by his work'.[2]

Depressing words. Muir wrote them in 1936. Hugh MacDiarmid published *A Drunk Man Looks at the Thistle* in 1926, Neil Gunn *Morning Tide* in 1930, Lewis Grassic Gibbon *Sunset Song* in 1932, William Soutar *Seeds in the Wind* in 1933 and Eric Linklater *Magnus Merriman* in 1934. Sorley MacLean, Sydney Goodsir Smith, Robert Garioch, Robert McLellan, to mention just a few, were all then at the begining of their careers. For Edwin Muir, in the middle of all this, to imply, as he does in the last page of the book, that Scotland was a 'barbarous country' because it had no 'autonomous literature' suggests that he was blind and deaf to all that was going on around him, to say nothing of the past.

Of course, the Open University do not suggest that Muir's book should be accepted as doctrine, but only as 'influential theses to consider, test and challenge'.[3] In fact, further on in the text, they speak of 'Muir's method of simply accumulating statements, rather than *arguing* any logical connection between them'.[4] Or, they might have added, without producing much evidence. But they are certainly right that Muir's book, in spite of these weaknesses, is an admirable stimulus to debate. No book since Macpherson's *Ossian* has produced so much literary controversy in Scotland.

Most of this argument since the day of its publication has been about Muir's theories about language and, in particular, his attack on the literary use of Scots which MacDiarmid regarded as an act of betrayal.[5] That is not my present subject. Nor is the inadequacy of Muir's book as a treatment of its ostensible theme, what Walter Scott had done for Scotland and what Scotland had done for him.[6] I have already discussed that elsewhere.[7] What I now want to consider are some theories about the nature of Scottish society which Muir drew from his study of Walter Scott's life and writing. Study is perhaps too strong a word; there is very little sign in Muir's book that he had read much more about Scott's life than John Buchan's biography to which he constantly refers. Every other source that he quotes is quoted also by Buchan. In another essay published a year later he does refer to Scott's *Journal* and says very justly that it is one of the most moving autobiographical documents in the language.[8] From internal evidence it is difficult to believe that he had read the *Journal* with much attention before he wrote *Scott and Scotland*.

It is a pity that Muir did not have the time or inclination to do a little more research because his theories about Scott and the Scotland of his day rest on a very shaky foundation. He quotes a passage which comes from the entry in Scott's *Journal* for 18 December 1825. It is a very long entry but Muir quotes only one sentence and he probably took it from Buchan's biography where it appears in almost the same form: 'What a life mine has been!' he wrote towards the end, (Buchan says, more accurately, 'in later years') 'half-educated, almost wholly neglected or left to myself, stuffing my head with the most nonsensical trash'.[9]

Muir bases much of his argument on these few words. He asks what Scott meant by being neglected or left to himself. He could not mean his early education, Muir says, because his mother introduced him to literature at an early age, nor his youth when 'he associated with people of intelligence in a city which prided itself on its intelligence', nor his adult life when 'he certainly never suffered from neglect'. Without any further attempt to discover what Scott meant, Muir concludes: 'all one can think is that in these words he expressed a sense of something lacking in the whole life of his country: that binding and directing power which would have given unity and meaning to his work'. Muir accepts Buchan's judgement that Scott 'mingled intimately with every class and condition of men', but he still believes that this life 'had no centre, no heart radiating a living influence which would have made it impossible for him to feel neglected'. He follows this immediately with another unsupported conclusion that the 'most nonsensical trash' was 'the scattered fragments of Scotland's past'.[10]

Muir is so struck with this phrase about 'nonsensical trash' that he repeats it more than once. He relates it to some striking phrases of his own: 'a broken image of the lost kingdom'[11] and 'a people who lose their nationality create a legend to take its place'.[12]

The theories which Muir erected on these two phrases from Scott's *Journal* 'neglected or left to myself' and 'stuffing my head with the most nonsensical trash' are very ingenious and plausible. It is on them that virtually the whole of his argument about Scott and Scotland depends, but in fact they rest on quite false assumptions. There is no need to speculate on what the phrases might mean because Scott provided very full explanations himself in the autobiographical memoir written at Ashestiel and printed as the first chapter in Lockhart's *Life* and in the General Preface to the Waverley novels which he wrote at about the same time as the entry in the *Journal*. In both of these he explains in some detail how an illness in his youth meant that he had to stay in bed for about two years. The reader will not be surprised, he says, 'that I was abandoned to my own discretion, so far as reading (my almost sole amusement) was concerned, and still less so, that I abused the indulgence which left my time so much at my own disposal'. He continues:

> There was at this time a circulating library in Edinburgh, founded, I believe, by the celebrated Allan Ramsay, which, besides containing a most respectable collection of books of every description, was, as might have been expected, peculiarly rich in works of fiction. It exhibited specimens of every kind, from the romances of chivalry, and the ponderous folios of Cyrus and Cassandra, down to the most approved works of later times. I was plunged into this great ocean of reading without compass or pilot; and unless when some one had the charity to play at chess with me, I was allowed to do nothing save read, from morning to night.[13]

So much, then, for being neglected and left to himself, but what was the nonsensical trash? He tells us in the General Preface that he could not describe 'the vague and wild use' which he made of his freedom to read 'better than by referring my reader to the desultory studies of Waverley in a similar situation; the passages concerning whose course of reading were imitated from my own'.[14] These passages are to be found in chapter 3 of the novel where Waverley is described as reading widely through early English, Italian, French and Spanish literature with a strong bias towards the chivalrous and romantic. There is no reference to any Scottish history or literature at all. Of his own reading Scott says in the Ashestiel memoir: 'All that was adventurous and romantic I devoured without much discrimination, and I really believe I have read as much nonsense [note the word] of this class as any man now living'.[15] By modern standards, one might think that Scott was unnecessarily harsh about this youthful indulgence, but he did take it very seriously: 'it is with the deepest regret that I recollect in my manhood the opportunities of learning which I neglected in my youth; that through every part of my literary career I have felt pinched and hampered by my own ignorance; and that I would at this moment give half the reputation I have had the good fortune to acquire, if by doing so I could rest the remaining part upon a sound foundation of learning and science'.[16]

I think that it is very clear from all these passages precisely what Scott meant by the remarks in his *Journal* on which Muir erects such an elaborate theory. There is no basis for speculation about hidden references to 'the scattered fragments of Scotland's past' and no need to search for an explanation, in this instance at least, in the inadequacies of Scottish society without a centre or a heart. The fact is that Muir's criticism is intuitive, not scholarly. It usually rests on his instinctive reactions, not on a careful and painstaking study of the evidence. His reaction, as I shall suggest later on, may not be to the writer or work which is the ostensible subject, but to something else which Muir is concerned about for some quite different reason. I am quite prepared to believe that sometimes his intuitions tell us more than volumes of careful research and that he can also sometimes be right for the wrong reasons. But his intuitions must be approached with caution because he can be quite wrong simply because he has not taken enough trouble to establish the facts.

In this particular case, it might be possible to argue that Muir was right about the main point even if he based his argument on a misunderstanding of his text. Is there not some truth in the proposition that Scotland, 'once proud and independent' (to use Scott's phrase which Muir quotes), had been reduced to a few 'scattered fragments' and memories of the past? The whole argument of *Scott and Scotland* is based on this assumption. He has three subsidiary theories which seem to follow from it although he does not give us much supporting argument or explanation of the terms he uses:

1. The 'complexity and exactness' of Scots law was superimposed on Scott's 'riotous imagination', not reconciled with it. 'It was a superposition, not a reconciliation such as might have been found in a whole body of experience radiating from a centre in an autonomous society'.[17]

2. Scott's response to his disappointment in love was 'inadequate' for a similar reason. 'Scotland was not an organic society with its own conventions of thought and sensibility; except in the ordinary commerce of daily life, it was trying to imitate England'.[18]

3. 'Scott can find a real image of Scotland only in the past, and knows that the nation which should have formed both his theme

and his living environment as a writer is irremediably melting away around him'. [19]

The common thread which runs through all of these ideas is that Scotland failed to give Scott the environment he needed because it was no longer an autonomous or 'organic' country with a living centre. The word 'organic', which Muir uses so frequently, is open to more than one interpretation. George Bruce in his essay in *The Age of MacDiarmid* expresses surprise that Muir should think that Scotland is less organic than England which has separate schools for the rich and the poor and a language barrier between the classes. [20] Bruce therefore assumes that the word means socially homogeneous, but I do not think that this suits any of the sentences in which Muir uses it. The sense which suits all of the contexts is autonomous, which he sometimes uses as an equivalent, or independent. By 'living centre', he seems to mean an effective political capital to which the country looks for guidance in matters of taste as well as politics. He is arguing, in fact, that Scotland can only be a healthy society, capable of sustaining a literature of its own, if it is independent.

He made the same point in less opaque language in *Scottish Journey*, published in 1935, only a year before *Scott and Scotland*:

> Scotland is as urgently in need of independence as Ireland was. More urgently, indeed, for if she does not get it she will lose her national consciousness, as Ireland would never have done . . . The remedy which Nationalists prescribe for the ills of Scotland is self-government. There is, to anyone who knows the state of Scotland, no serious argument against it . . . What stands in the way of Home Rule is simply apathy, the apathy of England, but chiefly the apathy of Scotland. [21]

He says something rather different in the conclusion to *Scott and Scotland*:

> I do not believe in the programme of the Scottish Nationalists, for it goes against my reading of history, and seems to me a trivial response to a serious problem. I can only conceive a free and independent Scotland coming to birth as a result of a general economic change in society, after which there would be no reason for England to exert compulsion on Scotland, and both nations could live in peace side by side. [22]

I suppose that what he is saying here is that Scottish independence is unobtainable unless it is accompanied by a socialist revolution in both countries, or perhaps he is running away from the logical conclusion of his own arguments.

Muir is on surer ground on two further points which he makes

in *Scott and Scotland*, that Scott was deeply disturbed by the erosion
of the Scottish identity and that he was torn between his Jacobite or
nationalist feelings and his acceptance of the established order which
included the Union. Muir quotes the famous passage from the end
of Scott's Introduction to the *Minstrelsy*:

> By such efforts, feeble as they are, I may contribute something to the
> history of my native country; the peculiar features of whose manners
> and character are daily melting and dissolving into those of her sister
> and ally. And, trivial as may appear such an offering to the Manes
> of a kingdom, once proud and independent, I hang it upon her altar
> with a mixture of feelings which I shall not attempt to describe.

Muir comments, very justly, I think, 'There is no mistaking the
emotion in these words'.[23] He goes on to discuss the conflict between
such feelings and Scott's support for the established order and the
British patriotism aroused by the Napoleonic Wars.

Here again, it is a pity that Muir had not read more deeply into
his subject. If he had read Scott's account in *Tales of a Grandfather* of
'that most obnoxious of measures the Union of the Kingdoms' or
'the sad and sorrowful Union'[24] he would have seen how powerful
Scott's feelings were about Scotland's loss of independence. If he
had read Scott's fullest statement of his political philosophy, the
Letters of Malachi Malagrowther of 1825, he would have discovered
that inhibitions about the established order did not prevent Scott
writing a powerful argument in favour of diversity and autonomy
and against English interference in Scottish affairs. It is the first
manifesto of modern Scottish nationalism.[25]

Muir might also have learned from the *Malachi* letters that the
erosion of the Scottish identity had gathered pace rather more
recently than he supposed. Scott argues, and modern scholarship
confirms that he was right, that during the eighteenth century, apart
from Culloden and its aftermath, the London government had left
Scotland severely alone. Scotland was left, in Scott's phrase, 'under
the guardianship of her own institutions, to win her silent way
to national wealth and consequence'.[26] English interference began
only in the early nineteenth century, especially in the atmosphere of
English triumphalism after Waterloo. Henry Cockburn says much
the same, that the Edinburgh into which Walter Scott was born was
still a metropolitan city with its own style and habits, its independent
taste, ideas and pursuits, and that it had not yet begun to feel the
pressures of centralism from London.[27] It sounds very much like a
description of what Muir was to call a 'living centre'.

Indeed, in *Scott and Scotland* Muir says very justly of the erosion
of the Scottish identity that Scott 'was nearer the beginning of

that process than we are, he saw its end more clearly, and had a more complete image of what was involved'.[28] In spite of this perception, throughout the second chapter of the book, which is the one about Scott, Muir seems to attribute to the Scotland of Scott's day the qualities which he found in the Scotland of the 1930s. He took a profoundly pessimistic view, summed up in that celebrated sentence in *Scottish Journey*: 'My main impression is that Scotland is gradually being emptied of its population, its spirit, its wealth, industry, art, intellect, and innate character'.[29] No one, I suppose, would dispute that such a process has been, and is, relentlessly going on. It gathered pace towards the end of Scott's life, but for most of it he was sustained by a much more vigorously Scottish community than we can now readily imagine. Without it, he could not have written the Waverley novels.

Finally a remark or two on what Muir was seeking to do in writing *Scott and Scotland*. There is an article by Douglas Dunn in the issue of *Radical Scotland* of June/July 1987 which turns on this point. He shows that Muir felt that he had to set aside his socialism in order to free his imagination to write poetry 'fed on dreams, myths, symbols, religiosity and an increasingly disenchanted surmise of the future of humanity'. For the same reason, he suggests that Muir 'had to escape from the demands of nationality'. His *Scott and Scotland* was a 'wholesale act of rejection . . . a gestural farewell to nationality as a shaping factor in the making of Muir's poetry'.[30] George Bruce makes much the same point when he wrote in *The Age of MacDiarmid* that Muir's 'concern was not with the survival of a Scottish identity, but with a personal identity'.[31] I think, in fact, that Muir's purpose is declared in a sentence or two in the introduction to *Scott and Scotland*: 'There is at present a general disposition in Scotland to blame Scottish writers who turn to the English tradition. I shall have to consider whether they should do so, or rather whether they have any choice but to do so'.[32] I suggest that the whole book is not really concerned with Walter Scott or even with the language question, but is an extended apologia for his personal preference and practice.

(Paper for Edwin Muir conference, St Andrews, June 1987.)

NOTES

1. *Scottish Literature: A Study Guide*, by William Donnelly and others. The Open University in Scotland (Edinburgh, 1984), p. 1.
2. Edwin Muir *Scott and Scotland: The Predicament of the Scottish Writer*, London, 1936), p. 15.
3. As 1, p. 1.
4. *Ibid.*, p. 73.

5. George Bruce, '1936 The Borderer and the Orcadian', in *The Age of MacDiarmid*, edited by P.H. Scott and A.C. Davis (Edinburgh, 1980), p. 101.
6. As 2, p. 9.
7. P.H. Scott, *Walter Scott and Scotland* (Edinburgh, 1981).
8. In his essay, 'Sir Walter Scott (1771–1832)', in *Edwin Muir, Uncollected Scottish Criticism*, edited by Andrew Noble (London, 1982).
9. As 2, pp. 141–2 and John Buchan, *The Life of Sir Walter Scott* (1932) edn of 1961 (London), p. 43.
10. As 2, p. 144.
11. *Ibid.*, p. 141.
12. *Ibid.*, p. 160–1.
13. Sir Walter Scott, General Preface to Waverley novels, edn of 1895, p.v.
14. *Ibid.*, p. vii.
15. Sir Walter Scott, Autobiography, printed as chapter 1 of J.G. Lockhart's *Life*, edn of 1900 (London), p. 35.
16. *Ibid.*, pp. 33–4.
17. As 2, p. 127.
18. *Ibid.*, p. 132.
19. *Ibid.*, p. 140.
20. As 5, p. 120.
21. Edwin Muir, *Scottish Journey* (1935), edn of 1979 (Edinburgh), pp. 29–30.
22. As 2, pp. 181–2.
23. *Ibid.*, p. 137.
24. Sir Walter Scott, *Rob Roy*, Introduction and Chapters 18 and 19.
25. Sir Walter Scott, *The Letters of Malachi Malagrowther* (1826), edited by P.H. Scott (Edinburgh, 1981).
26. *Ibid.*, p. 10.
27. Henry Cockburn, *Life of Francis Jeffrey* (1852), edn of 1872 (Edinburgh), pp. 150–4.
28. As 2, p. 140.
29. As 21, p. 3.
30. Douglas Dunn, 'Edwin Muir: Poetry, Politics and Nationality', in *Radical Scotland*, no. 27, June/July 1987, p. 27.
31. As 5, p. 107.
32. As 2, p. 14.

PART TWO

Cultural Independence

(A paper for the Scottish Centre for Economic and
Social Research, October 1989.)

Musis Respublica Floret (The nation flourishes by means
of the arts)

Motto of the Royal High School, Edinburgh
since at least 1578

'But if you *unscotch* us, you will find us damned mischievous Englishmen.'

Sir Walter Scott in a letter to J.W. Croker,
March 1826

'The Union has always been, and remains, a threat to the
survival of a distinctive culture in Scotland.'

A Claim of Right for Scotland, July 1988

19

Cultural Independence

I. THE HISTORICAL BACKGROUND

Scotland, although a small country on the northern extremity of Europe, has made a remarkable contribution to world culture and civilisation. One of the first of them is also one of the most characteristic, the Declaration of Arbroath of 1320. This statement, in resounding Latin prose, on behalf of the Community of the Realm of Scotland asserts both the virtues of national independence and of the sovereignty of the people. These are ideas which many historians seem to imagine emerged only with the French Revolution more than 400 years later. They run consistently throughout Scottish history and are to be found, for example, in the writings of George Buchanan in the sixteenth century and in the successive Claims of Right of 1689, 1842 and 1988. The same ideas, the same insistence on the values of national and individual freedom and concern for the community are reflected in Scottish poetry from its beginnings with John Barbour in the fourteenth century, to David Lindsay in the fifteenth, Robert Fergusson and Robert Burns in the eighteenth and to Sydney Goodsir Smith, Hugh MacDiarmid and Sorley Maclean in the twentieth.

In the fifteenth century William Dunbar, Gavin Douglas and Robert Henryson were writing in Middle Scots some of the finest poetry writen anywhere in Europe at that time. A hundred years later George Buchanan was recognised all over Europe as 'poeta sui saeculi facile princeps', the finest poet writing in Latin since the days of classical Rome. In more recent times, Scotland has produced some of the most influential writers in European and world literature, Walter Scott, Lord Byron, and paradoxically James MacPherson. Few poets in any country at any time have found a wider or more immediate appreciation than Robert Burns. In part he responded to, and in part helped to preserve, the incomparable body of traditional poetry and music which is one of the great riches of both Lowland and Highland Scotland. This close affinity between popular and high art, which at all periods refreshes Scottish literature, is found also in the architecture. The solid virtues of the vernacular tradition of building were reflected in the work of the great architects from William and Robert Adam to Charles Rennie Mackintosh.

There is a rich tradition of Scottish painting with such great names as Ramsay, Raeburn, Wilkie, McTaggart and Peploe. As with literature and architecture, our painters have always been receptive to developments in continental Europe. In the past, Scottish painting has been little known outside Scotland, but this is no longer true as the work of both past and contemporary Scottish painters is now widely appreciated internationally.

Scots law was one of the institutions left intact by the Treaty of Union, although it was then deprived of a legislature to amend it in accordance with its own logic and spirit, and it was further weakened and confused by becoming subject to appeals to the House of Lords. It still remains one of the great achievements of the Scottish mind. It is 'an admirably finished philosophical system', as Lord Cooper wrote in a classic essay, 'with a rigorous logic and a felicitous ingenuity which is a pleasure to study'. Scots Law is unique in combining elements of both the Roman and Anglo-Norman systems, but, Lord Cooper adds, 'it was not a case of wholesale or indiscriminate borrowing, but of critical picking and choosing, simplifying, adapting and rationalising.'[1] External influence is only useful when it can be subjected to just such a process of selection and discrimination.

Some of the most fundamental and important scientific discoveries have been made by Scots. John Napier of Merchiston's discovery of logarithms in the early seventeenth century is the root of the subsequent development of calculators and computers. James Watt's improvement of the steam engine was as vital to the age of steam as the work of James Clerk Maxwell to the present electronic age. Scottish inventions have made life safer and more comfortable with such things as anaesthetics, antiseptic surgery, penicillin, the pneumatic tyre and television. Almost every branch of science and technology and enquiry about man and society owes an enormous debt to the ideas developed in the Scotland of the Scottish Enlightenment. The English historian, H.T. Buckle, said of Adam Smith's *The Wealth of Nations* that it is 'probably the most important book which has ever been written whether we consider the amount of original thought which it contains, or its practical influence'.[2] This is true, even if Smith's ideas are now being misappropriated and distorted by propagandists of the right.

Scottish energies have not been confined to Scotland itself. Before the parliamentary Union of 1707 Scots made important contributions as scholars, diplomats, administrators, soldiers and merchants in the whole of North Western Europe, including Russia. Since the

Union they have made a massive contribution to the development of Australia, India and Canada and the other countries of what used to be called the British Empire. Scottish thought had a decisive influence on the American Constitution and on the evolution of American education.

Some centuries before most other countries, Scotland aspired towards education of the whole population in the same spirit of democratic egalitarianism which has characterised Scottish political thought. James IV was a true renaissance prince in his encouragement of the arts and sciences, printing and the universities. From the time of Knox's *First Book of Discipline* of 1561, there was a determined effort to establish a school in every parish and a college in every substantial town. As Andrew Lockhart Walker said in a recent article, it was by far the 'most comprehensive national scheme' for education of any country at that time and for long afterwards. 'It saw education as the right of all. There was a rational organisation of the universities without snobbery or special privileges for the rich.'[3] Successive Scottish parliaments passed Acts to give effect to these aspirations. Of the effect of the Act of 1695, the historian, Lord Macaulay, said 'it began to be evident that the common people of Scotland were superior in intelligence to the common people of any country in Europe . . . Scotland made good progress in all that constitutes civilisation, as the Old World had never seen equalled, and as even the New World has scarcely seen surpassed. This wonderful change is to be attributed, not indeed solely, but principally to the national system of education'.[4] The Scottish universities maintained a close association with those in Italy, France, Holland and Germany from the fifteenth century. They developed a belief in an inter-disciplinary approach to learning, widely accessible to all classes of the population which George Davie has called the Democratic Intellect.

From this merest sketch of Scottish intellectual and artistic achievement, I think it is possible to understand why an American scholar, Harold Orel, said of Scotland, 'no nation of its size has contributed so much to world culture'.[5] Another of his countrymen, J.K. Galbraith, has suggested that our only serious rivals in this respect are the Jews.[6] Yet another, Harold Thompson, said that to find 'comparable achievements by so small a nation in so short a time we should need to go back from the age of Mackenzie (1745–1831) to the age of Pericles'.[7]

And yet all of this has been achieved against very substantial odds. Not only is Scotland small and mountainous with a comparatively harsh climate, but it is unfortunate in its neighbour. The English people have many virtues but it is difficult to share an island with them. In earlier times they were aggressive and acquisitive to the point where they attacked and endeavoured to subjugate almost every country within reach, Wales, Scotland, Ireland and France. In more recent times they have been not so much aggressive as insensitive to other points of view. Their attitude to Scotland has varied between hostility and indifference.

Scotland, although much smaller than England, successfully defended her independence for more than 300 years, the longest war in European history. This was a great achievement, but the cost was high. The defeat at Flodden inflicted damage on Scotland from which we never fully recovered, especially as towns, villages and churches in the whole of Scotland south of the Forth and the great Border Abbeys were sacked or destroyed by English armies in the following decades. The centuries of English attack had one beneficial result. Scotland turned for alliance and support towards the rest of Europe and especially France. All aspects of Scottish life from the wine trade to philosophy and poetry and the law developed a close association with the European mainstream.

The succession of James VI to the English throne was another serious reverse. At that time the Royal court was the source both of patronage of the arts and of control over the Executive with the disposal of all state appointments. Scotland lost all of this when the court moved to London. James's successors were increasingly under the influence of their English ministers. Scotland became only nominally independent and no longer had direct diplomatic relations with other countries. She contributed men and money to wars fought in pursuit of English policy although they destroyed Scotland's established foreign trade. For the whole of the seventeenth century, in the words of Hume Brown, 'Scotland was a severed and withered branch, and her people knew it'.[8] The religious and dynastic wars of the seventeenth century contributed to the decline. This too was partly in consequence of the removal of the Court to London which enabled the Kings, backed by English power, to try to impose an unpopular church settlement on Scotland.

The removal of royal patronage to London was not the only adverse consequence of the Union of the Crowns. Since the monarch and his immediate advisors remained the sole source of state pensions and posts, the only means of gainful employment for the nobility and gentry, it was necessary for the politically and socially ambitious to make themselves acceptable to court circles in London by aping English speech and manners. At the same time, the adoption by the Kirk of the translation of the Bible authorised by James VI powerfully contributed to the acceptance of the English language for serious purposes. Scots, which had been the language of the poets as well as of the court, government and the people at large outside the Highland line, began to be regarded as socially and intellectually inferior.

To about the middle of the eighteenth century, Gaelic was the language of about half of the land area of Scotland, roughly west of a line from Dumbarton through Blairgowrie to Nairn. Gaelic too went into retreat, especially after the attack on the Highland way of life in the brutal suppression of the Rising of 1745.

Both Gaelic or Scots are languages with a long history, deep roots and a rich poetic inheritance. Like all languages they reflect the attitudes and states of mind of the people who speak them. Over the centuries they have acquired nuances and associations which defy adequate translation. There are things which can be said in Gaelic or Scots which cannot be said with equal effectiveness in any other speech. For either of them to be lost would be an impoverishment of the diversity of human communication. When children are forced by schools to abandon their native speech, as has been the practice in Scotland, they are liable to lose all confidence in self-expression. What R.F. Mackenzie said of Buchan Scots in his last book has a more general application: 'when we lose our native speech, a birthright, we lose something of our character, our integrity. We have too easily accepted the prevailing argument that north-east speech is a picturesque anachronism, a hindrance to progress. We have to balance up the profit and loss again. Maybe the accompanying alienation affects our mental health more than we had supposed.'[9]

Recently there has been a strong move towards reconsidering the profit and loss. Both the schools and the broadcasters are beginning to reflect on the damage which they have done. Gaelic and Scots are now more highly esteemed than they have been for some two or three hundred years. They are fighting a vigorous rearguard action and are being equipped with the scholarly tools to give intellectual substance to their struggle. It is noticeable, however, that these initiatives are supported more by the agencies of the European Community and international organisations such as PEN than by the British Government. Edward Gibbon said of the Roman Empire, 'so sensible were the Romans of the influence of language over national manners that it was their most serious care, to extend, with the progress of their army, the use of the Latin language'.[10] In this, as in other ways, the British Empire followed the example of the Romans.

The decline of the seventeenth century meant that by the beginning of the eighteenth, Scotland was in a weak position to resist English demands for an incorporating Union. The Scottish Parliament struggled for four years to re-establish Scottish influence but yielded in the end to intimidation and bribery. They accepted the Treaty of Union although the population at large demonstrated by every possible means that they were bitterly opposed to it.[11]

Although the traditional pattern of Scottish trade and diplomatic alliance was destroyed by the Union of the Crowns, intellectual contacts were not immediately curtailed. Scots continued to study and teach at continental universities and to keep abreast of new movements in European thought. David Hume, for instance, was as much at home in Paris as in Edinburgh, but he disliked London and, in his own words, 'the barbarians who inhabit the Banks of the Thames'.[12] Dugald Stewart attributed the sudden burst of genius in the Scotland of the Enlightenment to the fact that 'from time immemorial, a continuous intercourse had been kept up between Scotland and the Continent'.[13] The Scottish Enlightenment, when Scotland was the intellectual power-house of the world, found many of its origins in Dutch science and French philosophy. Scotland in turn influenced many other countries.

For most of our history, Scotland, although very much part of Europe, had very little contact with England except on the battlefield. The effect of the association with England from 1603 onwards was naturally to increase English influence and diminish or remove contacts with other countries. This was a slower process than one might suppose. Even by the end of the eighteenth century there was very little intercourse between England and Scotland. As Walter Scott pointed out in *The Letters of Malachi Malagrowther*,[14] Westminster interference in Scottish affairs, apart from the suppression of the Highlands after the '45, really only began after the Napoleonic wars. This coincided with, or caused, a collapse of Scottish self-confidence and a decline into provincialism between the 1830s and the end of the century.[15]

No doubt, some of the influence from England, as from other countries, was beneficial. But to benefit from such an influence it is not necessary to be under the same political control. A point which E.F. Schumacher made in his book, *Small is Beautiful*, about trade applies also to cultural influence: 'whether a market is outside the political boundaries or inside, makes on the whole very little difference. I am not aware, for instance, that Germany in order to export a large enough number of Volkswagens to the United States . . . could only do so after annexing the United States.'[16] In fact, it is much better that we should be free to pick and choose whatever cultural influence happens to suit our particular tastes and needs. When a smaller country falls under the political hegemony of a larger one, as in the case of Scotland and England. the risk is that the larger by the sheer force of size forces a suffocating pressure on the smaller.

When this happens, the Elephant in the Bed syndrome,[17] there is a very serious danger that the identity, distinctiveness and creativity of the smaller country is smothered and dies. This is precisely the danger to which Scotland has been exposed since the elephant started to roll about in this particular bed from about 1830. It seemed likely to have fatal consequences in the following fifty years or so.

But in George Davie's words, 'the characteristic national inheritance was . . . brought to the very brink of ruin only to be saved at the last minute by a sudden burst of reviving energy'.[18] By 1895 Patrick Geddes was able to speak about a Scottish Renaissance. William McTaggart in painting and R.L. Stevenson in writing, and both of them very distinctly Scottish, were at the height of their powers. As always, the cultural revival was part of a general quickening of national consciousness, expressed both in a demand for self-government and in the formation of new Scottish institutions. In the 1880s, the Scottish National Portrait Gallery, the Scottish Text Society and the Scottish History Society were formed.

With the interruption of the two World Wars, this revival has continued ever since in a series of surges and ebbs, but with each surge building on the advance of the one before. The first of the surges was in the '20s and '30s with the literary movement associated with Hugh MacDiarmid and Sorley Maclean, the formation of the Scottish National Party, the National Library of Scotland, and such organisations as the Saltire Society. This resumed after the War and built up to a climax of intense intellectual and artistic activity in the late '70s encouraged by the prospect of a measure of self-government through the Scotland Act. The Advisory Council for the Arts in Scotland and the Association for Scottish Literary Studies were only two of many new bodies which emerged at this time. Literature, the theatre, painting, music, historical scholarship and publishing were all part of a general ferment of thought and activity. For a time all political parties, including the Conservatives, were committed to a measure of Scottish self-government. Support for the SNP grew strongly. There was a striking recovery of feelings of national identity, self-confidence and optimism.

The swindle, the disappointment, the humiliation of the Referendum of 1979 seemed for a time to kill the hopes. The Conservatives had campaigned, not against the principle of devolution, but against the particular bill on offer and they promised to introduce a better bill with stronger powers. They reneged on all of this when they came to power on English votes in 1979. The Scots were faced with the first of a series of Conservative governments which they had overwhelmingly rejected at the polls. It was symptomatic of the change in atmosphere that the BBC abandoned their plans to build a large new studio complex in Edinburgh close to the aborted Scottish Parliament in the old building of the Royal High School. Abandonment and curtailment of projects and aspirations seemed to be the order of the day.

In fact, the loss of confidence was more apparent than real. The political parties committed to constitutional change had more than 75 per cent of the vote at the succeeding elections and Conservative support continued to decline. The debate on the future of Scotland in conferences and seminars resumed. The writing and publishing of Scottish books expanded. New Scottish plays began again to be written and produced. New research and new revaluation of Scottish history became more active than at any previous time. The world at large became aware of the vitality of Scottish painting. In 1988 a new *Claim of Right for Scotland* exposed the inadequacies of the constitutional position of Scotland with clarity and force, and with more general agreement than would have been imaginable even a few years earlier. Once again, cultural activity and achievement are rising along with a recovery of political confidence and assertiveness. At the same time, there are many less encouraging signs under a Government particularly hostile to Scottish aspirations. I shall return to the present position after looking at some more general aspects of the situation in which Scotland finds itself.

II. 'THE NATION THAT FORGETS ITS PAST IS DEAD'

J. A. Froude, the English historian and biographer of Thomas Carlyle, wrote of Scotland: 'No nation in Europe can look with more just pride on their past than the Scots, and no young Scotchman ought to grow up in ignorance of what that past has been'.[19] I think that this is a fair and just comment. No sensible person would want his countrymen to become obsessed with the past nor to use it as a pretext for xenophobia or triumphalism; but a healthy society needs a decent pride in its past achievements as a basis for self-confidence and a spur to emulation. As Froude said, few other European nations have as much justification for such a feeling. The past of Scotland is remarkable not only for a heroic resistance to 300 years of sustained attack, but for a great contribution to the arts and sciences and to liberal and egalitarian ideas. Buckle is not the only outside observer to have remarked how striking it is that so small a country should have produced so many men of genius.[20]

But in Scotland we have not followed Froude's advice. We have done the opposite. With a perversity which is probably unique in the world, we seem to have done our best to prevent our children from learning anything about the history of their own country or its literature. It is possible to go through the whole educational system in Scotland's schools and universities, and emerge with the illusion that Scottish history and literature do not exist. Marinell Ash was an American who died, tragically young, in December 1988. She was a historian who became fascinated by Scottish history and was astounded to discover that the Scottish people allowed themselves to be kept in ignorance of it. As she said in an article in *The Scotsman* in 1985: 'Scotland must be the only nation in the world that does not require its own history to be taught in its schools and universities. It is certainly the only western nation in which a majority of its citizens are effectively licensed to be ignorant of their own past.'[21]

The position of Scottish literature in our schools and universities is improving, largely because of the efforts of such bodies as the Saltire Society and the Association for Scottish Literary Studies. Some very good work in this field is now being done by most of the Scottish universities, but there is still no established chair in the subject in any of them. In the schools, even now, Scottish literature is still regarded as something optional and unimportant. When Scottish books are read they are nearly always contemporary. It is good that modern work is no longer ignored by the schools, as it used to be; but the complete neglect of older literature contributes to the feeling of rootlessness which is a consequence of the suppression of history. In a well known passage, R.L. Stevenson wrote about 100 years ago: 'For that is the mark of the Scot of all classes: that he stands in an attitude towards the past unthinkable to Englishmen, and remembers and cherishes the memory of his forebears, good or bad; and there burns alive in him a sense of identity with the dead even to the twentieth generations.'[22] There is a sense in which that is still true. A feeling of identity with the past is still there, but it is not informed by any precise notion of history. It tends to be based on a mixture of half-remembered legend, inaccurate fact, and downright distortions of the truth often derived from deliberate English or unionist propaganda. To give one example, many Scots seem to be persuaded that Scotland in the past was a particularly violent and unruly country. From this, it is a short step to believing that tranquillity and civilisation came in with the Union. In fact, mediaeval Scotland was a good deal less turbulent than many other European countries and England in particular.[23] Independent Scotland never evolved into a police state, like Tudor England, or taxed and organised itself for aggressive war. The Scottish Parliament was often ahead of its time in legislating, not only for education, but for such matters as the care of the poor, the protection of the citizen from arbitrary imprisonment and the restriction of the death penalty.[24]

One reason for this sort of distortion of the Scottish past is that the Scots have become accustomed at looking at themselves through English eyes. This is encouraged by the English domination of television and a large part of the press, but it begins with the teaching of so-called British history and of English literature in the schools. It may be argued that since Scotland is part of Britain, Scottish history should be adequately covered within that of Britain. There are two reasons why this does not work. In the first place, Scottish historical development, even after 1707, is so different from the English that it is very difficult to explain them together. An expert in one probably knows very little about the other. Most books on British history are in fact on English history with the occasional brief, and usually condescending or hostile, glance at Scotland. Secondly, the attitude of English historians confuses the issue. The Scots for about 200 years made a conscientious effort to act in accordance with the Treaty of Union and to believe that the words of the Treaty meant what they said when they abolished England and Scotland and replaced them with a new entity called Great Britain. The English have never really believed this. They assumed that England carried on as before except that it had now annexed Scotland. Britain and England became for them interchangeable terms for the same thing, and they seem to be genuinely incapable of grasping the distinction. Similarly for most English historians, British history is merely English history, under a different name. They have also tended to inherit the traditional anti-Scottish prejudices of their predecessors and to write about Scotland habitually in derogatory terms. When it comes to Scotland, most English historians, even those of a creditable academic reputation, have a remarkable tendency to descend to prejudice and something close to racialist hostility.

A Cambridge historian, H.W. Wrightson, recently contributed a very frank discussion about this to a book of essays on Scottish society. English historians, he says, have shown 'a marked tendency to ignore the Scottish dimension of British history'. They have shown both 'insularity and on occasion blinkered anglo-centricity', and have been hampered by 'the distorted excesses of English national feeling'. Scottish historians 'have been far less indifferent to the existence of their closest neighbours' but have been forced by the English attitude to the ambivalence of insisting on Scottish uniqueness and at the same time trying to relate to 'processes of historical development which the English persist in regarding as essentially their own'.[25] For such reasons as these, British history (as distinct from English history under another name) has hardly ever been written. In any case, Scotland historically was always closer to the European norm than to England, and it would be better to study each in a European context than simply in relation to each other.

The anglo-centric bias of most British history means that teaching it in Scottish schools not only gives the pupils a distorted view of their own country, but one that is damaging psychologically. They are encouraged by it to believe that everything of importance happened outside Scotland and that their own country is inferior and of little account in the world. This is very destructive of self-confidence and it tends towards an attitude of helplessness and despair. It is likely to encourage emigration or a tendency to despise your own country or to ape other people. So far from cultivating a decent pride and an incentive to emulation, it is a recipe for social disaster. It is not surprising that a sociologist recently wrote of 'the almost schizophrenic nature of many Scots: aggressively asserting the superiority of their country whilst hiding a deep-rooted feeling of inferiority'.[26] I do not know if the ideas of superiority are relics of dim memories of past achievements, but there can be little doubt that the virtual suppression of Scottish history and literature in our schools might be designed to create feelings of inferiority.

The Newbolt report of 1921 on *The Teaching of English in England* had an important influence on the curriculum in schools and not only in England. 'For English children', it concluded, 'no form of knowledge can take precedence over a knowledge of English, no form of literature can take precedence over *English* literature to form the only basis possible for a national education.' With the imperial confidence of the age it tended to be assumed that what was good for the English must necessarily be good for the Canadians, Australians, Indians, Irish and Scots. Almost everywhere a desire for cultural independence has now asserted itself and most countries (although this has not yet happened to any great extent in Scotland) now give precedence to their own literature. This is a healthy development, as long as it does not become too exclusive, because the literature which is likely to mean most to people as they grow up is the one which deals with their own background and surroundings. Again, if we encourage our children to believe that all the best books have been written elsewhere, by and about people of quite a different background, we are instilling in them a feeling of alienation and inferiority.

The wide-spread ignorance within Scotland itself of Scottish history, literature, the other arts and sciences and of our achievements generally has many effects apart from the undermining of self-confidence. One of the purposes of the study of history is to help us to understand the present. If we know virtually nothing about our own past, we cannot expect to understand the present very clearly either. In a state of ignorance we can be persuaded to believe almost any nonsense about our own country, even that nothing of any great value has ever been written, produced or invented in it. Some of us can ultimately be persuaded to become ashamed of our own country, to accept another as superior and be ready to accept its direction and control.

For some years, the Saltire Society has used the slogan, 'The nation that forgets its past is dead'. I do not know who originally said this, but I have no doubt that it is true, and that Scotland is in danger of succumbing to just such a case of forgetfulness.

III. CULTURAL COLONIALISM

The way in which Scottish culture has been denigrated and suppressed is so obvious, both in its methods and effects, that some investigators have concluded that it is the result of deliberate policy. In 1975 an American sociologist, Michael Hechter, published his *Internal Colonialism*, a study of the relationship between England and what he called the Celtic Fringe, Scotland, Ireland and Wales. He noted that for centuries England had tried, with varying degrees of success, to impose control over her neighbours. Cultural policy was an important part of this process. To establish English control it was necessary to disparage the other cultures so as to undermine their will to resist the colonial régime. Hechter noted also that this policy of anglicisation was greatly assisted 'through the voluntary assimilation of peripheral élites'.[27]

More recently, Craig Beveridge and Ronald Turnbull in their book, *The Eclipse of Scottish Culture*, have independently reached very similar conclusions. They apply to Scotland the work of Frantz Fanon who had studied colonial methods in the Third World. 'It is through the undermining of the native's self-belief and the disintegration of local identity that political control is secured. . . . Every effort is made to bring the colonised person to admit the inferiority of his culture.' One consequence of this pressure is that some of the native population try to do well for themselves by co-operating with the colonising power. These are the people whom Hechter called the 'peripheral élite'. Fanon calls them the *évolués,* 'those natives who try to escape from their backwardness by desperate identification with the culture of the metropolis'.[28] Every subjugation of one country by another produces such a class. In Norway during the German occupation they were called Quislings.

We have certainly had such a class in Scotland at least since 1603. As Beveridge or Turnbull say: 'Many of our intellectuals seem motivated by the fear of being considered, by metropolitans, to be like the rest of the natives, and consequently try to out do each other in decrying the practices of those still sunk in their aboriginality. What such behaviour testifies to is cultural colonisation'.[29] It is dangerously easy for the Quislings to get away with such a line since most Scots have been kept in ignorance of their own history and culture.

As I have already remarked, the transfer of the Court and then the Parliament to London obliged the socially and politically ambitious to ape English speech, manners and attitudes. They tended to send their sons to the English boarding schools and universities quite deliberately to make them grow up sounding and behaving like Englishmen. In his recent Donaldson lecture, George Rosie described the results of this process: 'The anglicisation of the Scottish upper classes, the social élites if you like, is a syndrome with which we have been living for almost 400 years. It is now more or less complete. That stratum of Scottish society is now almost totally anglicised, episcopalian in religion, south-ward looking, and politically conservative. And as their politics seem to have been rejected by about 80% of the Scottish people, the Anglo-Scottish ascendancy are beginning to look increasingly at odds with the rest of the population'.[30]

But, as Rosie went on to point out, this minority has an influence out of all proportion to its size. Because of their wealth and prominence they tend to set a style which the ambitious imitate. They tend also to be appointed to the boards of public and voluntary bodies. This is especially true of public bodies under the Thatcher Government which has been quite ruthless in pushing forward the few political friends which it has in Scotland. On these bodies, they have an influence over appointments and naturally tend to favour people of their own kind and education.

This last factor is one of the reasons for a very remarkable phenomenon which has recently caused a great deal of concern, the fact that the people in charge of many, even most, of the institutions of Scottish life are English and educated in England. This was the subject of George Rosie's celebrated television programme of August 1988, *The Englishing of Scotland*. He has said that the more research he made on the subject, the more he was astonished by the extent and scale of the English take-over. Their take-over is at its most threatening when it applies, as it does almost completely, to the leading posts in cultural institutions. Such posts as the Directors (and many of the senior staff) of the National Galleries and Museum of Scotland, Scottish Opera and Ballet, the Scottish National Orchestra, the Scottish Arts Council are in the hands of people who were neither born nor educated in Scotland and had very little knowledge of Scotland when they were appointed to their posts. From the nature of the appointment, they are supposed to give a lead to an aspect of the cultural life of Scotland and to act as a spokesman for the Scottish point of view. It must tend to misrepresent the Scottish identity when these leaders and spokesmen are in fact the products of a quite different cultural tradition.

In the late 19th century the Scottish universities were among the best in the world and were in the forefront of innovative thought. With their European traditions, their democratic accessibility, their broadly based approach to learning and the importance which they attached to philosophy, they were quite different in nature and function from the two universities which then existed in England. This did not protect them from what Andrew Lockhart Walker has recently called a 'determined, prolonged and cumulative effort' to bring them into conformity with English practice. This pressure, which began about 150 years ago, continues and is now in its final stage. For years the Scottish universities have been removed from Scottish control and from the rest of the Scottish educational system. They have been subjected to detailed interference, cuts have been imposed on their staffing and many whole departments have been abolished. A large proportion of their academic staff and their students are now English. 'Is there any other country in Europe'. Walker asks, 'which allows its universities to be run by academics from a bigger and more powerful neighbour or their policies to be largely decided by the neighbour's government? Simply asking the question lays bare the appalling situation we find ourselves in.'[31]

In broadcasting the situation is very similar. J.M. Reid wrote in 1959: 'when regular broadcasting began in 1922, Scottish self-confidence was at its lowest ebb. It is impossible to believe that, at any other time, a people who had long had most other cultural media in their own hands – church, schools, newspapers – would have accepted a monopoly in a new form of communication over which Scotland had no sort of control'.[32] Reid was thinking, of course, of BBC radio, but the situation has become very much worse since television became the dominant medium and by far the most powerful influence that exists over minds, speech and attitudes. As with sound radio, some programmes are made by Scots in Scotland, but the overwhelming majority come from London, where control also rests. Not only is this a powerful means of spreading English influence, but the Scots are obliged to contribute substantially to the cost. Of the money collected to pay for television, both through licence fees and the commercial profits which fund advertising, about 10% comes from Scottish pockets, but only some 2 or 3% returns to Scotland for programme making. This is one of the many ways in which money is extracted from Scotland to subsidise the South-East of England.

The distortion of the Scottish cultural tradition is aggravated by two other developments. Large numbers of English people are settling in Scotland to take advantage of the disparity in house prices between Scotland and the South-East of England and of the less congested and tormented style of life. At the same time, emigration from Scotland continues at a very high rate particularly of the young and energetic who cannot find jobs in Scotland to give scope to their abilities. After 1745, the persecution of the Highlanders, followed by the Clearances, led to the virtual destruction of the whole Gaelic way of life. The pressures which now face Scotland as a whole threaten the survival of the national identity.

IV. NATIONAL IDENTITY AND SELF-DETERMINATION

Whether or not we should worry about these intense pressures on our national identity depends on the value which we place on distinctiveness and diversity. There are those who would argue that such a concern is now out of date, as David McCrone does in a recent book. Also, he says, we should note that the English cultural *imperium* collapsed with the burgeoning of indigenous literature in Canada, Australia, South Africa, New Zealand, the United States and Ireland.[33] This is precisely the point; Scotland, like these other countries, is rejecting a form of cultural colonialism. It is an assertion of a preference for distinctiveness and diversity.

Of course this is happening all over the world. In this century, the Ottoman, Austro-Hungarian, British, French, Dutch, Belgian and Portuguese Empires have all broken up and the same thing is now happening to the Soviet Union. One of the first people to argue, since the Union, not only for Scottish control over Scottish affairs but for the principle of diversity was Sir Walter Scott. In *The Letters of Malachi Malagrowther* of 1826, he suggested that it was a perfectly natural preference: 'The degree of national diversity between different countries, is but an instance of that general variety which nature seems to have adopted as a principle through all her works, as anxious, apparently, to avoid, as modern statesmen to enforce, anything like an approach to absolute "uniformity".'[34] Scott was convinced that diversity was preferable to imposed uniformity and self-determination to external control. Uniformity is monotonous and stifling to spontaneity and inventiveness. Self-determination brings with it self respect, responsibility and free expression.

This conviction, generally called nationalism, is so widespread that it seems to correspond to a general human need. It has done more than other political idea to shape the modern world. Even when it has been suppressed for generations or centuries it can survive and reassert itself, as at present in eastern Europe. In Scotland it has perhaps deeper roots than anywhere else because it not only emerged here in the 14th century but it was the motive force behind the struggle of 300 years to preserve independence. In the words of Dewar Gibb: 'In all history there is surely no more striking example of an unquenchable national spirit than that of Scotland before the Union. Time after time, despite heavy defeat and despite the frightful destruction which normally went with an English invasion, Scotland rallied, ousted the invaders and set herself to building up again what had been torn down. The resilience seems at times almost inexplicable'.35 The first major work of Scottish literature, Barbour's *The Bruce*, written about 1375, is also the first in any country since the time of classical Greece or Rome, to celebrate the solace of national freedom and the misery of 'foule thyrldome'.36 A recent writer, C.J. Watson, is not alone in finding in modern Scotland the psychological consequences of the denial of national freedom: 'the sense of weariness, of the absence of hope, and of lacerating self-contempt which is a marked component of the psyche of "colonised" peoples'.37

This sense of nationhood, thus so powerfully allied to human satisfaction, and to contentment or discontent with the system of government, is difficult to define. Peter Alter in a recent book on the subject defines a nation as 'a social group . . . which because of a variety of historically evolved relations of a linguistic, cultural, religious or political nature, has become conscious of its coherence, unity and particular interests. It demands the right to political self-determination'.38 In spite of all the pressures during the last 400 years towards anglicisation and assimilation, the Scots are clearly such a group. Every opinion poll since polls on the subject began has confirmed that this feeling of nationhood exists among the great majority of Scots and that it expresses itself in a desire for a measure of self-government.

The awareness of a sense of cultural identity is the essential ingredient of a sense of nationhood. By itself, as everywhere else in the world, it is a sufficient reason for self-determination. Without it, any proposal for self-government would be a matter of administrative convenience without any great significance or emotional impulse. In other words, the cultural aspect is not incidental to the case for constitutional change, but its essential core and purpose.

V. SCOTTISH CHARACTERISTICS

It is difficult to define the characteristics of the Scottish, or any other, national cultural. As long as they are alive, they are multifarious and changeable. As Roderick Watson said recently, 'a fully defined psychology is a static psychology and hence a dead one'.39 Even so, there are some Scottish characteristics which are so persistent and conspicuous that they are readily recognisable.

In the first place, there is the democratic and egalitarian spirit which, as I have mentioned, runs through Scottish literature from the earliest times to the present. Even in feudal times, the Scottish belief was that kings existed to serve the community, not the other way round. The Scottish Reformation was based on the conviction that all were equal before God. Since the extension of the franchise to the mass of the people, the Scottish vote has overwhelmingly gone to parties concerned with liberal and community values. The firm rejection of Thatcherism is another example.

Pomposity and social pretension are distrusted and subjected to reductive humour which can be ruthless. At the same time, there is a strong feeling for suffering humanity and an identification with the oppressed, even among animals, as, for instance, in Henryson and Burns.

A high value is placed on logic and in following thought to its logical conclusion, even if this is inconvenient and makes compromise impossible. There is a tendency towards rationalism and scepticism. Importance is attached to general principles and to moral values. The Scots, as Sir James Mackintosh remarked, are a 'wrong-resenting race'.

There is a preference for the historical approach to problems in the belief that they can only be understood by an analysis of their origin and development. As David Hume said, 'this is the historical age and this the historical nation'.41

There is an urge towards internationalism, travel and the exchange of experience with other countries. Andrew Fletcher of Saltoun, for instance, was both a firm opponent of an incorporating union with England and one of the first people to suggest a political structure embracing the whole of Europe.

Self-indulgence and excessive wealth, ornament and ostentation are distrusted. Value is placed on education, hard work and solid effort. In these, as in most other respects, allowance has to be made for what Gregory Smith called the Caledonian Antisyzygy, 'the contrasts which the Scot shows at every turn'. This has often been interpreted as a sort of Jekyll and Hyde split personality, but Smith saw it rather as a reconciliation, an adaptability and an 'admission that two sides of the matter have been considered'.[42] It is a recognition that Scottish attitudes combine rationalism and scepticism with an appreciation of the fantastic and imaginary. R.F. Mackenzie and others have suggested that this is a reflection of the combination of Lowland and Highland qualities.[43]

In spite of a reputation, especially in England, for truculence and violence, the Scots are in fact an excessively tractable and law-abiding people. When William Cobbett came to Scotland in 1832, he remarked on the 'docile and cheerfully submitting labourers of Scotland'.[44] History is full of examples, such as the accept-ance of the Highland Clearances and of the reneging on prom-ises by both Government and commercial firms in the present decade, which show how right he was. It is this fatal docility which has tolerated outrageous neglect and exploitation for too long.

It is striking that these qualities, which have their weaknesses as well as their strengths, are in almost every point diametrically opposed to the qualities most typical of the English, with their resistance to general principle and their preference for pragmatic compromise. (The ideological obsessions of the present Govern-ment are, I think, an aberration from the English norm.) There is no point in considering which set of attributes may be prefer-able to the other, but there is no doubt that they are very dif-ferent. The value of sustaining both of them derives from this difference. They contribute to the diversity of humanity which is both a relief from monotony and the source of the richness of our common civilisation. T.S. Eliot, consciously or unconsciously echoing Walter Scott, argued that it was to the advantage of all four nations of these islands that each should retain their national culture. 'It is probable', he wrote, 'that complete uniformity of culture throughout these islands would bring about a lower grade of culture altogether.'[45] And this would be a loss to the world as a whole.

Diversity is of value for its own sake, but the particular blend of qualities in the Scottish tradition has contributed so much to civilisation that it is even more important in the general interest to see that it survives. As an editorial in the *Times Higher Education Supplement* of January 1988 said: 'In the face of the frightening integration of the world's economy, intellectual as well as material, the uniformity of mass attitudes, the conformity of our values, there is an urgent need to reassert the claims of cultural pluralism. For on cultural pluralism is built the capacity to imagine otherwise that is the root of freedom and science. Scotland is a better place than most to start.'[46]

VI. THE PRESENT

As I said above, there is a good deal that is encouraging about the present state of Scottish culture. Many aspects of it, especially literature, writing and historical scholarship, are showing more vitality than they have done since the decline of the 1830s. At the same time, one is left with the anxiety that this revival may be precarious because of public ignorance and Government hostility. The public is ignorant of these matters, at least partly because their attention is directed elsewhere by the schools and the broadcasters. The Government expresses its hostility by cuts in the funding of education and the arts, by its philistinism and by its centralist refusal to listen to Scottish opinion and aspirations. There is an essential contradiction between the vitality of Scottish culture and centralising policies. Each is a threat to the other.

For many years Scottish writers have expressed the conviction that the Union of 1707, and the educational system that reflects its ethos, have been inimical to Scottish culture and character. I quote some examples:

Edwin Muir in 1935: 'Scotland is gradually being emptied of its population, its spirit, its wealth, industry, art, intellect, and innate character . . . A distinctly marked style of life is now falling to pieces, for there is no visible and effective power to hold it together . . . Scotland is as urgently in need of Independence as Ireland was. More urgently, indeed, for if she does not get it she will lose her national consciousness, as Ireland would never have done.'[47]

Eric Linklater in 1935: 'By reason of its association with England, Scotland became insular. Its political frontier was broken down, and its mind was walled up. Geographical or political enlargement, beyond certain limits, is nearly always accompanied by intellectual shrinkage.'[48]

William Soutar in 1937: 'A general meanness of national spirit [has been] accumulative since our loss of nationhood. By the severance of our continental ties, our linguistic roots, our traditional heritage, it was inevitable that parochialism should spread like a national blight, so that ultimately our national traits have withered into idiosyncrasies and our types degenerated into "characters".'[49]

DeLancy Ferguson, a biographer of Robert Burns and the editor of his letters, in 1953: 'Had he [Robert Burns] received a formal

education, it would have been in the anglifying mould that was
standard in late eighteenth-century Scotland. So trained, the poet
might have become another Thomson, but he would have been
taught to despise the folk tradition which has made him immor-
tal.'⁵⁰

Trevor Royle in 1977: 'The Union of 1707 had been an awkward
way of doing things and many Scots still smarted with shame at the
nature of the joining together of the two very different peoples.'⁵¹

A Claim of Right for Scotland in 1988: 'The Union has always
been, and remains, a threat to the survival of a distinctive culture
in Scotland.'⁵²

Whatever argument there might be about the case for self-
government in other respects, there seems to be general agreement
that the cultural case is unanswerable. If you attach importance to
the survival of a distinctive Scottish culture, it is clear that the
present constitutional arrangements are damaging to it. It is a
system which ensures that the great majority of radio and television
broadcasts received in Scotland are produced in England and that
has placed the control of our universities and the key posts in most
of our institutions in English hands. The cultural distinctiveness of
Scotland survived the loss of political independence, although it was
weakened and distorted by it; but the pressures against survival have
greatly increased, especially under the Thatcher administration with
its xenophobic English nationalism and aggressive centralisation.
   One of the problems of anglicisation is that the Scottish and
English character do not blend very happily, presumably because
they are so different. 'If you *unscotch* us', said Walter Scott in a famous
phrase, 'you will find us damned mischievous Englishmen.'⁵³ Edwin
Muir in his *Scottish Journey* has a description of the process, in which
we may recognise such types as Michael Forsyth and Teddy Taylor:
'Everybody knows that the Scotsman who tries to be English
takes on the worst English qualities and exaggerates them to caricature. And the vowel-clipping, flag-wagging, Empire-trumpeting
Scotsman is, I think, not a fantastic example of what the Scottish
race in general might become if it were submitted unconditionally
to English influence. For the Scottish character has a thoroughness,
or in other words an inability to know where to stop, which is rarely
found in Englishmen, who make a virtue of compromise. When
Scotsmen become English they do it with this thoroughness; they
work out the English character, which has the vaguest connection

with logic, to its logical conclusion, to something, in other words, which only formally resembles it, and is in spirit completely different. They do this on insufficient knowledge and with the aggressive confidence which is one of the curses of the Scottish character, and produce with elation a botched copy of a warped original. This process is called Anglicisation, and it is going on rapidly among the upper classes in Scotland. It is clearly harmful to both countries, and it is bound to become more harmful as it continues.'

Muir goes on to say that the great mass of Scotsmen and women have not reached this stage. 'They are not English, and they are ceasing to be Scottish for lack of encouragement. They live in the sort of vacuum . . . which exists in places that have lost their old life and not yet found a new one. A certain meaninglessness and despondency hangs round such places; they are out of things, they do not know the reason for their existence; and people emigrate from them readily, without knowing why. The increasing centralisation of all vital energies in London has turned Scotland more and more into a place of this kind.'54

Muir wrote these words in 1935. In the fifty-odd years since then much has changed for the good and the bad. There has been the cultural revival, of which Hugh MacDiarmid was the chief instigator, and the movement for constitutional change, largely stimulated by the SNP. At the same time, it is impossible to read the passage without recognising that what he says is still true and that the process of decline is in many ways more advanced.

Writing in the *Glasgow Herald* on 25 March 1989, William McIlvanney, more than fifty years after Muir's book, found the same division in the Scottish community: 'On the one side an Anglicised minority whose motivation was their own well-being and for whom the cost . . . was accepting the materialistic values that made sense of the English connection . . . On the other side a more radically Scottish majority whose motivation was the maintenance of a distinctly Scottish identity and for whom the cost . . . was adopting the deeper, non-materialistic values that were needed to make sense of their determined Scottishness.'

In the *Observer Scotland* on 14 May 1989 Ian Bell examined the state of the arts in Scotland and reached a depressing conclusion:

'While Scotland's cultural life continues to decline, the Scottish Arts Council, shaped by London, transforms itself into a Thatcherite sponsorship machine, placing the future of cultural life in the hands of the economic system which has reduced the country to a province, with provincial attitudes and provincial art. Our cultural institutions, meanwhile, are run by men and women from England. In a healthy, cosmopolitan society such imports would go unremarked. Scotland, on all evidence, is far from being a healthy society. For all the achievements of individuals there is neither cohesion nor a sense of momentum in our cultural life.'

The main reason why the situation is even more precarious now than at the time when Muir wrote is the centralising policy of the Thatcher administration. It makes no secret of its intention to ignore the votes and wishes of the Scottish people and to do all it can to transform Scottish society and force us to dance to the tune of the South-east of England. Previous British Governments have treated Scotland with indifference and neglect. They have introduced measures of Anglicisation more by accident than with deliberate intention and because they have assumed that everything English is best and what is good for England must be good for everyone else. Even so, they have generally accepted that the Treaty of Union provides some (but grossly inadequate) safe-guards for Scottish institutions and the national identity. The Thatcherites have no patience for any of this or for any views which are different from their own.

This is the most deliberate and sustained attack to which our identity has ever been subjected. Stephen Maxwell has described it in these words:

'The Government's project in Scotland is one of breath-taking audacity and I don't think that Scottish opinion has yet fully appreciated just how radical the Government's aim in Scotland is. It is also a project that is packed with ironies. Here we have a party, a Government, committed to the market and to a market-based concept of freedom, using the full power of the state to re-structure Scottish society, to re-build Scottish society in its own image. It is a piece of social engineering by a Government whose ideologists are contemptuous of the very idea of social engineering. It is also, of course, a project which flies in the face of democracy.'[55] In other words, the Thatcher Government is determined to ignore the advice of Walter Scott and do everything in its power to 'unscotch' us.

How are we to defend ourselves against such an attack? How are we to escape from 'the increasing centralisation of all vital energies in London' and the 'provincial attitudes and provincial art'? The answer must obviously include taking responsibility for our own affairs into our own hands. As Eric Linklater said, 'people degenerate when they lose control of their own affairs To any nation the essential vitamin is responsibility'.[56] This has been demonstrated whenever a colony or submerged nationality has been liberated from external control. A great surge of creative energy almost invariably follows. We have the talent in Scotland, but much of it is frustrated and has to emigrate because we do not have the centres of decision-making in Scotland to create the opportunities. Imagine a Scotland where we had the right to make our own decisions, to run our own broadcasting services and universities and to decide on our own priorities. Imagine having a Government responsible to the Scottish people and working for our interests, instead of one opposed to our wishes and indifferent or hostile to us.

Andrew Fletcher was right in 1703 when he argued that parliamentary Union would draw to the South-east of England the riches and political power which 'should be distributed in due proportion to the rest of the languishing body'.57 With political power goes not only riches but cultural influence. With the loss of these, self-confidence and self-respect are eroded and the result is a demoralised society that does not expect to succeed.

It might be argued that to achieve cultural emancipation it would be sufficient to have a devolved or limited Scottish Parliament responsible only for certain functions as long as they included all those of cultural significance, education, broadcasting and the like. I think that it is true that this would be a great deal better than our present impotence. On the other hand, there would still be haggling over finance with London and some limitation over our freedom to decide our own priorities. Ultimate responsibility would still be denied to us. We should not have our own voice and votes in Brussels which is vital if we are to play a full part in Europe. We should still be second-class citizens, cut off from direct contact with other countries, and invisible to the rest of the world, until we are as independent as Ireland or Denmark. I do not think that we should settle for less.

It is often assumed by supporters of limited autonomy or 'devolution' that it is self-evident that defence and foreign affairs should be left to the Westminster Parliament. This is a highly questionable proposition because it leaves to others some of the most important decisions which affect all aspects of our lives. We need, for example, to be able to decide for ourselves whether we are prepared to permit a massive concentration of nuclear weapons on our territory. They make Scotland a priority nuclear target and expose us to the risk of catastrophic accident without any conceivable advantage. The money spent on our share of their cost would be far better spent on our educational and cultural activities.

VII. CULTURAL POLICY

1. AdCAS

In the '70s the mere prospect of even a limited measure of autonomy brought about a marked change in the intellectual climate in Scotland. There was a surge of confidence and optimism and much activity in thinking and planning about the new opportunities which would be open to us when we had control of our own affairs. As part of this, the Saltire Society in September 1977 held a conference in St Andrews to discuss the consequences for the cultural life of Scotland. I proposed a resolution, which was passed, inviting the Society to get in touch with all the cultural organisations of Scotland to see if there was a general demand for a joint body to pool ideas and evolve proposals for the cultural policies which they would like a Scottish Government to adopt. With Professor John MacQueen as Convener and Mr A.C. Davis as Secretary, the Society then undertook extensive consultations with about 200 organisations, governmental, professional and voluntary, involved in diverse aspects of the artistic and intellectual life of the country. A conference, at which many of these organisations were represented, was held in February 1979 with Sir Kenneth Alexander in the chair. It approved a Manifesto for the Arts which suggested priorities in the cultural field for the Scottish Government. This included a recommendation for the election of an Advisory Council for the Arts in Scotland (AdCAS) which would continue to act as a joint think-tank and a means of exchanging ideas between the organisations and the new administration.

Shortly afterwards, there was a radical change with the Referendum, the election of a Conservative Government and the repeal of the Scottish Act. The new ministerial team in the Scottish Office declined an invitation to appoint representatives to take part in the work of the proposed Advisory Council, but said that the Government would 'recognise the value of its advice'. On this basis, AdCAS was established at a further Conference in June 1981. Since then, it has continued to keep policies towards the arts under review and has made frequent submissions to the Government, Committees of Enquiry and others. It has successfully pressed, for example, for a greater Scottish content in the Edinburgh Festival and for paperback reprints of important Scottish books. It has held public conferences on such matters as a Scottish National Theatre.

I mention all of this because I find that points made in the 1979 Manifesto and in subsequent discussions in AdCAS closely coincide with what I should like to say about the cultural policies which I think are urgently needed in Scotland. These proposals therefore reflect a wide consensus of agreement among people who are informed and involved. At the same time, I have not shown this paper in draft to my colleagues in AdCAS and it rests entirely on my personal responsibility. Most of these proposals could be introduced without constitutional change but they are not likely until we have established control over our own affairs.

2. Ministry for Cultural Affairs

Scotland already has a formidable range of cultural institutions and organisations although some others are still needed. Those which are funded by the State, such as the National Library of Scotland and the Scottish Arts Council, suffer at present from two disadvantages. They are being progressively starved of funds because of the Tory obsessions with privatisation and sponsorship and the reduction of Government expenditure. Also, since some are funded through the Scottish Office and others through Departments in Whitehall, it is difficult for them to follow coherent policies. There is an urgent need for a Ministry to bring together responsibility for the funding of all of these organisations, such as the National Library, Museums and Galleries, the Scottish Arts Council, the Scottish Film Council and so on. A Scottish Government would certainly wish to fund all of them more generously than in the past, and to encourage optimism and development, not, as at present, resignation and despair.

Several important Scottish institutions, such as the National Portrait Gallery and the National Library, were established by private generosity with the Government afterwards accepting responsibility for running costs. Successive British Governments have tended to avoid responsibility for cultural institutions in Scotland. It is, for example, scandalous that such things as the Dictionary of the Older Scottish Tongue, the School for Scottish Studies and a long overdue proposal to establish a Chair of Scottish Literature in Edinburgh University, and indeed now the entire university system, should have to appeal to public generosity for their very survival. It would be one of the functions of the Cultural Ministry to ensure adequate funding in all such cases.

The Ministry would also be responsible for establishing institutions which are still needed. The most important of these are:

i) A Scottish Broadcasting Corporation and a Broadcasting Authority to regulate the conditions under which independent broadcasting operates. They would ensure the continuation of public service broadcasting and that independent franchises are awarded on merit, not (as proposed in the recent White Paper) merely to the highest bidder.

ii) An organisation, which might be called Scotland International, which would promote cultural exchange, in both directions, with other countries. In particular, it would encourage co-operation within the European Community.

iii) A Scottish National Theatre. It is anomalous that we should have national companies for opera and ballet, but not for drama which is precisely the form of the performing arts in which we have made the most valuable distinctive contribution. Experience in virtually all other European countries has shown that a national theatre is an effective stimulus to the general cultural life of the country. The AdCAS Conference in May 1987 was the largest and most representative meeting of those involved in, and concerned about, the theatre in Scotland, and was an impressive demonstration of an urgent and wide-spread desire for a National Theatre. It adopted a resolution virtually unanimously that there was a 'pressing need' for a National Theatre and elected a Working Party to pursue the matter. They issued a Report on 30 November 1987, but there was a serious set-back when the Scottish Arts Council almost simultaneously allowed the Scottish Theatre Company to collapse. Active attempts are being made to find an alternative approach.

All of these new institutions, like those which already exist, would be autonomous with their own councils or boards. They would operate openly and encourage public discussion of their policies. AdCAS, reinforced by government participation and assistance, could act as a channel for ideas about policy.

Funding of the arts, crafts and films, through their appropriate councils, would be particularly directed at new creative work in Scotland and to the revival and performance of important work from the Scottish past, including the great wealth of Scotland in traditional music, song, poetry and dance.

In a more directly governmental role, the Ministry in association with other appropriate departments would explore means of encouraging the arts by suitable taxation policies or by purchase and distribution. They would look for useful examples in the policies of this kind already followed in other countries and encourage measures for cultural co-operation and exchange within the European community.

3. *Education*
There is such a close relationship between education and the arts and sciences that it is arguable that all should come under the same ministry. Probably, however, this would be too much for one department and it would probably be far preferable to have a separate Ministry of Education and Science, working in close collaboration with the Ministry of Culture. Education at all levels should be integrated into one coherent system. It should be accorded a high priority for government expenditure with a tendency towards expansion and development instead of the cuts and closures of the last ten years. Education will be freely available as a life-long process for people of all ages. Newbattle will be re-opened as an adult residential college and other colleges of a similar nature will be opened in other parts of Scotland.

The anglicisation of Scottish universities has proceeded relentlessly since the early nineteenth century, as George Davie has described in his great book, *The Democratic Intellect*. This has now reached the point where very little remains of the broad philosophical approach, which was the essential characteristic of the Scottish universities, and an excessive proportion of staff and students are English. Under the Thatcher Government savage cuts have been imposed which have meant large reductions in staff and even the abolition of whole departments. Angus Calder scarcely exaggerates when he said in the summer of 1989 issue of *Cencrastus*: 'the drive from London seems to be towards a situation where elderly English academics in decimated departments teach an Anglo-centric view of culture and history to English public schoolboys amid the ruins of the broad Scottish curriculum'.

There are also serious causes for concern for the school system as a result of the recent government policies. In May 1989 SCESR published *Scottish Education: A Declaration of Principles*, a report by a group of distinguished educationalists invited by AdCAS to consider the position. They concluded that the system was 'being savaged and destabilised on ideological grounds irrelevant to Scotland'.

A Scottish government will therefore be faced with the urgent and vital task of repairing the damage inflicted on our education at all levels. In Scotland we have traditionally placed great value on education and at one time gave a lead to the world. The restoration of the democratic intellect with all that it implies must be a major objective of an independent Scotland.

Scottish history, literature and languages will be given their proper place in the curriculum at all levels and in broadcasting. There should be no attempt to enforce linguistic change by legislation, but an independent and self-confident Scotland is likely to make greater use of its native forms of speech, and reverse the decline which external influences have imposed on them.

4. *Science*

The Scots are an inventive people with a particular aptitude for science and technology. We should build on this strength by encouraging research in areas likely to be useful to Scottish industry, agriculture and fishing as well as in pure science. One of the objects should be to increase the number of intellectually demanding jobs in Scotland and counter-act the process under which well qualified Scots are forced to seek employment elsewhere. For this purpose a Research Council should be established responsible to a Department within the Ministry of Education.

5. *Important Posts*

Applicants for important posts in the cultural institutions of Scotland should be required to show a good knowledge of the Scottish background in their own field. One might think it self-evident that anyone seeking the post of, let us say, the Director of the National Gallery of Scotland would be expected to have a good knowledge of Scottish painting and an enthusiasm for it. In fact, the extraordinary thing is that this has simply not been so in recent times. This is one of the reasons why our cultural identity is under the risk of disappearing from sight behind a solid phalanx of people from elsewhere (and nearly all of them English) with little previous experience of Scottish achievement and Scottish attitudes. We obviously want to avoid intolerance or unfair discrimination and we welcome the greater freedom of movement within the European Community, but it is the sheer scale of the influx from a single source which threatens suffocation. England has more than ten times the population and we are therefore highly vulnerable. We have, therefore, to face up to this very real and embarrassing problem. The simple answer seems to be an insistence on appropriate knowledge or experience in all job specifications for posts which are important for our cultural identity.

6. *Conclusion*

The entire cultural life of Scotland will be enlivened by the attainment of responsibility for our own affairs. This has been the experience of other countries which have obtained or regained independence.
By itself it is of sufficient importance to justify all our efforts to secure constitutional change.

Cultural policy is uniquely involved with national identity. However thoroughly the European Community may integrate and pool sovereignty in other matters, it will always be essential in the general interest that cultural policy remains a national responsibility. For the same reason, this is the area in which it is most urgent that we liberate ourselves from London control. This does not mean that we should not encourage wide cultural exchange and co-operation. On the contrary, one of the advantages of taking control of our own affairs is that we can then establish direct contact with other countries. It is the bottle-neck of dependence on London which is the real separation.

We should not set our sights too low. Scotland has many natural advantages but chief among them are the qualities of its people and the abilities which they have shown in everything from gardening to philosophy. We should make a conscious effort through our educational system and all the institutions of our cultural life to encourage the full development of this potential and to give satisfying careers to our people in their own country.

When Francis Jeffrey gave evidence to the Royal Commission on the Scottish universities in 1826, he praised our traditional system which encouraged students to argue about the basic questions of 'history, literature, physics, metaphysics and everything'.[58] This is a tradition which we should repair and restore. As Professor Peter Jones suggested in the *Glasgow Herald* on 8 March 1989, Scotland should not hesitate to become again 'unashamedly intellectual, the thinking nation', open to new ideas, sceptical of current understanding, recognising all ideas as provisional and resistant to 'narrowing categories of established boundaries of investigation'. But we should not only be intellectual, but enjoy the refreshment and enlargement of the spirit to be found through the arts. Here too we should be open to the world, but with a firm base in our own traditions. We should avoid slavish imitation, because as Ramsay of Ochtertyre said in one of his letters, 'professed copying ever implies inferiority'.[59]

All of this lies within our grasp if we make the effort. It will enable us to escape from the miserable position of being 'neither quite alive or quite dead', neither quite Scottish or quite anything else.[60] It will free us from agonising doubts about our identity and make us self-confident citizens of the world. By being more Scottish and more universal we shall make Scotland an infinitely more agreeable and stimulating place for our people and make a more useful contribution to the common civilisation of humanity. By becoming a full and active member of the European Community we shall recover the role which in the past brought so much benefit to Scotland and the rest of Europe.

NOTES

1. Lord Cooper *The Scottish Legal Tradition* (Saltire Society, Edinburgh, edn of 1982), pp. 11, 26, 8.
2. Henry Thomas Buckle *On Scotland and the Scotch Intellect* (editor H.J. Hanham, Chicago, 1970), p. 264.
3. Andrew Lockhart Walker 'The Democratic Intellect Under Threat', in *Radical Scotland*, no. 41, October 1989.
4. T.B. Macaulay *History of England* (London, 1858), vol. IV, pp. 82–3.
5. Harold Orel, editor, in *The Scottish World: History and Culture of Scotland* (London, 1981), p. 12.
6. On BBC Television in 1977.
7. H.W. Thompson, *Henry Mackenzie: A Scottish Man of Feeling* (London and New York, 1931), p. 1.

8. P. Hume Brown, in *The Union of 1707* (Glasgow, 1907), p. 4.

9. R.F. Mackenzie, *A Search for Scotland* (London, 1989), pp. 25–6.

10. Edward Gibbon, *The Decline and Fall of the Roman Empire*, abridged by Dero A. Saunders (Harmondsworth, 1988), p. 60.

11. See my *1707: The Union of Scotland and England* (Edinburgh, 1979).

12. David Hume, *The Letters of David Hume*, edited by J.Y.T. Greig (Oxford, 1932), vol. I, p. 436.

13. Dugald Stewart, *Collected Works* (Sir William Hamilton, Edinburgh 1884), vol. I, p. 551.

14. Sir Walter Scott *The Letters of Malachi Malagrowther* (1826), edited by P.H. Scott (Edinburgh, 1981), and in the collected editions of Sir Walter Scott's miscellanous prose.

15. See my essay, 'The Last Purely Scotch Age', in vol. III (1988) of *The History of Scottish Literature*, general editor, Cairns Craig (Aberdeen, 1987–8).

16. E.F. Schumacher, *Small is Beautiful* (London 1974), p. 60.

17. This is the subject of my Saltire Pamphlet, *In Bed with an Elephant* (Edinburgh, 1985).

18. G.E. Davie, *The Democratic Intellect* (Edinburgh 1961), p. xvi.

19. J.A. Froude, quoted by Gordon Donaldson in his Inaugural Lecture at Edinburgh University, 1964.

20. H.T. Buckle, *op.cit.*, p. 359.

21. Marinell Ash, 'The Fibs and Fables of Scottish History', *The Scotsman*, 23 November 1985.

22. R.L. Stevenson *Weir of Hermiston*, Chapter 5.

23. See, for example, Alexander Grant *The New History of Scotland*, (vol. 3), *Independence and Nationhood, Scotland 1306–1469*, p. 172, and a lecture by Gordon Donaldson, reported in *The Scotsman* of 6 October 1989.

24. James MacKinnon, *The Union of England and Scotland* (London, 1907), p. 468.

25. H.E. Wrightson, in *Scottish Society 1500–1800*, edited by R.A. Houston and I.D. Whyte (Cambridge, 1989), pp. 245 and 260.

26. Tony Dickson, in *The Making of Scotland: Nation, Culture and Social Change*, edited by David McCrone, Stephen Kendrick and Pat Straw (Edinburgh, 1989), p. 61.

27. Michael Hechter, *Internal Colonialism: The Celtic Fringe in British National Development, 1536–1966* (London, 1975), pp. 64, 73, 80, 81.

28. Craig Beveridge and Ronald Turnbull, *The Eclipse of Scottish Culture* (Edinburgh, 1989), pp. 5 and 6.

29. *Ibid.*, p. 58.

30. Report in *The Scotsman* of 25 September 1989.

31. As 3 above.

32. J.M. Reid, *Scotland Past and Present* (London, 1959), p. 167.

33. In *The Making of Scotland: Nation, Culture and Social Change*, edited

by David McCrone, Stephen Kendrick and Pat Straw (Edinburgh, 1989), p. 171.

34. Sir Walter Scott, *The Letters of Malachi Malagrowther* (1826), edited by P.H. Scott (Edinburgh, 1981), p. 144.

35. Andrew Dewar Gibb, *Scotland Resurgent* (Stirling, 1950), p. 64.

36. John Barbour, *The Bruce*. This is from the celebrated passage beginning, 'A fredome is a noble thing', in Book I, lines 225 to 250 (pages 20–1 in the selection edited by Alexander Kinghorn for the Saltire Society (1960).

37. C.J. Watson, in *Literature of the North*, edited by David Hewitt and Michael Spiller (Aberdeen, 1983), p. 140.

38. Peter Alter, *Nationalism* (1985) English translation (London, 1989), p. 17.

39. Roderick Watson, in *Nationalism in Literature*, edited by Horst W. Drescher and Hermann Volkel (Frankfurt, 1987), p. 137.

40. Sir James Mackintosh, quoted by David Murison in 'Nationalism as Expressed in Scottish Literature', in *Government and Nationalism in Scotland*, edited by J.N. Wolfe (Edinburgh, 1969), p. 194.

41. David Hume. As 12, vol. II, p. 230.

42. G. Gregory Smith, *Scottish Literature: Character and Influence* (London, 1919), p. 4.

43. As 9, p. 63.

44. William Cobbett, *Tour in Scotland* (1832), edited by Daniel Green (Aberdeen, 1984), p. 29.

45. T.S. Eliot *Notes Towards the Definition of Culture* (London, 1948), p. 58.

46. *Times Higher Education Supplement* of 29 January 1988.

47. Edwin Muir, *Scottish Journey* (1935), edition of 1970 (Edinburgh), pp. 3, 25, 27.

48. Eric Linklater, *The Lion and the Unicorn* (London, 1935), p. 130.

49. William Soutar, *The Diaries of a Dying Man*, edited by Alexander Scott (Edinburgh, 1954), p. 115.

50. DeLancey Ferguson, in his introduction to his edition of *Selected Letters of Robert Burns* (London, 1953), p. x.

51. Trevor Royle, in his essay, 'The Children in the Apple Tree', in *Jock Tamson's Bairns*, edited by Trevor Royle (London, 1977), p. 133.

52. *A Claim of Right for Scotland*, Report of the Constitutional Steering Committee (Edinburgh, 1988), para. 2.2.

53. Sir Walter Scott, *Letters*, edited by H.J.C. Grierson (London, 1932–7), vol. IX, p. 472.

54. As 47, pp. 26–8.

55. Stephen Maxwell, in *Politics and Power in Scottish Education* (Newbattle, 1989), p. 13.

56. As 47, p. 26.

57. Andrew Fletcher of Saltoun, 'An Account of a Conversation', in *Selected Writings*, edited by David Daiches (Edinburgh, 1979), p. 135.
58. Francis Jeffrey, quoted by John Gross, in *The Rise and Fall of the Man of Letters* (Harmondsworth, 1973), p. 19.
59. James Ramsay of Ochtertyre (1799–1812), *Letters* (Edinburgh, 1966), p. 204.
60. Edwin Muir, *Selected Letters* (London, 1974), p. 64.

PART THREE

Scotland Today

20

The Age of MacDiarmid

Stephen Maxwell, in his contribution to *The Age of MacDiarmid*,[1] said that 'MacDiarmid's impact on Scottish political opinion has been slight'. In the terms in which Maxwell was speaking that was a perfectly accurate statement. MacDiarmid had been active in at least four parties, the National Party of Scotland, the ILP, the SNP and the Communist Party and at various times he was expelled from two of them. In 1922 he was elected as an Independent Socialist Councillor in Montrose, and in 1928 he was one of the founders of the National Party of Scotland. He stood as an Independent Scottish Nationalist for Glasgow Kelvingrove in the General Elections of 1945 and 1950 and as the Communist Candidate in Kinross and West Perthshire in 1964. But in spite of all that activity, MacDiarmid was not really a party man. He was always too much of the individualist, too committed to extremes and contradictions, too incapable of compromise. He was not comfortable in any party and no party was comfortable with him. He has left no permanent imprint on the character or policy of any party.

And yet, I think, MacDiarmid has done something more important and fundamental than that. He has changed the atmosphere not only of literature but of politics in Scotland by transforming the assumptions against which they are carried on. Just after his death on 9 September 1978 *The Scotsman* said in its first leader: 'There is very little written, acted, composed, surmised and demanded in Scotland which does not in some strand descend from the new beginning he made'. Two months later, David Murison wrote of him in *Lines Review*: 'There is one other Scot, at first blush an unlikely candidate for comparison, who is his spiritual ancestor – John Knox; in him we have the same uncompromising aggression, the same extremist absolutism, the same unrestrained vituperative argumentativeness . . . After MacDiarmid, as after Knox, Scotland will never be the same place again'.

Very often, it might be more the aggression and the argument-ativeness of the expression, and its energy and persistence, than the originality of the ideas which has had this effect. As one who has lived through it, for I was born at about the time that Grieve invented

MacDiarmid, I have been a witness and I do not doubt that the effect is there. That is why I think that it is appropriate to call the period through which we are still living *The Age of MacDiarmid*, a phrase which I first used in an article in *The Economist* in October 1977.

What I am talking about has very little to do with the subtlety, complexity and confusion of much of MacDiarmid's thought and writing. It is quite a simple set of opinions and attitudes which MacDiarmid held and expressed through most of his life. Amid all the contradictions they are continuous and consistent. They are at their most explicit in his prose writing, although of course they are also expressed implicitly or otherwise in much of his poetry. They have made a major impact on the way that we think because he expressed them so often and with such force, but also simply because most of us were already disposed to agree, even if we needed MacDiarmid to articulate them. They have spread widely through Scottish society, including of course people who have never read a line that MacDiarmid wrote.

Let me give some examples from early and late in MacDiarmid's life. The first is a passage from *Scottish Eccentrics* published in 1936. It was one of the first of MacDiarmid's books which I came across because there happened to be a copy in the school library which suggests that the High School of Edinburgh was probably an exception amongst Scottish schools.

> If Scotland is to survive, where is the impetus to come from, what invisible reservoir secretes such a startling potentiality? No glimpse of anything of the sort is to be found in the conception of the Scottish character almost universally accepted to-day; certainly nothing seems to be further from the minds of the vast majority of Scots themselves. So far as they are concerned the long centuries of Scotland's national life have long ago been brought to nothing; they are totally unaware of them. Their 'race memory' only goes back to the day before yesterday. It is strictly confined to those aspects of the past which have contributed to the present happy state of affairs and are commendable on that account. Every consideration is abjectly adjusted to that. . . .
>
> All that every other European nation strives at whatever cost to retain and further means nothing to Scotland. The Scots attempt to compensate themselves in the fervour of their protestations for what they willingly relinquish in actual fact. They have allowed their languages . . . Gaelic and Scots and the literatures in them, to lapse almost completely, though every other European nation or national minority has fought most desperately to keep and use its distinctive language. The Scots alone have never generated any effective or even considerable Nationalist movement. No serious Scottish issue has induced them to put up more than a very temporary sham

fight. They have acquiesced in the progressive depopulation and relegation for sporting purposes of what now amounts to over a third of their country. They have since the Reformation or since the Union with England failed to erect distinctive national arts on the splendid foundations their ancestors had created for them; and they become irritated and indignant when this is pointed out to them. Scottish literature and history (even in those accepted forms which so carefully leave out of account all that would suggest that the present state of affairs is not highly creditable, and, blessed word, inevitable) are taught only to a negligible extent, if at all, in Scottish schools and Universities. . . .

As Mr R. B. Cunninghame Graham says: 'For a century Scotsmen have been content to remain pale copies of our "ancient enemy from beyond the Tweed". Some degenerate sons of Scotia, even today, attribute the economic progress of Scotland to the Act of Union and forget their own share in the job. When you have said Act of Union there are still sporadic Scots who put on the same kind of long face as they assume on reading aloud the genealogy of King David. Mercifully they are becoming rare, as rare as those who think John Knox invented Scotland, almost without the assistance of the Deity.' Scottish History is indeed being rewritten, but it is necessarily a long and difficult task, so massive is the overgrowth of error that encumbers it.

Reading that again today, and remember that it was written more than fifty years ago, I think that we can see how much remains to be done, but also how much progress has been made in the direction that MacDiarmid wanted to go. In particular, we have developed a nationalist movement and more pioneering work in Scottish history has been done in the last thirty years or so than in any previous period.

In a letter of 22 September 1967 to the Rev. Anthony Ross, MacDiarmid summarised his objectives which remained essentially the same as thirty years before:

I have devoted many years to seek to overcome the inability of the academic authorities and literary circles in many countries to recognise that Scotland is a separate and a very different country from England, that Scotland has an independent literary tradition at odds in many vital respects with the English tradition – and that it has always been, and remains, the aim of the latter to eliminate the former and assimilate Scottish standards completely to English. Government agencies like the Arts Council, the British Council, British consulates, etc. have pursued this policy and been largely responsible for the general identification abroad of what is merely English as British, and these agencies have actively endeavoured to frustrate my efforts

to give foreign countries a true sense of Scotland's difference, of the
need for Scotland to build on its own separate traditions without
regard to England, and in particular to revive our native languages,
Scots and Gaelic.

I think you will agree that I cannot lend my name and influence to
a project which does not accept as of prime importance the encouragement of Scots and Gaelic, the necessity of Scottish Independence, and
the recognition that in contradistinction to the situation in England
a deep-seated Radicalism is the chief, and an irreversible, element of
the Scottish political tradition and a prime requirement of Scottish
conditions today and henceforth.

Shortly afterwards in a speech at Glasgow University on 6 April 1968
he developed the same line of thought:

> These denationalised Scots have killed the soul
> which is universally human; they are men without souls;
> All the more heavily the judgement falls upon them,
> Since it is a universal law of life they have sinned against.

There surely is the answer to the particular kind of treachery found
in those Anglo-Scots intellectuals who bleat of a false antithesis,
internationalism, not nationalism, as if it were possible to have the
one without the other. They sin against the universal law of life
which invests life in individuals not conglomerations. Yes, even
in the ant hill. In the place of living separate identities, having
mostly their differences in common, these ghouls would reduce all
to a horrible international, characterless, abstract fog, a devitalised
nonentity, but their internationalism in fact equals 'English', and
behind the pseudo-internationalism of the Anglo-Scots lurks the
face of 'The Auld Enemy', English imperialism. The greatest Scots
have always deplored the union with England. The common people
had no say in the matter, but they protested violently against it.
But the greatest Scots, Burns, for example: 'Alas,' he wrote in
one of his letters, 'I have often said to myself, what are all the
boasted advantages which my country reaps from the union that
can counterbalance the annihilation of her independence and even
her very name?' The question is put in a way that implies that the
answer must be that there are no such advantages. I have put the
same question to myself insistently for nearly half a century, and
I have been unable to discover any merit in the connection with
England whatsoever. Sir Walter Scott summed up the intolerable
character of our relationship with England when he said: 'There
has been in England a gradual and progressive system of assuming
the management of affairs entirely and exclusively proper to Scotland
as if we were totally unworthy of having the management of our
own affairs.

He recognised that there had been some progress:

> Scotland is emerging again, culturally at any rate, into the modern
> world as a separate entity with something of its own to say, some
> contribution to make to the common pool of culture that no other
> people can make . . .
>
> It is the cultural questions, the language and literary questions, that
> have been the decisive factor in the national regeneration movements
> of many European countries, and it will not be otherwise with
> Scotland.

Of course, one could quote endlessly to the same purpose, but I
think that I have given enough examples to show the nature of this
long campaign. It was part of a universal struggle against conformity
imposed from the outside which threatens to destroy diversity and
vitality. The power of money and technology is on the side of the
external pressures but every movement of resistance is a sign of life
and hope. That is why MacDiarmid's campaign is important and of
far greater significance than to Scotland alone.

I think that the essence of this MacDiarmid campaign can be
summarised quite briefly. He believed that Scotland had a distinctive
culture which was vitally important to Scotland but which had
something to offer to the rest of the world as well. This culture
had flourished particularly in the Renaissance of the fifteenth century
in close conjunction with the rest of Europe. Scotland had lost its
way, especially as a result of the Union. Since then it has been under
Anglicising pressure which threatens to replace everything Scottish
with a pale imitation of their English equivalent. Scotland therefore
had to fight back by re-establishing control over its own affairs,
by re-opening direct contact with the rest of Europe, and above
all by the study and cultivation of its own languages, literature
and history.

In the sixty years or so since MacDiarmid opened this campaign
how much has been achieved? From one point of view, you might
think very little. We now have in London the most centralising and
most aggressively English nationalist government since the Union.
It appears to be determined not only to deny us a Scottish Parliament
but even to reduce the power of local government to insignificance.
Scottish universities and the distinctiveness of Scottish education are
under severe threat. But in doing all this it is significant that the
main agent of this government in Scotland, Malcolm Rifkind, finds
it necessary to make a speech saying that he attaches importance to
maintaining the character and distinctiveness of Scottish institutions,
including the universities. While doing the opposite, he pays lip
service to the spirit of MacDiarmid.

He finds it necessary to do this because he knows that the great majority of informed opinion in Scotland now agrees with MacDiarmid that the cultural distinctiveness of Scotland is important and that it should be cultivated and extended. Scottish literature, theatre, music and historiography have never been more flourishing. Gaelic and Scots are fighting back. If MacDiarmid was right in saying that cultural revival must always lead the way in national regeneration, then we should not despair. According to the opinion polls only 35 per cent are in favour of independence, but it is a percentage which is steadily increasing and about 80 per cent are in favour of some form of self-government. The new *Claim of Right* with its proposal for a constitutional Convention offers a practical way forward.

Tom Scott once wrote: 'To MacDiarmid the English ascendency was a historical iniquity with no right but might behind it, and to be overthrown by all good men and true'. Ten years after his death, the battle goes on.

Paper for MacDiarmid Conference,
Richard Demarco Gallery, Edinburgh, 21, 22, 23 August 1980)

NOTE

1. Edited by P.H. Scott and A.C. Davis (Edinburgh, 1980).

21

The Auld Alliance

It is very curious, almost incredible, that an alliance with France which came to an end 400 years ago should still affect our feelings and attitudes in Scotland. How else can you explain the special affection and affinity which the Scots, or many of them at least, feel for France? I know that I felt it myself long before I ever went there and still, after more visits than I can count, I cannot go to France without an excitement that applies to no other country. Perhaps Stevenson was right when he said of the Scottish feeling for the past: 'For that is the mark of the Scot of all classes: that he stands in an attitude towards the past unthinkable to Englishmen, and remembers and cherishes the memory of his forebears, good or bad; and there burns alive in him a sense of identity with the dead even to the twentieth generation.' Whether Stevenson is right about this or not, it is certainly true that the Scots and the English feel quite differently about France. To the Scots, France is the old ally and friend, even if Scotland suffered as well as gained from the Alliance, including our worst disaster on the field of Flodden. All the sentiment of nostalgia, of regret for our lost independence, clings to the Scottish idea of France. To the English, France is the old enemy and rival, with whom, even now, all relationships are tinged with memories of distrust and hostility.

If most people in France have forgotten the Auld Alliance, there are exceptions. Once, years ago, when I was staying with a family in Paris to improve my French, I was taken to have tea with the Secretary of the Academy. He was a historian, whose name, I am ashamed to say, I have forgotten. He was very conscious of the Auld Alliance. 'When I went to Scotland,' he told me, 'I went as a Frenchman always should, direct from Dieppe to Leith without putting a foot in England.'

There have been other instances of the old spirit during many of the Edinburgh Festivals, and not only in 1985 when the Auld Alliance was the theme. Indeed, French theatre, painting, music and ballet have been at the heart of almost all them. At the very first one in 1947 there were two French orchestras and Louis Jouvet's Company from Paris in Molière's *L'Ecole Des Femmes*, which Robert Kemp translated superbly into Scots as *Let Wives Tak Tent*. There have been very few Edinburgh Festivals without Molière.

The 1951 Festival had a memorable closing ceremony. The whole thing might have been conceived as symbol of the Auld Alliance. The script had been written by the same Robert Kemp. The guiding spirit of the proceedings was Duncan Macrae, the comic genius of the Scottish stage with many great performances of Molière in Scots to his credit. At the end, André Barsacq of the Théâtre de l'Atelier read a poem which he had written about the Auld Alliance and about Edinburgh and the Festival, 'Merci à toi, Ecosse fidèle'. The emotional effect on the audience was plain to be seen, and it takes a lot to do that to an Edinburgh audience. No one who was there can have any doubt about the continuing resonance of the old friendship with France.

Perhaps after all it is not really surprising. The Franco–Scottish alliance was one of the earliest, longest lasting and closest in European history. Its origins are lost in the distant past. The earliest surviving treaty is one of 1295, but the association between the two countries is probably even older than that. It remained a constant factor in the European scene, and a corner-stone of the foreign policy of both France and Scotland for the next 300 years without interruption. It was so close that the two countries exchanged citizenship and, for a brief period, virtually became one country with the same King. For centuries, the Kings of France entrusted their lives to their Garde Ecossaise. At least once, a Scottish army saved France. This was at the Battle of Baugé in 1421 when the Scots defeated the English and prevented them from crossing the Loire and occupying central France. From such feats as these the Scots acquired a reputation in France for daring and dependability. 'Fier comme un Ecossais', proud as a Scot, became proverbial.

In its origin the Alliance was defensive, a means of mutual help against aggression, like a mediaeval NATO. The aggressor in this case was England, lying between Scotland and France and constantly striving to conquer and control both of them. Wallace, the first hero of the Scottish resistance to English aggression, was also one of the architects of the Auld Alliance. He was in France for the purpose in 1298. Since England failed in her long, sustained endeavour, the Alliance achieved its immediate purpose. In its formal military and diplomatic aspects it came to an end in the sixteenth century, when the Reformation brought Scotland and England closer together in policy and the European balance of power had changed.

Since it was the Reformation which radically changed the political relationship between Scotland and France, it is a strange irony that it was a Frenchman, John Calvin, who was the major intellectual

influence on the Scottish reformers. The logic and clarity of his
doctrine, and his emphasis on education, exercised an irresistible
appeal on the Scots. But, as so often, the influence was in both
directions. When Calvin was a student in Paris, one of his teachers
was the great Scottish scholar, John Mair, regarded in his time as the
'veritable chief of the scholastic philosophy' and 'the prince of Paris
divines'.

The Jacobite risings in the eighteenth century were, in effect, an
attempt both to restore the Stuarts and to return to the traditional
policy of the alliance with France. They failed, of course, but they
forged a new link between the two countries, when Jacobites took
refuge in France after Culloden. Many joined the French service.
James Johnstone, for example, was a private secretary to Prince
Charles during the campaign of the '45. He reappears in history
as an ADC to Montcalm who opposed Woolfe in the battle for
Quebec. Most of Woolfe's troops were Gaelic-speaking Highlanders,
for whom French was the tongue of an ally, and this may well
have something to do with the survival of the French language in
Canada.

But the association between Scotland and France was by no means
only military or diplomatic. It affected virtually every aspect of life
through personal contact and the exchange of scholars, merchants
and craftsmen as well as soldiers. These influences have proved
much more enduring than the changing current of international
politics. A good example is the wine trade, 'the blood stream of
the Auld Alliance'. The 'Fresche fragrant Clairettis out of France'
were celebrated in Scottish poetry and song centuries after the formal
diplomatic alliance had come to an end.

It was so, too, with other more solid, if less convivial, influences.
The Scottish Universities grew up largely under French influence,
even if they also had important connections with Italy and with
Holland at a later period. This worked in both directions, because
Scots went to France to teach as well as learn. George Buchanan,
for instance, the greatest of all neo-Latin poets, taught at Paris and
Bordeaux where Montaigne was one of his students. Buchanan's
Latin tragedies were performed all over France, as indeed all over
Europe, for at least 200 years. He has an important place in the
history of French, as well as Scottish, literature. In language, both
Scots and Gaelic naturalised words borrowed from French. Even the
title of the great sixteenth century Scottish play, *The Thrie Estaites*,
derives from the Etats Generaux of France. It was in Paris in 1580
that James Crichton, 'The Admirable', first startled the Universities
of Europe by his public challenge to debate any subject in any of
twelve languages and either in verse or prose. Scots law acquired the

philosophical basis in Roman law, which it has never lost, through the French example. The French influence in architecture is obvious to anyone who looks at Holyrood or Falkland. The Royal Courts of France and Scotland developed a delightful tradition of courtly music and song.

This long and close association seems to have developed an intimate intellectual affinity between Scotland and France. Take, for instance, Sir Thomas Urquhart's translation in the seventeenth century of Rabelais's *Gargantua and Pantagruel*. This was described by Wyndham Lewis as 'a miracle of a kind that could happen only once or twice in the history of letters; the translation that is not a translation, but a transmutation'. Urquhart is so close to the spirit of his original that he performs the nearly incredible feat of out-Rabelaising Rabelais. You may savour a more recent instance of the affinity between the French and Scottish mind in Tom Scott's translations of François Villon. It is remarkable, too, how readily Molière translates into Scots and how popular these translations are with Scottish audiences.

The intellectual cross-fertilisation between France and Scotland reached one of its highest points in the Enlightenment of the eighteenth century, of which Paris and Edinburgh were the two great capitals. Montesquieu's book *De l'Esprit des Lois* was the inspiration of much of the Scottish exploration of the human condition; David Hume was lionised in the literary salons of Paris. Dugald Stewart, the first and more eloquent historian of Scottish philosophy, had no doubt about the origins of the intellectual explosion in Scotland in the eighteenth century. It was, he wrote, because 'from time immemorial, a continual intercourse had been kept up between Scotland and the Continent'. Italy, Holland and Germany all played a part in this interchange, but the earliest and strongest influence was from France. French intellectuals returned the compliment by their enthusiastic response to Scottish thought. De Remusat said that there was in Scotland a unique combination of poetry and reason. 'This nation takes its place among the most enlightened of the world. Politics, religion and literature have made Scotland incomparable.' Stendhal, in a similar spirit, said that Edinburgh was 'the Capital of reason and of humanity'.

The French Revolution brought a new dimension to the relationship. In Scotland the authorities took fright at the spread of revolutionary ideas from France. Thomas Muir and others were tried for sedition and sentenced to transportation to Botany Bay. He escaped on an American ship and, like the Jacobites before him, took refuge in France. Robert Burns, although an excise officer at the time, sent four cannons to France as his personal contribution to the Revolution. On the whole, however, Scotland was caught up in the fervour of the war against Napoleon, of whom Sir Walter Scott wrote the first major biography.

Scott had an enormous influence in France as indeed throughout Europe and America, and not only on literature but on painting and music as well. By 1840 the publishers of one of the French translations of the Waverley novels had sold two million copies. At least eighteen new operas based on the novels were first performed in Paris. Boildieu's opera, *La Dame Blanche*, based on *Guy Mannering* and *The Monastery*, was so popular at the Opéra-Comique that Délibes wrote a parody, *L'Ecossais de Chatou* about a Frenchman who boasted that he had seen it 666 times. Delacroix in painting and Victor Hugo in literature took the lead in France in responding to the influence of Scott, but they were by no means the last. Stendhal in a letter to Balzac called him 'nôtre père', a remark echoed by Georges Simenon in our own century when he said 'he invented us all'.

The term 'Scottish Renaissance' to describe the revival of the arts and intellect in Scotland after its nineteenth-century decline was not invented, as many suppose, by Hugh MacDiarmid but by Sir Patrick Geddes. He was a man of diverse interests in the true Enlightenment spirit. It is entirely appropriate that one of his last acts was to found a College des Ecossais at Montpellier as a conscious attempt to re-establish the Scots College of Paris. In the last century or so, innumerable Scottish painters have studied in France and reveal the influence both in their style and subjects. William McTaggart seems, indeed, to have reached the same conclusions as the French Impressionists by a separate route of his own, and it is natural enough that those same Impressionists found some of their first admirers and collectors in Glasgow. Again in exchange as it were, it was a French critic, Denis Saurat, who first gave international recognition to the achievement of MacDiarmid and wide currency to the idea of a Scottish Renaissance. One of the most detailed studies of the Scottish novelist John Galt is also by a Frenchman, Henri Gibault. A contemporary Scottish poet, Kenneth White, belongs more to the French than the Scottish literary scene.

Sacheverell Sitwell in his book about Edinburgh said that the Scots and the French, however different in some respects, shared national characteristics which always drew them together. Moray Maclaren said much the same: 'This Franco-Scottish alliance is something far more profound in the characters of both nations than just the old political alliance. The two nations have always had as common qualities an antipathy for the English and a love of clear logical thought . . . Occasionally the wildness, the Celtic mistiness of Scottish verse or song, may appeal to some Gallic strain in the French . . . French art can always be relied on to appeal in Scotland. It is half because of a sense of affinity, half the sense of contrast. In some hidden way, the Celt speaks to the Celt, and for the rest it seems that the Scots love the ordered skill which he perceives in the French spirit . . . He loves to cool his hot hands on the smooth polished metal of the French mind'.

Scottish painters, even more than the philosophers and writers, have been stimulated and enriched by the French example. One of them, J.D. Fergusson, once wrote in a letter from Paris: 'Vive la France; let us never forget the Auld Alliance'. He was not referring to the diplomatic and military alliance which came to an end 400 years ago, but to the less tangible form which it has assumed since then, a nexus of intellectual and artistic influence and the affinity which derives from it. When James VI flitted to London in 1603 to become the English as well as the Scottish King, Scotland began to lose control over its own foreign policy. This was completed by the Union of the Parliaments in 1707 when Scotland even lost the power to legislate over its own internal affairs. Since then, Scotland has been a curious hybrid, a nation which is not a state but which has its own distinct character and its own church and legal and educational systems.

Politics and diplomacy are, after all, not everything. There is a famous remark in a pamphlet of 1704 by Andrew Fletcher of Saltoun, a political thinker much in advance of his time. He was long known in Scotland simply as 'the Patriot', because of his vigorous defence of Scottish independence. In this pamphlet, *An Account of a Conversation Concerning the Right Regulation of Governments for the Common Good of Mankind*, one of the characters says that he knew a very wise man who 'believed if a man were permitted to make all the ballads, he need not care who should make the laws of a nation'. Scotland has survived as a nation precisely on this principle. It has lost the capacity to make the laws, but not to write the ballads and novels and paint the pictures. It is a precarious kind of survival, but survival nevertheless.

The situation would, of course, be quite different if the Scottish National Party succeeds and Scotland recovers its independence. This is by no means impossible. Public opinion polls have shown a steady increase in support for independence. It is now at about 30 per cent, compared to support for a more limited degree of autonomy at about 50 per cent. The last three general elections have shown very clearly that the Scots think differently from the English and that the Thatcherite appeal to materialistic greed finds little sympathy in Scotland. If the Thatcher Government continues to disregard Scottish aspirations, the demand for independence may well become irresistible. The opponents of the SNP often accuse them of 'separatism'. In fact, the opposite is closer to the truth.

One of the impulses behind the desire for independence is the urge to recover direct Scottish participation in the affairs of the world. The great periods in Scotland have been those when Scotland was most closely involved with the rest of Europe. To this day, the Scots do not share the insular instincts of the English. An independent Scotland would be eager to resume the old ties with Europe and to give a new reality to the Auld Alliance.

(*Autrement, Ecosse*, Paris, September 1988.)

22

Commercialism: The Fashionable Religion

Adam Smith, in a famous passage, said that there was 'a certain propensity in human nature to truck, barter and exchange one thing for another'. This is a useful instinct. It allows us to satisfy our basic needs and the whole of our material civilisation has derived from it. Without buying and selling most of us would soon starve or freeze to death. Commercialism, in decent moderation, is therefore an essential part of life. The trouble is that it has been allowed, or encouraged, to go beyond all reasonable proportions. Commercialism is becoming our master instead of our servant and is threatening and destructive instead of beneficial. It degrades the whole of life into a sordid pursuit of money.

An enormous amount of human talent and energy now goes into efforts to persuade us to buy things that we do not really need or want. We should be better off without most of them. In order to supply us with these unnecessary things, the resources of the planet are being exhausted and the environment in which we and our descendants have to live is being poisoned and destroyed.

America with its energy and inventiveness set the pace in most of this, but Europe has been an eager pupil. There is much that is admirable about America; it is a more open and egalitarian society compared to Britain with its obsessions over state secrecy and class. Unfortunately we tend to imitate the worst features and ignore the best. The Thatcher Governments (and there is not much sign of improvement with Major) were especially guilty of this. Three British institutions were widely admired by other countries before Thatcher attacked them: broadcasting, the health service and the universities with their system of student grants. Thatcher did her best to reduce all three to the much inferior, and more commercialised, American model, just as she uncritically and automatically accepted American leadership in foreign policy.

So-called 'privatisation' (an ugly word for an ugly process) is commercialism at its most flagrant. We are asked to believe that services which from their nature are monopolies or near-monopolies, like the telephone or electricity, can be entrusted to private companies. Profits and not public service become the reason for their existence. Inevitably they remodel themselves to make as much money as they can by selling us more, or at least charging us more, on every possible pretext.

This spirit begins to infect everything else. Banks, which used to offer us a remarkably disinterested service, now try to sell us insurance or press credit upon us at every opportunity. The friendly and helpful bank manager has become a salesman like nearly everybody else. Even public institutions, like museums or art galleries, devote a large part of their space and energy to running shops and restaurants. Sport is increasingly turned into another money-making business. It is curious that anyone can identify with a team which consists of paid employees who are bought and sold like commodities.

An aspect of the exaltation of the profit motive is a belief that businessmen are likely to be better than anyone else in running everything from the arts to the health service. This is an article of faith of those right-wing conservatives who profess to be disciples of Adam Smith, and is among the many proofs that they have not actually read much of his work. The *Wealth of Nations* is full of warnings about the dangers of allowing businessmen, or merchants and master manufacturers as he called them, to get their hands on anything except their own businesses. Smith thought that their judgement was not to be trusted because their thoughts were commonly exercised only in the interests of their own branch of business. Any proposals which they made about public policy should therefore be examined 'not only with the most scrupulous, but with the most suspicious attention'.

The commercial attitude to life has even been exalted into a pseudo-academic discipline called 'marketing'. This is the highly anti-social practice of studying means of inducing people to buy more than they actually need. There is the new witchcraft of public relations and advertising which are devoted to serving this purpose, not by rational persuasion, but by the exploitation of greed, lust, snobbery, fear and social insecurity. The object is to manipulate people in the interests of profit.

It is even more dangerous when it is applied to politics. Here again the Americans have provided the model and the Conservatives have imitated them slavishly. Rational argument is out. In are photo opportunities, image-making and television devised by the advertising men. This favours the parties with the money to pay for it. The Conservatives collect millions of pounds from business looking for legislative favours or knighthoods, and Labour is not far behind with its access to trade union funds. To avoid corruption by money, a more innocent age introduced restrictions on expenditure by candidates in their constituencies. There is no restriction on expenditure at the centre where the real corruption exists.

Commercialism has become the fashionable religion of the age with a pernicious influence spreading into every aspect of our lives. But it is something which we can resist. The country of David Hume should cultivate the virtue of scepticism, be on constant guard against manipulation and exercise a robust consumer resistance.

(*The Scotsman*, 9 March, 1991.)

23

Notes on an Italian Journey

I was asked recently to take part in a conference in Lucca which had the title, 'Towards a new urban system in western Tuscany'. For some time I resisted the idea on what seemed to me the strong grounds that I had no special knowledge of the subject and that there was no shortage of people with far better qualifications. They told me that they had plenty of experts, but they wanted a view from outside from someone who knew Tuscany and Lucca in particular, but also had fairly wide experience of towns in other parts of the world. This left me with little excuse. Just over ten years ago I was British Consul-General in Milan and Minister (in the diplomatic sense) with responsibilities in the north of Italy including Tuscany. I know Lucca quite well because I have good friends who live in a delightful old farmhouse a few miles away. Nor could I deny that in the course of my career I had lived in many towns in Europe and North and South America. Thus deprived of an excuse, and, of course, happy to have an opportunity to visit Italy, I was rash enough to agree to write and deliver a paper.

The more I thought about what I was going to say, the more convinced I became that the major problem in towns in Tuscany, as elsewhere, is the motor car. Italy is full of towns of great beauty which have survived, at least in their old centres, since mediaeval times. They grew up at a time when Italy, with the advantage of its climate in an agricultural age, was the wealthiest part of Europe. It also had an energetic and talented population with a particular genius for architecture, sculpture and painting. (Music and poetry as well, but that is another story.) The towns were not only full of works of art, but were themselves great artistic creations. They have survived partly because of the good sense of the people, but also because the industrial revolution came late to Italy. They escaped the nineteenth-century urge, which affected countries to the north, to destroy anything which stood in the way of industrial development. By the time industrialisation reached Italy on a large scale, they had learned something from the mistakes of others. Like the rest of us, they have now surrounded most of their towns with industrial and urban mess, but they have still spared the historic centres.

The centres of these towns are wonderful places to live, places like Florence, Siena, Lucca, Parma, Bologna, Ravenna, Ferrara, Venice and scores of others. Some are quite small, even more unspoilt and hardly known to the tourist. All of them have centres which are small and compact enough for everything to be within walking distance. Walking in them is a source of endless pleasure in the vistas, the architectural detail, the colour and flair of the shops, the attraction of the bars and restaurants, the animation of the people.

More often than not that pleasure is denied, or heavily restricted, by an inescapable problem. That is motor traffic, including the motor cycles and scooters which are a particular hazard of the Italian streets. In 1959 Mary McCarthy wrote a book about Florence. In it she said that many of the buildings had become quite literally invisible because there was now nowhere to stand to look at them without a high risk of being run over. If you drove a car in the town, you ran the risk of killing somebody. If you stood or walked, you were quite likely to be killed yourself. That was written more than thirty years ago and since then the number of cars and lorries on the roads has everywhere increased and is still increasing. There is not only death and injury from collision, which is on a scale equivalent to a continuous civil war, but also the effects of air pollution, which is a less obvious but no less effective killer. Buildings and works of sculpture, which have survived for centuries, now deteriorate before our eyes for the same reason. Few places are free from the stress of traffic noise. The demands of the motor vehicles for road and parking space lead to the destruction of large areas of both town and country. Cars have in any case become self-defeating because there are already so many that they choke the streets and it is often quicker to walk.

It is now becoming more and more obvious that drastic action will have to be taken to discourage the use of cars in town centres and to transfer as much long distance traffic as possible from the roads to the railways. For years many governments have being doing the opposite with taxation and road-building policies that were a positive incitement to the use of the car and the lorry. By far the worst offender has been the Conservative Government under Mrs Thatcher. Because of the constitutional inadequacies of the present British system, any Prime Minister who is ruthless and power-hungry enough can assume virtually unlimited personal power and inflict their personal whims and fancies on the rest of us. Mrs Thatcher likes cars ('our great car economy') but dislikes trains, probably because of her prejudice against public ownership. The result has been twelve years in which our railways have been forced into a decline which has made them probably the worst in western Europe. With the change of leadership there has been a confession of error; but it will take years to restore our railways to an acceptable standard.

In this matter, Lucca is a town which has special advantages. It not only has an old centre of great charm and beauty, but it is surrounded by one of the most impressive walls in the whole of Europe. There are only six gates and it would therefore be unusually easy to restrict the entry of cars. In addition the railway station is just outside the walls. Italy has suffered no Dr Beeching, the man who reduced our system to a sorry fragment. You can still go almost anywhere in the country by trains which are fast, frequent, comfortable and cheap. Lucca is therefore ideally placed to set an example to the rest of Europe by removing cars from the city centre entirely, with suitable provision for ambulances, deliveries and the like, and with car parks (preferably underground) outside the walls.

This, briefly, was the proposal which I proposed to argue in Lucca. I expected some opposition because it has always seemed to me that the universal love affair with the internal combustion engine is more intense in Italy than elsewhere. After all, no other country has so many boys and young men (and a few girls) who career about on very noisy motor cycles apparently for the sheer pleasure of the movement and the din. But, at least among adults, the love affair seems to have lost its sparkle. The motor car is a cuddly pet that has grown up into a monster.

In Lucca I found that I was pushing against a door that was very nearly open already. The conference was supported by the Commune and Province of Lucca, the Chamber of Commerce and the Military Region of Tuscany and sponsored by two banks. Behind them was the driving force of what one of the speakers called the improbable troika of a Scottish linguist, a Professor of Geography and a military sociologist. The Scottish linguist was my old friend, Ian Inglis (long resident in the neighbourhood, but still retaining a flat in the New Town of Edinburgh); the Professor was Berado Cori of Pisa University, and the military man was Colonel Guiseppe Caforio, the Commander of the Military Region. They were all in substantial agreement and I found that Prof. Cori had written an excellent paper against the tyranny of the motor car with strong arguments based on research in several countries. The Prince of Wales sent a message to the conference in which he too suggested that Lucca should be taken as a model town for the rest of Europe. There was a general feeling that a strong consensus was emerging in favour of curbs on the use of cars and for a more rational transport policy.

After Lucca, I took the opportunity to visit a few more of my favourite places, Florence, Venice and Bergamo, by means of these convenient Italian trains. Florence seemed somehow to have reduced the clutter of cars in the streets, but this was partly because most of the shops and offices were closed for a local holiday. Venice is, of course, the one place where you can walk as much as you like without any harassment from cars. They say that Venetians live longer than other people, simply because they walk more. Whether this is true or not, there is no doubt that building a town with canals instead of streets is a splendid solution to the problem of urban transport.

The major exhibition in Venice this year is one on the Celts, devoted to the theory that they were the first Europeans. This is running from 24 April to 8 December in Palazzo Grassi, a truly magnificent building, lavishly restored by Fiat. They are also financing the exhibition at a cost of £5 million and, to their credit, without any sign of commercial exploitation of the fact. (Ironic after Lucca that this generosity should come from an Italian car manufacturer.) There are more than 2,000 astonishing objects from twenty-four countries, including some from the National Museum of Scotland.

In view of all this, and the evident care, skill and scholarship with which the exhibition has been mounted, it is a pity to have to record that the impression is given that Scotland does not exist or has nothing to do with the subject. We are told about Great Britain which is said to have been occupied by the Romans, as if it were a homogeneous political entity which has existed since Roman times. We are told that Celtic literature continues in Ireland and Wales, without even a nod in the direction of Sorley Maclean or any other of our contemporary Gaelic poets. Perhaps we should not blame the organisers. It is only one more example of the extent to which Scotland will remain invisible to the outside world until we reassert our political identity.

(The *Glasgow Herald*, 27 July, 1991.)

24

Ireland and Scotland: A New Alliance

A visit to Dublin is for me a strange and disturbing, as well as a delightful, experience. Other Scots with whom I have discussed this tell me that their reaction is similar. Nearly everything in Ireland is familiar and reminiscent of Scotland, but at the same time subtly different. It is rather like looking at Scotland through distorting glasses. You can see what I mean most obviously in such things as traditional music and dance. They are more like one another than the music and dance of any other country, but they are distinct as well. So are our whiskies. The Gaelic languages of Ireland and Scotland are essentially the same, but again they have their differences. So also with architecture. We have at least one round tower in Scotland of a kind which is otherwise unique to Ireland. Both of us have tower houses which are more alike than the castles of any other country. There are many doors in the New Town of Edinburgh similar to the famous Georgian doors of Dublin, columns at the side and fan lights above, but in Edinburgh they are chaste and restrained in contrast to the colour and exuberance of those in Dublin. It is the opposite with eighteenth-century ceilings. They are similar in their classicism, but here the greater restraint is with the Irish.

This extraordinary blend of similarity and difference runs through virtually everything. It applies also to the ideas and attitudes of the people. In Scotland we have been egalitarian for centuries (as that greatest of all Scottish plays, *Ane Satire of the Thrie Estaites* reminds us). So too are the Irish, who have a special talent in the expression of it with charm and without truculence. We both dislike pomposity and pretension and are quite good at deflating them. Certainly we have been far apart in matters of religion, but the increasing secularisation of both countries is making this much less important than it used to be.

Both of us suffer from derogatory labels applied to us by the English as part of the process of asserting the supposed superiority of the coloniser over the colonised. The Irish are said to be stupid and illogical and the Scots mean and truculent. Both of these allegations are the opposite of the truth, but their persistence in stage types and jokes are proof of the efficacy of centuries of propaganda.

Altogether Scotland is more like Ireland, and Ireland more like Scotland, than they are like any other country. The basic similarities are not surprising when you consider our shared historical experiences. Scots from Ireland were one of the peoples who formed Scotland in the distant past and gave us both the name of the country and the Gaelic language. In the fourteenth century Robert Bruce's brother, Edward, was invited to Ireland to help to expel the English invader. At the time Robert sent a letter to the Kings and people of Ireland in which he referred to our shared national ancestry, common language and common customs. For centuries Scotland and Ireland were both subjected to repeated attempts by the English to invade and subdue them. Such episodes as Cromwell's bloody sacking of Drogheda are paralleled, not only by Edward I's sacking of Berwick, but by repeated invasions of Scotland over 300 years when Edinburgh and the south of Scotland were put to the fire and sword.

England also used more subtle methods. A recent history of Ireland[1] says of the country in the eighteenth century: 'Ireland was legally an independent country. But the King of Ireland was represented by a lord lieutenant nominated by the British Government, and the lord lieutenant selected and controlled the Irish executive, which is turn controlled the patronage . . . peerages, places, and pensions that influenced the outlook of many MPs'. This is precisely the system used by the English Government to frustrate the nominally independent Scotland in the period before the Union of 1707. England had failed to impose their King on Scotland; but after the succession of James VI to the English throne in 1603, the effect was much the same. The book which I have already quoted goes on to say that after the British Government failed to secure the agreement of the Irish Parliament to a parliamentary union in 1799, they 'set to work to obtain a majority, partly by propaganda and persuasion, partly by trying to gratify the crudely personal objectives of many peers and MPs'. These are the tactics, propaganda, bribery and intimidation, which the English Government used to secure Union with Scotland in 1707. The Scottish Parliament held out for four years; but, although quite unrepresentative in a democratic sense, it was more genuinely national than the Irish, which consisted solely of members of the Anglican Church of Ireland, or in other words of the English establishment and fellow travellers.

In many ways Ireland suffered even more than Scotland from English ambition and exploitation. This was because Ireland was defeated by force of arms, occupied and colonised. In fact, this happened twice, incompletely in the fourteenth century and more thoroughly under the Tudors between 1534 and 1603. English attempts to do the same to Scotland failed. The consequence was that Scotland, until this century at least, did not have a strong English settlement on its territory, nor penal laws designed to curb trade and land ownership to England's advantage. The imposition of English Protestantism on Ireland, which again failed in Scotland in the seventeenth century, was at the root of much subsequent difficulty. Catholicism (as towards the Russians in Poland) became the expression of resistance to alien control.

With so much that is similar in our origins, attitudes, and historical experience, and so much interchange of population, why is it that we now seem to be so much out of touch? On the Scottish side, there is a natural hesitation to show interest in Irish affairs because of a fear that it might mean becoming associated with the sectarianism and violence of Northern Ireland. From the Irish side, the fact that Scots were planted in Ulster as a continuation by James VI of the Tudor policy of colonisation gives us a share of the guilt. Also we have to face the fact that when Scotland lost its independence, it became invisible on the international stage. Only independent countries are entities both in international law and popular conception. Like the rest of the world, the Irish naturally tend to share the widespread illusion that Scotland long ago ceased to exist and is now no more than part of Britain which is another name for England. They simply do not think of us as a country, either actually or potentially.

This estrangement and mutual ignorance between two so closely related countries seems to me a pity. I think that we could both learn from the other and give each other mutual support. Anyone who has doubts about the advantages for Scotland of independence and full membership of the European Community should go to Dublin and talk to the Irish. I was talking recently to a man who has experience of both countries about the greater self-confidence and optimism which is evident in Ireland as compared to Scotland. Of course, he said, that is what seventy years of independence do for you.

In the 1940s a magazine was published in Edinburgh called *The New Alliance* because it aimed at developing the natural affinity between the Irish and the Scots. It did not survive the War, but it had the right idea. The exchanges promoted by the Scottish Arts Council between writers in the two countries are a move in the right direction. So is the new association between *Scotland on Sunday* and the *Sunday Tribune* of Dublin. The Scottish National Party has long proposed that an independent Scotland should aim at a close association with the other small countries of north-west Europe, particularly the Scandinavians. When we all become members of the European Community we could exercise a powerful and constructive influence within it. Ireland, with experience as an independent member of the Community, would have a key role.

The historian, Gordon Donaldson, recently wrote a book, *The Northern Commonwealth*, about the Nordic civilisation which once spread over this whole northern area, including Dublin. We may be moving towards a new grouping of countries with size, climate, geography and much else in common. Our first priority should be to strengthen our relations of every kind with the country with which we have the closest affinity of all and that is Ireland.

(*Scotland on Sunday*, 8 September 1991.)

NOTE

1. *The Course of Irish History* edited by T.W. Moody and F.X. Martin (Mercier Press).

25

Lord Mackay in Arbroath

The Lord Chancellor of England, Lord Mackay of Clashfern, recently made a long and elaborate speech against any idea of change in the constitutional relationship between Scotland and England. It is highly unusual for a Lord Chancellor, even if he happens to be a Scots lawyer, to make a frankly political speech, especially in Scotland and on the central issue of Scottish politics. Both the timing and the place of the speech were significant. It was on 18 September 1991, the first day of the SNP Conference, and it was in Arbroath, the town invariably associated with the Declaration in 1320, one of the most eloquent and powerful statements ever made of the case for national self-determination. All of these circumstances suggest that the Government is in a high state of panic over the demand for a Scottish Parliament.

As appears from the opening passages of the speech, one of the reasons for the panic is the encouraging example of the Baltic republics. Lord Mackay would have us believe that any parallel with Scotland would be 'ludicrous'. There are obviously great differences between their situation and ours; but the example of small, ancient nations escaping from the grip of a large and once powerful neighbour inevitably provokes the thought that surely Scotland can now achieve the same result. The similarities between the two situations were made explicit by a Latvian representative at the SNP Conference.

Lord Mackay thinks that we should be content with the measure of democracy permitted to us under the present system. He does not mention that this has allowed us to be governed for twelve years by a party with less than a quarter of the Scottish votes and which imposes policies on Scotland which the Scottish people have clearly rejected. This is surely undemocratic by any standard.

He tells us also that the Union is supported by 'the vast majority of our fellow Scots'. The fact is that for decades every opinion poll on the subject has shown about 80 per cent of Scots in favour of a Scottish Parliament and therefore of a fundamental change in the arrangements made in 1707. He describes the Union as a 'voluntary partnership' between the two nations. In fact, it was imposed by

England by means of bribery and military intimidation against the outraged indignation of the Scottish people.

Lord Mackay then goes on to make some perfectly valid points about the Constitutional Convention. As he says, the *Claim of Right*, the document on which it was based, asserted the sovereignty of the Scottish people and rejected that of the Westminster Parliament. He seems to be shocked by this; but the doctrine that in Scotland the people are sovereign is as old as the Declaration of Arbroath, and even in England the idea of parliamentary sovereignty is much more recent than he seems to suppose. He rejects the Convention proposals, to which Labour and the Liberal Democrats are committed, on the grounds that they would reduce Scotland to a region, be no more than a level of local government and leave all the important decisions to Westminster.

This argument would seem to lead logically to a preference for the SNP policy of independence and membership of the European Community, but Lord Mackay rejects this as well. He says that it would mean Scotland becoming a 'small, inward-looking nation, languishing on the fringes of Europe'. He has failed to notice that, on the contrary, a desire to become once again a fully participating member of the international community is one of the most powerful motives behind the demand for independence. Until we are independent, we have no real existence either in international law or in the minds of most people abroad. Independence will have enormous benefits in trade, regard for our interests, self-esteem and a healthier relationship with England.

Lord Mackay thinks that as a member of the European Community in our own right we shall be a 'mere bystander'. Would he say the same to Denmark, Ireland or even Luxembourg? International organisations bring greater benefits to small member states than to large ones. This is because they curb the unbridled exercise of power due to sheer size and ensure that the views and interests of even the smallest member state have to be taken into account. But you have first to be independent before you can be a member state. This is why the Baltic states (and the SNP) want both independence and the pooling of part of their sovereignty in the United Nations and the European Community. As part of the United Kingdom, the interests of Scotland can be, and they usually are, ignored.

Lord Mackay thinks that history is on the side of the Conservatives (a curiously Marxist phrase) and that the SNP is 'out of step'. Once again, the truth is the precise opposite. During this century, and now increasingly, the empires and the multi-national states have been dissolving into their component parts and the liberated nations have been coming together in international organisations. The United

Kingdom is one of the discredited multi-nationals which belongs to the past.

In internal matters, Lord Mackay (or whoever drafted the speech) is also quite wrong about the SNP. His suggestion that it is rent by 'internal contradictions and tensions' (this from a Tory!) is as fanciful as his pretence that there is something in common between SNP policies and those now discredited in eastern Europe. SNP policies, which have been consistent for many years, reflect the egalitarianism and the social concern for mutual wellbeing which are instinctive in Scotland. Like our legal system, they are very close to the European norm. That is an additional reason why independence and full membership of the European Community is the natural and proper role for Scotland.

(*Scotland on Sunday*, 29 September 1991.)

26

The 'Boasted Advantages'

In a letter to Mrs Dunlop in April 1790 Robert Burns said that he had often wondered, 'what are all the boasted advantages which my country reaps from a certain union that can counterbalance the annihilation of her Independence, and even her very name?'. As far as we know, no one attempted to give Burns an answer. It is still, and in fact now more than ever, one of the great unanswered questions. Not only the Conservatives, but Labour and the Democrats as well, often talk about the benefits of the Union. They talk as though these benefits were self-evident, but they never tell us what they are. Recently Ian Lang made a speech in which he promised to spell out in the months ahead the moral, patriotic, democratic, financial, social and economic advantages. He will need a lot of imagination.

Of course, we have to remember that, unlike the SNP, the Conservatives, Labour and the Democrats are all UK parties. They have to look at all questions from a UK, which means a predominantly English, point of view. Labour and the Democrats want to keep Scottish members at Westminster because they have a better chance of influence, or even power, in a UK, than they would have in an English, Parliament. For the Conservatives, the opposite is true, as several of their English back benchers have begun to realise. On the other hand, the Conservatives have an English nationalist reluctance to relinquish power and territory. Also, whatever their propaganda may say, I have no doubt that their advisors constantly remind them of the advantages to England of keeping a grip on Scotland. Where else would they keep their nuclear submarines and process nuclear waste at a comfortable distance from their own back-yard? Where else would they find the oil revenues which in the years of the Conservative Government have amounted to about £100 billion, or £20,000 per head for everyone in Scotland?

But are there any advantages to Scotland? That is a much more difficult question. This is a question that has to be considered historically, because the effects of the Union have been different at different periods. Many of the preconceived attitudes are influenced not by present conditions, but by what historians, politicians or propagandists have thought were the effects at various times in the past.

In the first place, we have to clear our minds from any notion that the Union was a negotiated bargain in which the Scots bartered their independence for trade advantages, meaning admission to the English home and colonial market. This is a rationalisation, invented in the nineteenth century, which has been handed down since then as accepted wisdom. The Union, in fact, was a political arrangement, not negotiated but imposed by a mixture of bribery and military intimidation. Any trading advantages were on the side of England which had a stronger economy and was able to treat Scotland as a captive market. The Scottish trading community was well aware of this and petitioned against the Union for that reason. It is true that the Scottish economy was stimulated by the wealth generated by the Glasgow tobacco trade, but the Scottish traders were perfectly capable of carrying it on in defiance of English laws, as they had done before the Union. Such advantage as there was in trading legally with an English colony, disappeared with American independence.

The Scottish economy only began to recover from the adverse effects of the Union about the middle of the eighteenth century. This was due to Scottish efforts, not aided by the Union, but by agricultural and industrial improvements in which Scottish inventions played a major part. In Walter Scott's phrase, Scotland was left 'under the guardianship of her own institutions, to win her silent way to national wealth and consequence'. For most of the eighteenth century the Government in London hardly intervened in Scotland at all, except for the brutal suppression of the Highlands after the '45.

By about the end of that century, however, Scotland became involved, as a direct consequence of the Union, in the development of the Empire. The Empire became a major source of employment for Scots as soldiers, civil servants, doctors, engineers, farmers and traders. Many of them had brilliant careers and made major contributions to the development of India, Canada, Australia and the rest of the once vast Empire. Their talents and energy were, of course, lost to Scotland itself. At the same time the products of Scottish engineering were aimed at an Empire market for which Scotland built most of the ships and most of the locomotives.

In these ways, the prosperity of individual Scots who emigrated, and of Scottish industry at home, were both intimately bound up with the Empire. Without the Union, Scotland would not have been part of it (unless, of course, we had carried out more successful versions of the Darien scheme on our own). It was this fact which reconciled many Scots to the Union and led politicians and historians in the nineteenth century to conclude that it had been beneficial to Scotland. Even then it was doubtful whether the Empire connection did not do more harm than good by causing the loss of talented people and the neglect of Scotland itself. There was, however, an investment of Scottish pride in the Empire, because of the Scottish contribution to its development. Michael Lynch in his recent history of Scotland writes of a 'rapturous embrace' made by the Scots, not of Britain, but of a British Empire which opened up in the 1780s and disappeared after 1945.

In the days of the Empire, Britain was the most powerful and prosperous country in the world. Of course, the British Empire is now as dead as the Dodo. Britain is now a minor and declining power and its standard of living is well below that of many of the smaller countries of western Europe; but, in the minds of many people, the old attitudes still linger on. Until about the time of the Second World War, there was a general belief in the British Empire as a magnificent and benevolent creation and that therefore the Union was beneficial to Scotland because it made us one of the senior partners. This was endlessly repeated or implied in countless speeches, newspaper leaders and school textbooks. We were so thoroughly indoctrinated that many people are still conditioned for this reason to approve of the Union, long after the Empire has gone. Approval of the Union is a relic of the imperialist past.

It has also been argued in the past that the Union was advantageous to Scotland because it gave us access to a wider market, once the Empire and then at least the United Kingdom. This was always a fairly dubious argument. The famous economist, E.F. Schumacher, said in his book, *Small is Beautiful*: 'whether a market is outside the political boundaries or inside, makes on the whole very little difference. I am not aware, for instance, that Germany in order to export a large enough number of Volkswagens to the United States could only do so after annexing the United States'. In any case, this argument too is completely out of date. The market is no longer the Empire or the UK but the European Community plus EFTA and Scotland will remain part of that European market inside or outside the Union with England.

The existence of the European Community adds several new dimensions to the debate. The unionists in all three UK parties commonly argue that Scotland has more weight when represented by the UK Government in the EC than we would have as a distinct member in our own right. This is absurd. As part of the UK, Scotland has none of the rights and privileges of a member state. If our interests and ideas are in conflict with those of England, as they frequently are, they are simply not expressed at all. Nor is it true that only the larger countries have any real say in the affairs of the EC. Tell that to the Danes, the Luxembourgois or the Irish and ask them if they would rather be represented by the Germans or the English than by themselves. The fact is that even weighted voting is so arranged that no majority is possible without the agreement of at least some of the smaller countries. International organisations like the EC or the UN are more beneficial to the smaller countries than to the large, because they tend to neutralise the power of mere size. In most respects, all member states, no matter how small, are treated as equals and their views have to be taken into account. This would apply to an independent Scotland as a member in her own right. Without independence, we have no recognised international existence at all.

The EC has made it easier for Scotland to achieve independence because it removes all the old arguments about the size of the market, custom posts on the border and so forth. It has also made it more urgent because otherwise our interests largely go by default at the level which increasingly matters which is the European. We should be free to follow our own European policy, free of the 'Little Englander' attitude which so often distorts UK policy and makes her a reluctant and troublesome partner in Europe.

To return then to the question with which we started – what are the 'boasted advantages' of the Union, if any, now that the Empire has disappeared into the mists of time? Let us look at them under the headings suggested by Ian Lang (with one extra which he seems to have forgotten):

Democratic
One of the strongest condemnations of the Union is precisely that it is a denial of democracy. It allows Scotland to be governed by a party which we reject by a large majority at the polls and which repeatedly imposes on Scotland policies of which we clearly disapprove. We shall not have democracy until we have an independent Scottish Parliament elected by a fair and proportional voting system.

Financial
The Tories will repeat their old con trick of trying to persuade us that Scotland is subsidised by England because 'identifiable expenditure' per head is higher in Scotland (a reflection, of course, of comparative economic disadvantage). This conveniently ignores the revenue from Scottish oil which has kept the UK economy afloat and the many forms of massive subsidy to the south-east of England through mortgage tax relief, road and rail infrastructure, Docklands and all the rest of it. Even before the Union Treaty was ratified in 1707, Andrew Fletcher said that its effect would be to suck the wealth of Scotland into the south-east of England. He was right.

Economic
Another major disadvantage of the Union is that it imposes on
Scotland economic policies designed for conditions in England, as
in the high interest rates designed to cool the over-heated economy in
the south-east. It has deprived us also of any means of resisting (as all
independent countries do) the steady erosion of Scottish ownership
and control of companies and therefore of senior decision-making
jobs. It may make sense from a UK perspective to 'rationalise' by
concentrating in the south; it is disastrous from a Scottish point
of view. An independent Scotland will have a government able to
concentrate on our own economic needs and opportunities.

Defence
Strangely enough Ian Lang did not mention this which is perhaps
a recognition that it has lost all urgency because of the collapse of
the Soviet threat. Even when that existed, the presence of nuclear
submarines on the Clyde did not make us more secure, but more
vulnerable, because we were a priority target for nuclear attack.
Now they are an expensive irrelevance with a potential risk of a
nuclear accident, and a massive waste of money.

   In the past, as part of the UK, we have repeatedly been involved
in wars in which Scotland has contributed a disproportionately large
part of the cost in blood. We should be far more secure, and less liable
to be involved in war, as a small, northern European country bound
by a relationship of mutual interest to the rest of Europe.

Social
Within the Union we are free to move freely across the Border.
This will be no different in an independent Scotland in Europe for
freedom of movement now extends over the whole of the European
Community.

   As for social policy, Scotland has always been in the forefront of
enlightened thought. As an independent country, we shall be once
again able to address our needs in accordance with out own instincts
and aspirations. We should also be free to develop and express our
own cultural identity, free from distortions imposed from outside.

Patriotic
According to Ian Lang, who is doing his best to re-write Scottish
history, 'it is not anti-Scottish to be for the Union'. Another
Conservative (who is, in fact, a historian), Michael Fry, is more
honest. He has described the Scottish Conservatives as unique among
Conservative parties elsewhere in the world, because it is unpatriotic.
It is alone in 'telling its country that nationhood counts for nothing'.

Patriotism can be carried to excess, but the irreducible and essential minimum is commitment to the freedom and prosperity of one's own country. Independence will make Scotland more prosperous, but that is not the most important point. The Conservatives insult Scotland when they assume, as they always do, that money is the only thing that matters.

In Eric Linklater's words: 'people degenerate when they lose control of their own affairs'. When they recover that control, they gain immeasurably in satisfaction, self-esteem and achievement. That has been the experience of every country that becomes independent. Scotland will be no exception.

(*Scotland on Sunday*, 5 January 1992.)

27

The Scottish Book of the Year

The Saltire Society was founded in 1936 as a response to both pessimism and hope about the state of Scotland. The pessimism had been expressed in a series of books about the parlous state of Scotland both economically and culturally. A Principal of St Andrew's University, J.C. Shairp, echoing a very similar remark by Sir Walter Scott, had once written: 'Anglicised Scotsmen are generally poor creatures and an Anglicised Scotland will be a contemptible country'. It was widely felt that this was precisely what was happening to Scotland, that it was being absorbed and assimilated into extinction. In his *Scottish Journey*, published in 1935, for example, Edwin Muir said that the distinctive national identity of Scotland was 'falling to pieces, for there is no visible and effective power to hold it together'. On the other hand, there were also reasons for hope. A cultural revival had begun at the end of the previous century and it reached critical momentum in the '20s with the Renaissance associated with Hugh MacDiarmid.

The visible and effective power of which Muir spoke requires a Scottish Parliament and to that end the Scottish National Party was formed in 1934. Almost simultaneously, the Saltire Society aimed at the improvement of the quality of Scottish life by the encouragement of the cultural revival. Its objective was no less than 'to restore the country to its proper place as a creative force in European civilisation'. We still have a long way to go, but there is little doubt that there have been great improvements since the '30s and that the Saltire Society has been at the bottom of many of them. It has used a great variety of means: publications, conferences and lectures, festival performances, award schemes to encourage achievements of many kinds. Anyone who shares the objectives can join, take part in the work and help to shape the policies.

If you have any ideas for the improvement of the cultural life of Scotland, put them to the Saltire Society. My own experience suggests that you will find them receptive. I have been a member for many years but I could play an active part only after I came back to Scotland in 1980. Within a couple of years several of my proposals had been adopted and carried out, including the revival of our publishing, the installation of the splendid work of Anne Carrick as a permanent exhibition in Smailholm Tower, and the setting up of a joint think-tank with many other organisations (AdCAS). Then there was the book award. Literature has always been important to the Society. It began the systematic publication of Scottish literary classics at a time when no one else was doing it. For years, especially during the Edinburgh Festivals, it has given readings of Scottish poetry of all periods. It has published the *Saltire Review* and the *Scottish Review* which have made notable contributions to Scottish letters. So why was there no book award, especially at a time when Scottish writing was in a very flourishing state? The Council of the Society readily approved proposals which I put to them in 1981 and almost at once we found a very generous and helpful sponsor in the Royal Bank of Scotland.

Of course, nothing is new under the sun. It was only afterwards that I discovered that there had been an earlier Saltire book award. The first award panel, which was appointed in 1937, consisted of Eric Linklater, Compton Mackenzie and Edwin Muir. One of the first books that they selected was Neil Gunn's *Highland River*. The war brought the scheme to an end with only a temporary revival in the '50s.

The new scheme, announced in September 1981, was for an award of £1,000 for the Scottish Book of the Year. Any new book by an author of Scottish descent or living in Scotland, or a book by anyone on a Scottish subject, was eligible. It might therefore be poetry, a novel, a play or other work of imaginative literature, or biography, literary criticism or a study of any Scottish issue. The year was to run from September to September with the announcement of the award in November. Literary editors of the leading Scottish newspapers, and the editors of magazines concerned with literature, were to be invited to submit nominations among books of which they had carried reviews.

The eligibility rules have remained unchanged since the beginning, but there have been changes in the amount of the award and the sponsorship. The Royal Bank of Scotland increased the prize to £1,500 in 1985. Their rules restrict them to sponsoring any one event to a maximum of six years and they therefore withdrew after the 1987 award. When this became known, Magnus Linklater of *The Scotsman* spontaneously offered to take over and proposed the addition of a new award for the Scottish First Book of the Year by a new author with a prize of £1,000. In 1990 Scottish Television joined in the sponsorship and the amounts of the awards were increased to £5,000 for the Book of the Year and £1,500 for the First Book. For reasons which I shall explain later, the announcements of the awards are now made in January.

We have been very fortunate in our sponsors. They have not only provided the funds for the awards and the administrative costs, but have also arranged the award ceremonies which have been notable and agreeable occasions. They have always accepted the judgement of the Awards Panel without the slightest hint of interference. Unlike some other sponsors for other things, they have never exploited the awards for blatant commercial publicity. The Panel has not hesitated to give the awards to books which some people might regard as controversial, as the following list shows:

Scottish Book of the Year
1982 Alastair Gray for *Lanark*.
1983 Shared by Derick Thomson for *Creachadh an Clarsaich* and Edwin Morgan for *Poems of Thirty Years*.
1984 Shared by David Daiches for *God and the Poets* and Tom Leonard for *Intimate Voices*.
1985 Norman MacCaig for *Collected Poems*.
1986 Stuart Hood for *A Storm from Paradise*.
1987 Muriel Spark for *The Stories of Muriel Spark*.
1988 Shared by Neal Ascherson for *Games with Shadows* and Tom Nairn for *The Enchanted Glass*.
1989 Allan Massie for *A Question of Loyalties*.
1990 Sorley MacLean for *O Choille gu Bearradh*.

Scottish First Book of the Year
1988 Raymond Vettese for *The Richt Noise*.
1989 Sian Hayton for *Cells of Knowledge*.
1990 Harry Tait for *The Ballad of Sawney Bain*.

I think that all members of the Panel would agree with what Angus Calder, one of the members, wrote in *The Scotsman* in 1988. He said that the list of winners gave him a great deal of satisfaction because between them they represented 'experiment, virtuosity, wit and intellect'. For some years, the Panel has consisted of Angus Calder, Ian Campbell, Douglas Gifford, Isobel Murray, Alan Taylor, Derick Thomson and myself as Convener. We have several times considered making more frequent changes, but have decided that the advantage lies on the side of continuity. The present membership brings together a wide knowledge of Scottish writing with sufficient diversity of taste and instinct to be fair to all comers. Above all, we work well together and combine a seriousness of purpose with a spirited discussion which we all enjoy. As is usual with Saltire Society activities, the members give up a good deal of their time without any reward apart from the satisfaction of doing something useful for Scottish literature. Often our discussion begins with quite strong disagreements, but we have always reached in the end a decision which we all accept. I think that something of this atmosphere came over in the BBC recording which was broadcast in 'Queen Street Garden' on the day of the last award ceremony.

Nomination by literary editors has two purposes. First of all it throws the net wide by including in the selection process most of the people involved in the reviewing of books in Scotland. On the other hand, it is a safety valve to exclude the scores of books which are not seriously in the running. We want to protect our judges from the superhuman task of reading, or pretending to read, every new book that appears. At the same time, we do not want to miss any book which deserves consideration. For this reason the judges can nominate any such book which might be missed. As a second line of defence, we go through a list of new Scottish books drawn up every year by the Book Trust.

When the Award was first introduced, I thought that there would probably always be a book which was so clearly outstanding that it would resolve the apparently impossible job of deciding between books of quite different kinds. Sometimes this happens, as with Sorley MacLean last time. Every year, I am happy to say, we have been faced with a rich choice of many excellent books of diverse types. So how do we decide between, say, a novel, poetry and a biography? Of course there is no scientific standard of measurement and in the end it is a matter of personal taste. The safeguard is that there are enough members on the Panel to rule out our individual prejudices and eccentricities and we have evolved a voting system which, we think, gives as fair a result as possible.

If imitation is the sincerest form of flattery, I suppose we should be gratified by the appearance on the scene of the McVitie's Award in 1987. Perhaps the organisers, a Glasgow PR firm on behalf of United Biscuits, had heard that the Royal Bank sponsorship was coming to an end and imagined that this would leave them a free field. At all events, without any consultation, they imitated the terms and conditions of the Saltire award very closely. The name of the award (Scottish Writer as opposed to Book of the Year) was almost the same, the definition of a Scottish writer was a close paraphrase and the timing (September to September with the announcement in November) was identical. The main differences were that unpublished theatre, cinema, television and radio scripts were eligible and that there was no restriction on the number of nominations by 'publishers or others'.

My first reaction was that two awards so similar in their terms and timing would be self-defeating and ridiculous. I suggested both publicly and privately that the two should be combined, but there was no response from United Biscuits. This was one of the reasons why we moved our award ceremony to January. The other was the purely practical purpose of allowing us more time to read and consider the books. I do not know how the McVitie's judges are able to cope with their unfiltered flood of nominations in so short a time.

I now think that I was probably wrong to worry about the effect of the duplication of the award. Literature tends to languish if it meets with indifference and lack of response, and to flourish in an atmosphere of interest and appreciation. The purpose of the Saltire Award is to help to encourage such an atmosphere. More than fifty years of experience of running awards has given the Saltire Society a firm reputation for fairness, integrity and seriousness in this activity and any Saltire award therefore carries a good deal of weight and influence. The award for the first book by a new writer gives encouragement precisely where it is most needed. At the same time, Scottish writing is now so vigorous and prolific that there is room for a number of awards and, of course, there are others. Perhaps it is a case of the more, the merrier.

(*Books in Scotland*, No. 37, Spring 1991.)

28

A Scottish National Theatre

In Scotland we have a National Library, three National Galleries, a National Museum, national companies for opera and ballet and an orchestra which, in spite of its unhappy change of name and present crisis of management, is still our national orchestra. They are the custodians of much of our national achievement, the flag-ships of our cultural life. Unfortunately, however, there is a conspicuous gap; we have no National Theatre.

This missing link is a very serious deficiency, especially for two reasons. In the first place, there is something about a National Theatre which in virtually every other country in Europe gives it a central role in intellectual and artistic life. It not only gives work, recognition and encouragement to dramatists, theatre directors, actors and designers, but it very often enlivens thought and artistic creation in many other directions. Perhaps this is because of the ability of the theatre, in Shakespeare's phrase, to hold a mirror up to nature, and sharpen our self-awareness, self-understanding and self-confidence. For this to be effective, it has to address itself primarily to our own society.

Secondly, the gap is unfortunate and paradoxical because, among the performing arts, drama is the one where we have most to offer which is valuable and distinctive. Scottish actors have a style and vitality of their own. We have a substantial corpus of plays which address themselves to Scottish life and experience. We have the work of such writers, to mention only a few from this century, as Barrie, Bridie, MacClellan, Kemp, Reid, Taylor, Campbell, Lochhead and the two MacMillans. Many of these plays deserve revival and reassessment. In the absence of a National Theatre company, which would regard old and new Scottish plays as its primary responsibility, there is no organisation to establish and develop a living tradition. Few plays are ever revived; new ones have a hard struggle to achieve production at all.

In opera and ballet we have much less of our own to offer. These are art forms which are largely imported from outside. There is nothing wrong with that, of course, except that new and distinctive creation is more valuable than mere imitation and reproduction. If this matter had been approached logically, a National Theatre would have been a higher priority than companies for opera or ballet.

It has not been for the want of trying. The Scottish National Players flourished from 1922 to 1934 and in that time produced 131 plays, and that was long before the days of public subsidy for the theatre. The Citizens in Glasgow and the Lyceum in Edinburgh have at various times seemed on the verge of becoming a National Theatre. Much more recently, the Scottish Theatre Company was very close indeed; but, after a great international triumph in Warsaw with the *Thrie Estaites*, was scandalously allowed to collapse through lack of funding.

In May 1987 the Advisory Council for the Arts in Scotland (AdCAS) held a conference to discuss this whole matter which was the largest and most representative meeting ever held of people involved in, or concerned with, the theatre in Scotland. It resolved unanimously that there is a pressing need for a Scottish National Theatre. In September of this year Scottish Equity, representing the actors, held a conference on the same subject and reached the same conclusion. So did a meeting in Stirling on 23 October organised by the Scottish Arts Council as part of their consultations for a Charter for the Arts. The Saltire Society regard the achievement of a National Theatre as a principal objective for the 1990s. In writing to them on behalf of the Labour Party, Donald Dewar said that there could be no opposition to the concept. The SNP have been committed to a National Theatre for years. As far as I know, the other parties have not expressed a view, but this should not be a party issue. The distinguished theatre director, Peter Brook, wrote recently to AdCAS; 'Of course, Scotland must have a National Theatre. This is so self-evident that it is shaming to feel that it has to be underlined'.

With so obvious a need and so much enthusiasm behind it for so long, almost the whole of the present century, why do we still not have a National Theatre? The Government spokesman who in 1949 introduced the Bill establishing the National Theatre in London in 1949 said that he hoped that Scotland would soon follow the example. More than forty years later we are still waiting.

As always, the problem is, of course, money. A National Theatre must be adequately financed to aim at the highest international stand-ards and be capable of large, as well as small-scale, productions. It should have research and training facilities which should be available to other theatres in Scotland. It should be able to tour in Scotland and outside and exchange productions with other theatres. The whole intention would be to improve the quality and prestige of Scottish theatre and to give it international reputation and involvement. All of these things would probably require a subsidy of about £2 million a year, or about the amount at present paid to the RSO.

It is probably this thought which explains the attitude of the Scottish Arts Council. In the '70s they seemed to be working towards a National Theatre, but under the financial pressures of the Thatcher years they have done their best to pretend that the question does not exist. Also, some of the existing theatre directors have resisted the idea. Possibly this is because some of them are English and do not feel at ease with Scottish plays; but their chief worry is that a National Theatre would eat up their own subsidy. In fact, the advocates of a National Theatre have always emphasised that it must not be financed at the expense of the other companies and that part of the function of a National Theatre would be to co-operate with the other companies and to help all of them by enhancing the reputation of Scottish theatre generally.

The opponents of the idea have fallen back on the argument, or excuse, that we already have a National Theatre in the sum total of all the theatre companies which already exist in Scotland. Every other country might have said the same, but that did not deter them. It is true that we have an encouraging number of diverse theatre organisations doing interesting work; but even all of them taken together do not aim at the functions of a National Theatre. None of them is committed to the cultivation of the corpus of Scottish plays as a priority nor to building up a team of Scottish actors capable of the appropriate style. None of them is funded adequately to aspire to the highest standards nor to produce plays which demand a large cast.

We need not, I think, contemplate the expense of new building. Several suitable sites already exist. Think, for example, of the Lyceum in Edinburgh. It was always a very beautiful theatre and has now been made into one of the most attractive you can find anywhere. Across the street they have another building with offices, rehearsal space and so on and even another small theatre. Almost next door, the Traverse Theatre will soon have a new home with two flexible performance spaces. Taken together these places and the resources of the Lyceum, Communicado (the highly successful travelling company which is part of the same organisation) and the Traverse (which has an international reputation as an innovative theatre), you would have a critical mass which could explode into a formidable theatrical force which could measure up very well to international comparison as a National Theatre. They would need extra financing, but not an amount which should present insurmountable difficulty. The Government should honour the implied promise of 1949.

Of course this is not a project which could be realised without the agreement of these theatre companies and a great deal of co-operation between them and with the other companies in Scotland. They all have their identities, their contractual rights, their own policies and ideas. They would have to be capable of unselfishness for the common good, vision and imagination to merge into something much more ambitious than any of them can now contemplate. They would have to be prepared to accept a sort of federal structure, perhaps headed by someone of the stature and vision of a Tom Fleming or a Bill Bryden.

Glasgow, and perhaps other places, will, no doubt, question the location in Edinburgh. As everywhere else in the world, the Capital is the appropriate place for the National Theatre, and Glasgow already has the Opera, the Ballet and the Orchestra. In any case, although a National Theatre needs a recognisable and worthy home, its responsibility should be to the whole of Scotland. It needs a base to provide the solidity and continuity to succeed, but it must serve the whole of Scotland by touring and exchanging productions and by making many of its facilities available to the theatre generally.

This is an ambitious and demanding project which has eluded us for nearly a century. I believe that the Scottish people now have the cultural assurance and self-confidence to insist upon it and achieve it.

(*The Scotsman*, 1 January 259 1992.
A version of the earlier part of this article was broadcast in 'Newsweek' on BBC Scotland on 30 November 1991.)

29

The Scottish National Galleries

Evidently in an attempt to justify the announcement by the Trustees on 30 November 1993, the National Galleries published simultaneously four pamphlets, designed in an eighteenth century style and printed on expensive hand-made paper. Strangely enough, the first of them opens with an eloquent defence of the policy which the National Gallery has followed since its foundation nearly 150 years ago. It quotes a statement by Sir James Caw, who became Director in 1907. He said that the largest part of the collection was the work of Scottish artists and that this was 'as it should be', since one of the chief functions of a National Gallery was to illustrate the 'development of the National School'. A policy statement shortly afterwards said that the ideal at which the Gallery should aim was a full representation of Scottish painting, set against examples of the more important schools of other countries. This is, in fact, the policy followed by national galleries in the other capitals of the world; they concentrate on the work of the country concerned, but hope to acquire adequate examples from elsewhere to offer comparisons and suggest affinities and distinctions.

The pamphlet then goes on to boast that the ideal has been achieved. The Gallery now has 'the finest collection of Scottish art in the world', and has also acquired masterpieces from all the European schools. 'Nowhere else save in Edinburgh can the full range and diversity of the Scottish school be seen to such advantage.' It comes as a shock after this proud statement to discover that the rest of the pamphlet is an apology for the dismantling of this great and balanced collection built up with such effort over more than 100 years.

I do not think that any other gallery in the world has ever proposed such self-destruction, comparable to the seizures of Napoleon or Goering as the spoils of war. The reason which they offer is lack of space. They have in the three galleries about 2,900 paintings of which 2,000 are Scottish. About 1,700 of the total and 900 Scottish are in store. This is a common problem everywhere in the world. There are several ways in which it could be solved without closing the Portrait Gallery (regarded by many people all over Scotland with a passionate pride and affection) and without removing two-thirds of the collections from the Gallery on the Mound and from the Modern Art Gallery. They would then have so few Scottish paintings that they could hardly claim to be National Galleries at all.

The Portrait Gallery should be removed from this equation. As many people have pointed out repeatedly over the last year, its purpose is quite different from an art gallery. It has more affinity with the National Museum and it would be logical to bring it under the same management. Of course, many of its portraits are great works of art and some of them could be lent from time to time to the art galleries. Although both the pamphlets and Ruth Wishart in a recent article have denied it, the SNPG has no problem of space. The removal of the Antiquities to the new museum will nearly double its capacity, and there is unused exhibition space in the York Building across the street and there is a fine empty building next door.

The proposal to remove the greater part of the art collections to a new National Gallery of Scottish Art would not do such violence to the principle of balance in an international context if the new gallery was close to the other two. The visitor could then walk from one to the other with fresh impressions in the mind. The removal of most of the Scottish paintings to another city would isolate them, as though we were ashamed of them. Also, many of the Scottish paintings have a close relationship with Edinburgh and they would lose something if they were removed from the context in which they have remained from the day they were painted.

The arguments advanced by Glasgow lobbyists do not stand up to close examination. Their declaration that they would lend pictures to a Gallery in Glasgow, but not in Edinburgh, suggests such a parochial and ungenerous spirit that it condemns those who made it. The claim that more people would visit a Gallery in Glasgow is very doubtful indeed. The Kelvingrove Museum has a large number of visitors, but most of them, in my observation at least, do not go there to look at the pictures. The McClellan Gallery is also agreeably uncrowded. The European money is a mirage. Its diversion from the infrastructure projects for which it is intended would require approval by the Scottish Office and the European Commission, and would have to be equally matched by the British Government. The deprived outer suburbs of Edinburgh have a similar financial status; but no one, as far as I know, has used this as an argument for a Gallery in Wester Hailes.

None of this means that the whole of the national collection should remain permanently in Edinburgh. Some paintings are already at Paxton and others are to go Duff House. Instead of 1,700 pictures staying in store, many could be circulated, both Scottish and others, to other towns in Scotland. They could be lent, with suitable guarantees for their safe-keeping, to the existing municipal galleries. Other out-stations could be acquired or built. The pictures belong to the people of Scotland and they should be given greater opportunities to see them, especially in places which so far have few pictures of their own.

(*The Scotsman*, 17 January 1994.)

30

Broadcasting in Scotland

In response to the Government White Paper, *The Future of the BBC*, the organisation itself has produced its own glossy booklet, *Extending Choice*, a title which betrays an anxiety to align themselves with Conservative dogma. In it they achieve the unlikely feat of displaying an even more centralist and London knows best attitude than the Government does in its recent publications. I have been comparing the documents with increasing incredulity.

Let us look first at the paper, *Scotland in the Union*, in which the Government gives us the results, such as they are, of its 'stock-taking' exercise. The first nine chapters set out proposals for some tinkering with the existing machinery, but the tenth and final chapter comes closer to an acceptance of the reality of Scotland. It acknowledges that a 'more concerted recognition of Scotland's status as a nation is necessary' and that the Scots 'want their Scottishness to be recognised, understood and respected'. It assures us that the Government will not hesitate 'to create, when appropriate, new bodies to take account of the distinctive Scottish identity'. We have yet to see the Government acting in full accordance with these principles, but the fact that they have been stated so clearly is significant.

Of course, a self-respecting nation, as the Government has now accepted that we are, wants above all the right to accept responsibility for its own government. The Government is misguided enough to deny that to us, but it seems to have accepted the need for cultural, if not yet political, self-determination. The transfer to Scotland of responsibility for university funding and the Scottish Arts Council are steps in that direction. We have already most of the institutions of a distinctive culture, apart from the all-important exception of a Parliament. The 'new bodies', in the Government's phrase, which are still lacking are a National Theatre and a genuinely autonomous corporation for public service broadcasting. Towards the first of these, the Scottish Arts Council have announced a feasibility study. The revision of the charter of the BBC, which expires in 1996, offers an opportunity for a new approach to broadcasting in Scotland.

J.M. Reid, in a book published as long ago as 1959, said that the position of broadcasting in Scotland was anomalous. 'When regular broadcasting began in 1922, Scottish self-confidence was at its lowest ebb. It is impossible to believe that at any other time, a people who had long had most other cultural media in their own hands – Church, schools, newspapers – would have accepted a monopoly in a new form of communication over which they had no sort of control.' The distinguished historian, Geoffrey Barrow, has said that the failure to establish a Scottish public service broadcasting was 'the most serious cultural disaster which Scotland had suffered in this century'. For decades, many individuals and organisations, such as the SNP, the Saltire Society and the Advisory Council for the Arts in Scotland, have been campaigning for autonomy in broadcasting.

In its White Paper, *The Future of the BBC*, the Government has responded to this demand. It says (p. 37): 'The special needs and interests of Scotland, Wales and Northern Ireland will need to be reflected in any new organisational structure for the BBC. The BBC services in the three countries could be given a larger measure of autonomy . . . It is essential that there should be sufficient radio and television programmes for each country, which reflect its culture, needs and interests'.

The BBC, I am sorry to say, have ignored this clear lead. There is no mention of autonomy for the three countries in the whole of their document of 88 pages. On the contrary, the recent establishment of a Resources, Engineering and Services Directorate under direct London control is a serious curtailment of the limited freedom which BBC Scotland already enjoys. It is true, of course, that the BBC paper makes a gesture towards what they choose to call regional broadcasting. It tells us (p. 47) that 'the BBC is the *British* Broadcasting Corporation, not the *London* Broadcasting Corporation. It should remain in touch with the views and priorities of its audience throughout the UK . . . It should reflect the regional and cultural diversity which so enriches Britain'.

Apart from a few passages like these, the paper uses language throughout which shows that the authors do not understand the question at issue. Where the Government speaks of the 'three countries', the BBC speaks constantly of one nation, Britain or the UK, as if it were one homogeneous unit, and not an artificial construct now in decline and with a very uncertain future. They declare, in fact, that they act, and propose to continue to act, as a propagandist for a controversial view of Britain which a large part of the Scottish population does not accept. They even speak repeatedly of 'British culture' in the singular, although not one but several cultures are involved. The matter is further complicated by the almost universal practice in England of using British and English as interchangeable terms. The confusion is very obvious at one point in the paper where they refer to 'national institutions like "Test Match Special"'.

I admire many things about the BBC and I think BBC Scotland does a remarkable job on very restricted resources. London control, however, has distinct disadvantages. It has an attitude of metropolitan arrogance. As Briggs, the historian of British broadcasting, says, it assumes that the best talent resides in London and that 'local culture' is inferior to the 'universal culture' of the metropolis. It also keeps an unfair proportion of the funds raised in Scotland from the sale of licences. In 1990/91 the audience in Scotland paid over £110 million. Less that half of this, £51.5 million, came back to finance programme-making in Scotland.

Market research by the independent television companies has shown that the Scottish audience wants more Scottish programmes. An autonomous Scottish Broadcasting Corporation, with the £110 million, could meet that demand. This would mean more jobs for broadcasters and technicians in Scotland, enhanced self-confidence and self-expression, more patronage of the arts, entertainment suited to the Scottish taste and more analysis of Scottish events. Of course, we should buy some programmes from England and other countries, but the choice would be ours. I think that they would be unlikely to include coverage of the test matches or the Oxford-Cambridge boat race.

No doubt we shall be told that a small country like Scotland cannot afford to run its own broadcasting. All the small independent countries in Europe, comparable to Scotland in size and other respects, manage perfectly well. Switzerland even maintains separate full-time services in three languages and part-time in a fourth.

The BBC proposals fail to come to terms with our need to stand on our own feet in this vital matter. The decision, of course, rests with the Government. It will be a test of the sincerity of chapter 10 of their paper on the Union.

(*The Herald*, 6 April 1993.)

31

The Scottish Historical Tradition

Modern scholarship largely agrees on at least one point about the great outburst of intellectual activity in Scotland in the eighteenth century. This is to dismiss as absurd, and contrary both to common sense and all the evidence, 'the hoary myth' (to quote the recent book[1] by David Allan) 'that the Enlightenment condensed, as it were, out of nothing'. No serious scholar now doubts the the Scottish Enlightenment was the consequence of centuries of development in Scotland and that it was marked by many characteristics which were uniquely Scottish.

This does not mean that there are not still some people who are uninformed or unscrupulous enough to claim that Scotland was an artistic and intellectual desert until the Union brought us the alleged blessings of English civilisation. Ian Lang is a case in point. In the famous Usher Hall debate he suggested that 'our greatest economic growth, our cultural flowering, our arts and our heritage' all followed the Union. He was dismissing, for his own narrow political purposes, centuries of history and many of our greatest achievements, including those of Duns Scotus, Henryson, Dunbar, Carver, Buchanan and Napier. It is a sad reflection on the state of Scottish education that anyone should imagine that he can talk like this without exciting general derision. The Usher Hall audience, to their credit, gasped with incredulity.

David Allan's book is an important contribution to this issue and to the understanding of the intellectual riches of the centuries before the eighteenth. He covers a vast range of unfamiliar territory, the work of Scottish historians, especially of the sixteenth and seventeenth centuries. As he says, 'Scotland had possessed a talented community of historians since at least the fourteenth century'. It began as early as 1370 with John Fordun and was 'sustained by a lineal succession of historians like Hector Boece, John Major and George Buchanan, unsurpassed, it was invariably claimed, in the field of European letters'. Among these, Buchanan was one of the most influential and many of his ideas became part of the Scottish tradition. He elevated public utility above self-interest, and believed that sovereignty belonged to the whole people. 'The people have the power to conferre the Government on whom they please'. He saw history as the best form of education, 'that sort of Writing, which tends to the Information of the Mind'.

These attitudes, which Allan sees as both a humanist and a Calvinist tradition, were shared by both presbyterian and royalist writers. History was seen as a guide to the future and as a means of encouraging virtue, of which public spirit was the essence. History was therefore regarded as the pre-eminent branch of learning and particularly appropriate for the education of social and political leaders.

The *literati* of the Scottish Enlightenment inherited what Allan calls 'the prodigious intellectual legacy of the Scottish past'. They shared many of the attitudes of their predecessors, including the importance attached to the historical approach. At the same time, they believed that they had introduced more scientific methods, although Allan thinks that they were much less innovative than they supposed. When Hume said that 'this is the historical Age and this the historical Nation', he was celebrating both the continuity of the Scottish tradition and the achievements of his own time.

It was, of course, a self-confident age, convinced of the power of its own rationality. In Scotland the very absence of a Parliament and Government, at a time when Westminster still took very little interest in Scottish affairs, meant that the professors, historians and philosophers had a higher reputation and more influence than was usual in other societies. For a time, reason was in charge and there seemed to be unlimited prospects of rational improvement in all directions.

Did it all end in the early decades of the nineteenth century and, if so, why? Allan points out that in fact Scottish intellectual influence continued to be widely felt for the rest of the century. Literature and ideas, he says, were 'Scotland's most durable and valuable exports'. Even so, he recognises a marked decline in intellectual self-confidence within Scotland itself. Partly he attributes this to the implications of the theory of 'unintended consequences'. This theory, that human affairs are determined as much by accident as design, like Adam Smith's invisible hand, can be seen as similar in effect to a belief in divine intervention and therefore destructive of confidence in the power of reason. Allan makes a brief reference to other factors such as the pull of industrial England and the British Empire and the distraction of the Disruption. Strangely enough he does not mention the most important one of all, the increasing interference of Westminster in Scottish affairs which progressively destroyed the *de facto* autonomy on which the self-confidence had largely depended.

David Allan has clearly read very widely in fields where few have recently ventured. He reports the results in language so densely packed with argument and unfamiliar fact that it makes heavy demands on the reader. It is an effort well worth making. The book opens up an impressive but neglected part of our cultural history and adds a new dimension to the study of the origins of the Scottish Enlightenment. It has many important implications, not least on the place of historical studies.

(*Books in Scotland*, No. 47, Autumn 1993.)

NOTE

1. *Virtue, Learning and the Scottish Enlightenment*, David Allan (Edinburgh University Press 1993.)

32

The Sentimental Unionist

In the first week of February (1992) *The Scotsman* carried a series of articles for and against independence. Those against, especially those by English academics, seemed to me to fail to make much of a case. Anthony Bradley appeared to think that the only purpose of independence was to avoid the West Lothian question. Nevil Johnson suggested that an independent Scotland would become 'introverted and isolated', although on the contrary one of the purposes of independence is to restore an international identity to Scotland with the ability to play its own direct part in international affairs. The rest of his remarks applied, not to independence, but to devolution. Since he has advised the Conservative Party in these matters, it is not surprising that their policy makes so little sense.

Allan Massie's article was another matter. He dismisses the 'arid and evanescent' arguments over financial statistics and (like John Major in his Glasgow speech) turns to feelings and sentiment. Very often a resort to sentiment is a sign of the lack of solid arguments, but it can also relate to the underlying feelings which in the last resort determine political attitudes. Whether we are for or against the Union may well depend on whether we feel predominantly British or predominantly Scottish. In fact, according to a recent opinion poll, only 15 per cent of us feel predominantly British, which is close to the 18 per cent or 20 per cent who usually support the status quo.

There are several very real weaknesses in a sentimental appeal to the Union. In the first place, even if Mr Massie for some unexplained reason thinks that it was not imposed, there is no doubt that the methods used were sordid and shameful. As the distinguished English historian, Christopher Hill, wrote recently, 'Scotland was bribed and swindled into union with England'. Secondly, it is very difficult to approve of a Union which only one of the two parties has ever attempted to take seriously. The Scots have tried, but without much encouragement from the other side. The English have always behaved as if the Treaty did not mean what it said and that what had happened was the annexation of Scotland with England otherwise continuing as before. They can hardly be blamed for that since, in practice if not in theory, that was very much the effect.

Then there is a sense in which the Treaty of Union no longer exists as a valid guarantee of Scotland's residual rights. Almost from its ratification, the Treaty has been so frequently violated by the British Parliament that not much remains. The Treaty contained no provision for amendment or the arbitration of disputes and it has been left to the tender mercies of the English doctrine of parliamentary sovereignty. This is a fundamentally undemocratic doctrine because it means that no Scottish rights, and indeed no human rights of any kind, can be safeguarded from arbitrary decisions by Parliament. Allan Stewart stated it during the recent meeting of the Scottish Grand Committee in Edinburgh when he said that a devolved Scottish Parliament could not be entrenched because no British Parliament could bind its successors.

Of course, sentimental unionists do not address their emotional appeal to constitutional technicalities, but to shared experiences, friendships and relationships which cross the border and freedom of trade and movement across it. They are on less sure ground when they appeal, as Mr Massie does, to the massive sacrifice of Scottish lives in war. We must surely hope that this is something which belongs only to the past.

The fact is, of course, that no one is proposing to rebuild Hadrian's Wall. Cross-Border co-operation and freedom of movement will remain with independence. Both Scotland and England will be part of the much wider area of free movement and free trade which is the European Community. In addition, our relationship with England will not be damaged but enhanced by independence. It is our subordinate status which causes resentment and tension. As two independent member states of the European Community we should be able to co-operate in a more equitable and friendly way.

This brings me to the question with which Mr Massie ended his article. Why do I think that Europe can hold together if the Union of Scotland and England cannot? The reason is that the two associations are quite different. Under the Union of 1707 Scotland has no rights that the Briitish Parliament cannot set aside, as it repeatedly has done. As a member state in Europe, Scotland, like the other member states, would have recognised status and recognised rights. The experience of other small countries is that this pooling of sovereignty has increased and not diminished their influence. The Union of 1707 was disguised annexation; the European Community is a negotiated arrangement for international co-operation and mutual benefit.

In a subsequent article Mr Massie quotes Edwin Muir's remark that Scotland, did not have a centre, 'but a blank, an Edinburgh, in the middle of it'. He meant, of course, that Edinburgh was not a real capital because it had no Parliament and no Government. Muir's conclusion in his book, *Scottish Journey*, was that 'Scotland is as urgently in need of independence as Ireland was. More urgently, indeed, for if she does not get it she will lose her national consciousness, as Ireland would never have done.'

(*The Scotsman*, 10 March 1992.)

33

Scotland at the Summit: A Dialogue with an Enquiring Visitor from Italy, in December 1992

E.V. I hear that your latest book is called *Scotland in Europe*. It is presumably not a coincidence that it is published just before the European Summit in Edinburgh. There was, as far as I know, no particular political significance in the fact that the previous one was held in Birmingham. Does the choice of Edinburgh for this one have any more point than that?

P.H.S.   Certainly. Even John Major has said that 'Edinburgh is a capital city and a capital city should be the scene of great events'. His chief representative in Scotland, the Secretary of State, Ian Lang, for his part has added: 'We must draw more on Scotland's status as a nation and on Edinburgh's status as a capital city'. So far they have refused to draw what I should regard as the obvious conclusions from these facts, but they acknowledge the essential point. It is because Edinburgh is not a provincial city, but the capital of an ancient European nation with close connections with the rest of Europe, that the Summit there has special implications.

E.V.   Forgive me, but this is where I begin to have difficulties. In my language, Italian, we use the same word, Inghilterra, for the whole of this island. We do not distinguish between what you call Britain or the United Kingdom and England. We have some vague ideas about Scotland in the past; but as our language reveals, we have assumed that it has long ago been absorbed in England. Is that not the position?

P.H.S.   I am sorry that there is no simple answer to that question. It confuses people not only in the rest of the world, but even some in Scotland itself and nearly everybody in England. To cut a long story short, the facts briefly are these. In 1707 the Scottish Parliament was induced by various means, including bribery and military threat, and against the wishes of the great majority of the Scottish people, to ratify a Treaty of Union with England.

The Treaty abolished the Parliament of both Scotland and England and replaced them with a new entity, the Parliament of Great Britain. At least that is what the Treaty said. In practice both Houses of the

English Parliament carried on as before, except that some Scottish
members were added. The Scottish Parliament ceased to exist.
England was hardly changed by the Union. Scotland lost the ability
to legislate for itself and it disappeared from view internationally.
Because of this, you could say that Scotland was absorbed in fact,
if not in law.

On the other hand, many other institutions in Scotland, such as
the legal system, the Church, the local administration and the Universities, not only continued in being but their separate existence was
guaranteed by the Treaty. Until quite recent times, these institutions
had far more effect on the lives of the people than the remote Parliament and Government. In a very real sense, therefore, Scotland was
not absorbed but continued to exercise its own distinctive national
existence.

E.V.   But Scotland, if I understand correctly, has been subject to
the London Parliament since 1707?

P.H.S.   That is true and it is a Parliament which has in the meantime
evolved the peculiarly English doctrine of parliamentary sovereignty.
That means that it claims the right to pass any law it chooses without
the restraint of a written constitution or constitutional court. It has
never hesitated to violate the Treaty of Union, although that is the
instrument to which it owes its own its own existence.

E.V.   So Scotland has a legal system, a Church and an administration, as well as its long history as an independent country, but
has no legislative body to exercise democratic control over its own
affairs. It claims to be a nation and has many of the attributes of
one, but it has no Parliament or legislative assembly of any kind.
That presumably means that it has less power than a region in Italy
or a land in Germany.

P.H.S.   Yes, that is the position.

E.V.   From the Scottish point of view, that seems to me unsatisfac-
tory, unstable and humiliating.

P.H.S.   I must agree again.

E.V.   Why then have the Scots tolerated this state of affairs for
so long?

P.H.S.   I find that difficult to understand myself. Part of the explanation is historical. Until about the middle of the nineteenth century
Scotland did very well under its own institutions with very little
interference from London. By the time the London Government
began to intervene, the situation was complicated by the existence

of the Empire and involvement in European wars. The population as a whole did not have the right to vote until this century, but there has been increasing agitation for Scottish self-government for more than 100 years.

E.V.   Well, you deserve credit for patience if nothing else, but was there not a referendum on the matter some time ago?

P.H.S.   Yes, there was a referendum in 1979 on a proposal for an Assembly with limited powers over internal Scottish affairs. The Conservatives campaigned for a 'No' vote with the promise that, if they succeeded, they would immediately call a constitutional conference to improve the government of Scotland. This confused the whole issue. In spite of it, the 'Yes' side had a majority of over 77,000 votes which was 51.6 per cent of the votes cast. Normally this would have settled the matter because every other decision in our political history has been taken in the belief that a majority of one is sufficient. In this case alone, however, the British Parliament had introduced the requirement that the result would be regarded as positive only if at least 40 per cent of the total electorate voted 'Yes', an impossibly difficult condition since the electoral roll contains many people who have died, moved away, gone on holiday or to hospital and so on. The Conservatives, who came to power shortly afterwards, repealed the legislation for an Assembly and have never honoured this commitment to call a constitutional conference. Under Edward Health they had been in favour of a Scottish Parliament, but Margaret Thatcher reversed the policy and John Major has followed her example.

E.V.   What is the evidence about the present state of Scottish opinion on this issue?

P.H.S.   Every opinion poll on the subject since polls began has shown between 75 per cent and 80 per cent in favour of a measure of self-government and therefore only 20 per cent to 25 per cent, or even less, in favour of the constitutional *status quo*. The division of opinion between independence and a Parliament with more limited powers has fluctuated. The latter has usually been in the lead, but independence has been gaining ground. The results of the last four elections have been consistent with these polls. The parties in favour of a Scottish Parliament have always had about 75 per cent of the vote and the Conservatives, the only party in favour of the *status quo*, 25 per cent or less. They have formed the Government at Westminster for the last thirteen years on the strength of votes in England and have used this position to impose policies on Scotland which the Scottish electorate have repeatedly rejected.

E.V.   But I have the impression from what I have read in the press that the Conservatives did rather better in Scotland in the last elections in April.

P.H.S.   They have worked hard to give that impression but the fact is that their vote in Scotland increased by only 1.7 per cent. This is a very small amount when you consider that John Major, who was at that time still quite popular, had replaced Margaret Thatcher who was generally detested in Scotland. Also many voters opposed to the Conservatives had removed themselves from the electoral roll because they wanted to avoid the poll tax. On the other hand, the Conservatives spent millions of pounds on an organisation which mobilised their vote very effectively. Any one of these factors could account for the small increase.

John Major had made the constitutional *status quo* a major issue which, he said, transcended the whole campaign. That point of view can take little comfort from the fact that it was, once again, rejected by 75 per cent of the Scottish votes. The votes of the Scottish National Party, the party of independence, increased by 7.5 per cent.

E.V.   From what you tell me there seems to be no doubt that the Scots have consistently demonstrated over many years that they want their own Parliament, but that the Conservatives since Margaret Thatcher became their leader have steadily refused to listen, and that John Major seems to be even more opposed to any constitutional change.

P.H.S.   Yes. In a speech in Glasgow on 10 September John Major said that he would defend with equal vigour 'the remarkable, magical Union' and the value of sterling within the ERM. Admittedly his strong commitment on the second of these lasted only about another week.

E.V.   The point about this which interests me most is that this is the same John Major who is always lecturing his EC colleagues about the importance of national identity and national decision-making and subsidiarity. He accepts that Scotland is a nation, but refuses to allow Scotland to make her own decisions about her own affairs. How can he simultaneously hold such different views towards the EC and towards Scotland? That looks to me like a high degree of hypocrisy and inconsistency.

P.H.S.   Exactly. That is what makes the Summit in Edinburgh so significant.

(*The Herald*, 4 December 1992.)

34

The End of Britishness

In Scotland there has long been profound discontent with the British constitution or system of government. Every opinion poll on the subject since polls began has shown a large majority in favour of constitutional change. What is new is the sudden collapse of faith in the system also in England. It is the culmination of long process. Robert Worcester, the chairman of MORI, whose polls have recorded the process, says that there is no doubt that for some decades there has been a decline of confidence in British institutions, 'in monarchy, in Westminster and Whitehall, in the judiciary and the system of government as a whole'.[1]

This steady decline has now reached the point of crisis with a collapse of morale and a widespread feeling of despair. Since 1962 Anthony Sampson in the successive editions of *The Anatomy of Britain* has given a detailed account of the state of British institutions. His latest book, published at the end of last year, *The Essential Anatomy of Britain*, reflects the new pessimism. It has the subtitle, *Democracy in Crisis*, and Tom Nairn has described it as 'a cry of mingled horror and alarm'.[2] As Henry Porter has said in *The Guardian*, 'Suddenly what seems to be at stake is not economic and material well-being, but the Britishness of being British'.[3] According to a recent poll, about half of the British public would emigrate if they could. A headline in *The Scotsman* concluded that the mood and morale of the nation (meaning Britain) has never been at such a low ebb.[4]

Of course, there have been many recent events which are likely to contribute to disillusionment and despair. Major's government has shown nothing but indecision, incompetence and confusion, with no apparent purpose beyond clinging to power. Even the Tory press finds it derisory. There is an unmistakable air of deceit and corruption. Ministers refuse to resign in circumstances where common decency, to put it no higher, would have demanded it in the past. Unemployment exceeds three million. Since the humiliation of Black Wednesday the Government has staggered from one muddle to another. The British economy has been in steady decline for decades. In 1960 the UK was ninth in terms of GDP per head out of the twenty-four members of the OECD; by 1991 it was eighteenth. The courts have had to release people who have been wrongly imprisoned for years. The despair of the young erupts in violence in the streets. The myth of the monarchy turns into a bedroom farce. The 'stock-taking' White Paper has shown again that the Government cannot, or will not, respond to the need for democratic normality in Scotland. The shambles of the Grand National was an apt symbol of the state of Britishness.

Some of these tendencies, although bad enough, may be checked or reversed and their effects may be only temporary. After all, the Government will change eventually; there will be some recovery in the economy, even if there is little sign of any escape from its fundamental weakness; the failings of the law courts and of the royal family may be forgotten and forgiven. These changes by themselves are, however, unlikely to halt the steady decline of confidence in the British system because its troubles are far more deep-seated than any temporary difficulty.

The British system has been in existence for nearly 300 years and has had far-reaching consequences. It is therefore surprising how little investigation has been made of its origins and nature. Historians have tended to regard it as the mere continuation of England under another name or have taken its existence for granted. In fact, one of the few serious attempts to explain what it is and how it came about appears in a book published only last year. This is *Britain: Forging the Nation, 1707–1837*, by the distinguished historian, Linda Colley. She has blind spots, particularly towards Scotland, but her book is the most thorough and penetrating account so far of the nature of Britishness.

Colley begins at the Union of 1707 when 'as a would-be nation, rather than a name, Great Britain was invented'. The Union was 'profoundly unpopular' in Scotland and there were 'profound cultural and historical divisions between the English, the Scottish and the Welsh'. This new nation was an artificial invention, 'forged above all by war', especially the long war with France from 1689 to 1815. Partly because France was the leading Catholic power, 'an uncompromising Protestantism was the foundation on which the state was explicitly and unapologetically based'.5

In spite of these unpromising origins, the idea of Britain became widely accepted in the course of the nineteenth century, even in Scotland. (In fact, one might say particularly in Scotland, because the English always seem to have had difficulty in understanding the distinction between England and Britain.) As Colley continues, 'an extraordinarily large number of Britons seem to have believed that, under God, they were particularly free and particularly prosperous'.

This is curious because, until recent times, both the freedom and the prosperity applied to only a very small part of the population. The idea of Britishness rested on a mass illusion which Colley calls an 'enormous conceit'. She identifies a number of factors behind it, apart from Protestantism. 'Aggression channelled into war and imperial expansion' led to the Empire which was a British, as opposed to an English, institution. 'A reverence for Parliament became an increasingly important part of elite attitudes, and a vital part of elite patriotism.' The myth of monarchy was part of it as well, although in the period of Colley's book it had not yet reached the height of apotheosis which it later achieved.[6]

It is not part of Colley's purpose to describe the consolidation of this system in the latter half of the nineteenth century or to speculate about how long it might last. She does allow herself to 'express the hope that if Britishness survives (and it may not) it will in the future find a more pragmatic and more generous form'. Britishness, as it emerges from her frank account, is not something which any fair-minded person would want to perpetuate. Its essential characteristics have been as 'an artificial nation, governed at the highest level by a predominantly landed and in the early decades especially an aggressively Anglocentric oligarchy', depending for its identity on war and on an irrational conviction of superiority.[7]

One of the virtues of this important book is that, although its period ends in 1837, it helps us to understand the nature of Britishness in its heyday and to see why it now inevitably faces collapse. No one would now dare to claim that Britain was vastly superior to her European neighbours in either freedom or prosperity, but the decline has been still more radical. The fact is that the four props, on which Britishness rested, have now all either disappeared or changed and weakened beyond recognition.

Protestantism may once have been a unifying force, although there have always been substantial differences between the Churches of England and Scotland. It no longer has any political weight in a society of diverse religions which is predominantly secular. The exception, of course, is Northern Ireland where seventeenth century attitudes have mysteriously survived and Protestantism is still equated with Britishness and the Crown. More profoundly than they probably realise, the loyalists of Ulster reflect the origins of the British idea. The great majority of people in mainland Britain regard their attitudes as no more than eccentric and distasteful sectarianism.

The Empire has disappeared into history. In its day, it was the major factor which made the British idea acceptable in Scotland, even if it benefited individual Scots, rather than Scotland as a nation.

As Michael Lynch said in his recent *New History of Scotland*, the Scots embraced, not Britain, but the British Empire.[8] For this reason, Scotland should logically have terminated the Union as soon as the Empire dissolved after the last War. Almost all of the component parts of the Empire have achieved independence. Scotland, which contributed greatly to their development, has still not recovered what Hamish Henderson calls 'the elementary civilised right of a nation to control over its own affairs'.[9]

The institution of Monarchy, although part of the British idea, does not affect the question of the Union very much one way or the other. It has been no obstacle to the independence of the other countries which used to be parts of the Empire. In any case, monarchy itself now faces a very dubious future. Within a few months it has declined from something apparently unassailable and sacrosanct to a questionable anachronism. It is not its cost nor the indiscretions of the younger members of the family which are the real objections to it, but again much more fundamental defects.

At the end of the seventeenth century, Andrew Fletcher of Saltoun said that a hereditary prince is as absurd as a hereditary professor would be.[10] Certainly, nothing could be more illogical than choosing a head of state, or the holder of any other important office, not by personal qualities, but by parentage alone. This involves a high risk that the accident of birth can land you with some one who is quite incapable of the job. This happens all the time with family businesses, which is why very few of them survive for more than two or three generations. It might be argued that this does not matter in the case of the monarchy which has no power, but then why preserve an expensive institution which does so little? The fact is that the role of the monarch in the British state, although residual in a constitutional sense, still has a pervasive influence on social and political attitudes, and this influence is wholly undesirable. It is probably one of the main reasons for the failures and decline of the British state.

In the first place, the monarchy by its nature endorses the mediaeval idea of inherited privilege which is repugnant to social justice and common sense. You cannot logically object to inherited privilege in the House of Lords, or any other British institution, if you accept it at the top. Consequently, a largely unconscious acceptance of this antiquated and pernicious principle runs through the whole of British life.

Apologists for the monarchy often tell us that it is an institution which is greatly admired abroad. We are told how lucky we are to have it and how good it is for the tourist trade. I have some experience in other countries and have had opportunities to witness reactions in this matter. My impression is that some people in other countries are titillated by the soap opera, but that most intelligent people regard it as a ludicrous survival which no modern society should tolerate. We are regarded with more pity than admiration.

But the worst thing of all about monarchy, and especially the British version of it, is that it cultivates an attitude of reverence and humility towards people of very ordinary capacity, which is an insult to intelligence and fills heads with nonsense. This has been wearing a bit thin recently in some quarters, but the British press still expects its readers to respond to royal photographs as to a mystical icon. This whole attitude of unreality introduces a large element of myth and make-believe into the process of government which conceals and confuses the reality of power.

This myth and make-believe badly corrupts the last of the four pillars of Britishness, the Westminster Parliament. Unionist politicians in the British parties speak much about the sovereignty of Parliament. According to this theory, Parliament is supposed to be the supreme authority which controls the Executive. The truth is the opposite. It is the Executive which controls Parliament. As long as the Prime Minister has the support of his own party and they have an overall majority, the Prime Minister has more individual and arbitrary power than any Monarch in history. Parliament fought long to curb royal power, but the result has been the transfer of the royal prerogative to the Prime Minister. This is true even of an inadequate Prime Minister like John Major. His power is secure until his own party turns against him.

Lord Hailsham has described this system as 'elective dictatorship' and Lord Home said in his autobiography: 'But now a party can be elected on a minority vote, and in spite of that gain a parliamentary majority, and use it to force down the throats of the electorate policies which the majority do not approve. This is a caricature of democracy. It was never meant to be like that'.[11] These two prominent Conservatives expressed their anxieties at a time of Labour rule, but the erosion of the checks and balances which once curbed Prime Ministerial power have proceeded at a much fiercer pace under Thatcher and Major. Anthony Sampson points out in his latest book that centralising power has been diminished all over Europe, but that Britain has done the opposite. 'The British in the last decade have seen concentrations of power which the Victorians never dreamt of.'[12] Every rival to the central power of the Prime Minister, particularly the local authorities and the trade unions, has been curbed and emasculated. All contrary opinion has been derided or ignored. Ruthless use of Prime Ministerial patronage has packed public bodies with yes men.

The British parliamentary system has always been liable to abuse.

There is no written constitution to curb the misuse of power, no guarantee of human rights and no freedom of information. The first past the post electoral system works with the reliability and fairness of a roulette wheel. In the absence of fixed terms, the Government can fix the date of elections to suit itself and manipulate fiscal policy to influence the result. In addition to the Honours system, the Government has at its disposal a large number of influential and lucrative appointments. There is no limit on the amount of money which political parties can spend centrally on propaganda and election campaigns. Parties have no legal obligation to publish their accounts, or information about donations from firms or individuals, domestic or foreign. The procedures of the House, as the Maastricht debate amply demonstrated, are arcane and absurd.

In the past, this ramshackle and easily abused system survived because of a tacit agreement between Government and Opposition to operate it with restraint and resist the temptation to exploit its weaknesses. Alternative centres of power and influence, such as the local authorities, the trade unions, the universities and the broadcasters were tolerated with very little interference by the Government. Patronage was shared between the parties and the quangos were not packed with Government nominees. Sophisticated and expensive publicity techniques had not yet been introduced into British elections and money therefore played a lesser role. The first past the post electoral system worked fairly well as long as there were only two major parties.

The remnants of this old system of fair play, mutual restraint and consensus (which is all that substituted for a written constitution to shield the British system from the risks of tyranny and corruption) were shattered by Margaret Thatcher. She despised consensus and was determined not only to impose her dogma but to curb all alternative centres of power. When it suited her, she had no hesitation in reneging on promises, such as the commitment to give a measure of autonomy to Scotland. She used the power of patronage to extend the influence of the governing party and to attract donations to party funds. Honours were given to compliant newspaper editors and to directors of firms who used their company funds to make large donations to the Tory Party. By these means and by the creation of artificial booms before she called elections, she seemed to be set on creating a permanent one-party state, at least in England. She was eventually sacked by her own party, not for any of these reasons, but because they thought she had become an electoral liability.

The semi-secret conspiracy between certain businessmen and the Tory Party has become even more flagrant, or at least more exposed, under John Major. It has long been evident that this Government tends to award knighthoods and peerages to directors of companies which have made substantial donations to the Tory Party. This is a misuse of money which properly belongs to the shareholders or customers, who are not consulted, for the purposes of private vanity. It is much more sinister when the rewards are appointments to senior, and often well-paid, posts in the new quangos set up by the Government to take over powers previously exercised by elected councillors. The most recent examples are the police authorities proposed for England and Wales and the water boards proposed for Scotland. It is still more sinister if the donations (which, as we have seen recently, can be from foreign businessmen of doubtful integrity) are intended to influence Government policy. This is difficult to prove, but is it a coincidence that the tobacco companies are large donors and the Government stubbornly refuses to ban tobacco advertising? Is the illogical and anti-social preference for road over rail unconnected with the donations from the car manufacturers and road builders?

The overall impression is of a thoroughly corrupt system under which businessmen finance the expensive election campaigns which keep the Tories in power and they repay the favour with policies designed to favour the private interests of the donors. Margaret Thatcher used to be fond of invoking the authority of Adam Smith, at least during her visits to Scotland. Her Party have conspicuously ignored his advice on this matter. He said in *The Wealth of Nations* that Governments should regard the advice of 'merchants and master manufacturers' with the most scrupulous and suspicious attention. 'It comes from an order of men whose interest is never exactly the same with that of the public, who have generally an interest to deceive and even to oppress the public.' In another passage he said that 'people of the same trade seldom meet together, even for merriment and diversion, but the conversation ends in a conspiracy against the public'.[13] Under the British system, Government has been reduced to exactly such a conspiracy.

This system has worked to the particular disadvantage of Scotland. Our evident desire for self-government has been disregarded. For more than a decade Scotland has been governed by a party which it rejects at the polls and which has imposed policies opposed by the great majority of the people. The Government makes promises to serve its immediate purposes, such as Lord Home's before the Referendum, and the 'guarantees' to Britoil, Ravenscraig and Rosyth; it then ignores them when they become inconvenient. Scotland has been treated with contempt like a helpless and despised colony. James VI boasted that he was able, with the backing of English power, to rule Scotland from London by the stroke of a pen. Ian Lang is under the same illusion. So far, he has got away with it, partly because the official Opposition has been feeble, which is inevitable as long as Labour have the majority of Scottish seats but are preoccupied by an ambition to win power in England. The Government may now have gone too far. The Scottish people are long-suffering to a fault, but even they cannot stomach the blatant breach of trust over Rosyth, followed so quickly by the gerrymandering (or langrigging) of the local government proposals, with their implied threat of the privatisation of water. The Government, by its own actions, has now destroyed all credibility in itself because its guarantees and promises have been exposed as worthless. A Government and a system in which hardly anyone now has any faith does not deserve to survive, and it is unlikely that it will.

But in Scotland we are fortunate because we have an alternative. As Government ministers have frequently acknowledged, we have an undeniable right to decide for ourselves that we want independence, and that would follow from a majority vote for the SNP in a General Election. With independence we can build a rational and prosperous state like one of our Scandinavian neighbours. This might well be an inspiration to the English. As many of them know only too well the British system is now so antiquated, perverse and corrupt that it cannot be saved by minor adjustments. England, like Scotland, needs radical constitutional reform. We are in a good position to give a lead.

(*Cencrastus*, No. 46, Autumn, 1993.)

NOTES

1. *The Scotsman*, 24/2/93.
2. *The Scotsman*, 18/11/92.
3. As 1.
4. As 1.
5. op. cit., pp. 11, 47, 53, 18.
6. op. cit., pp. 32, 43, 53, 50.
7. op. cit., pp. 9, 56.
8. op. cit., p. 14.
9. Hamish Henderson, *Alias MacAlias* (Edinburgh, 1992), p. 262.
10. Paul H. Scott, *Andrew Fletcher and the Treaty of Union* (Edinburgh, 1992), p. 11.
11. Quoted in Bruce Lenman, *The Eclipse of Parliament* (London, 1992), pp. 1, 260.
12. Anthony Sampson, *The Essential Anatomy of Britain* (London, 1992), p. 154.
13. Adam Smith, *The Wealth of Nations* (Everyman's Library edition, London, 1975), vol. I, pp. 232, 117.